The American History Series

SERIES EDITORS

John Hope Franklin, *Duke University*

A. S. Eisenstadt, *Brooklyn College*

Ralph B. Levering
DAVIDSON COLLEGE

The Cold War
A Post–Cold War History

SECOND EDITION

HARLAN DAVIDSON, INC.
WHEELING, ILLINOIS 60090-6000

 Address inquiries to Harlan Davidson, Inc., 773 Glenn Avenue, Wheeling, Illinois 60090-6000.

Visit us on the World Wide Web at www.harlandavidson.com.

Library of Congress Cataloging-in-Publication Data

Levering, Ralph B.
The Cold War: a post–Cold War history / Ralph B. Levering.— 2nd ed.
p. cm.—(The American history series)
Includes bibliographical references and index.
ISBN 0-88295-233-1 (alk. paper)
1. United States—Foreign relations—1945–1989. 2. United States—Foreign relations—1989– 3. Cold War 4. United States—Foreign relations—1933–1945. 5. World politics—1945–1989. I. Title. II. American history series (Wheeling, Ill.)
E840.L435 2005
909.82'5—dc22

2004017134

Cover photo: Chairman Nikita Khrushchev and President John F. Kennedy at a meeting in Vienna, 1963. Courtesy National Archives. ARC 193204.

Manufactured in the United States of America
07 06 05 04 1 2 3 4 5 VP

To John Lewis Gaddis and Arthur S. Link:
Exemplary historians, mentors, and friends

FOREWORD

Every generation writes its own history for the reason that it sees the past in the foreshortened perspective of its own experience. This has surely been true of the writing of American history. The practical aim of our historiography is to give us a more informed sense of where we are going by helping us understand the road we took in getting where we are. As the nature and dimensions of American life are changing, so too are the themes of our historical writing. Today's scholars are hard at work reconsidering every major aspect of the nation's past: its politics, diplomacy, economy, society, recreation, mores and values, as well as status, ethnic, race, sexual, and family relations. The lists of series titles that appear on the inside covers of this book will show at once that our historians are ever broadening the range of their studies.

The aim of this series is to offer our readers a survey of what today's historians are saying about the central themes and aspects of the American past. To do this, we have invited to write for the series only scholars who have made notable contributions to the respective fields in which they are working. Drawing on primary and secondary materials, each volume presents a factual and narrative account of its particular subject, one that affords readers a basis for perceiving its larger dimensions and importance. Conscious that readers respond to the closeness and immediacy of a subject, each of our authors seeks to restore the past as an actual present, to revive it as a living reality. The individuals and groups who figure in the pages of our books appear as real people who once were looking for survival and fulfillment. Aware that historical subjects are often matters of controversy, our authors present their own findings and conclusions. Each volume closes with an extensive critical essay on the writings of the major authorities on its particular theme.

The books in this series are designed for use in both basic and advanced courses in American history, on the undergraduate and graduate levels. Such a series has a particular value these days, when the format of American history courses is being altered to accommodate a greater diversity of reading materials. The series offers a number of distinct advantages. It extends the dimensions of regular course work. Going well beyond the confines of the textbook, it makes clear that the study of our past is, more than the student might otherwise understand, at once complex, profound, and absorbing. It presents that past as a subject of continuing interest and fresh investigation. The work of experts in their respective fields, the series, moreover, puts at the disposal of the reader the rich findings of historical inquiry. It invites the reader to join, in major fields of research, those who are pondering anew the central themes and aspects of our past. And it reminds the reader that in each successive generation of the ever-changing American adventure, men and women and children were attempting, as we are now, to live their lives and to make their way.

John Hope Franklin
A. S. Eisenstadt

CONTENTS

PREFACE

Preparing a new edition of a book permits the author to take a fresh look at what the work tends to focus on and what it tends to discuss briefly or omit entirely. Such a reevaluation is especially important in the case of a topic as large as the Cold War, which involved many nations and lasted for more than forty years. It also is important because recently released documents from archives in Moscow, Beijing, Hanoi, and other capitals of communist bloc nations have enabled scholars to write more authoritatively about these nations' policies during the Cold War. Several of the books published since the mid-1990s that are helping to develop a truly international history of the Cold War are included in the Bibliographical Essay.

Another important recent emphasis—again based partly on newly available sources—is the intensive study of the role of ideology in influencing policy on both sides of the conflict. As one of the authors of a recent textbook, *Debating the Origins of the Cold War: American and Russian Perspectives* (2002), I argued that the liberal internationalism espoused by leading Democrats and Republicans during World War II, plus most Americans' profound dislike of communism and communists, contributed greatly to America's decision to oppose postwar Soviet foreign policy. Following the lead of other scholars, I noted that President Woodrow Wilson was the most influential advocate of liberal internationalism. Wilson's ideas about how to achieve a peaceful and prosperous world greatly influenced the thinking of America's leaders in the 1940s. Similarly, many recent scholars have emphasized the role of Marxist-Leninist ideology in postwar Soviet and Chinese foreign policy.

Although these new directions in scholarship are worthwhile, I have concluded that the basic emphases of the previous edition are appropriate for this one as well. Because this book is in a series designed to increase students' understanding of American history, it is appropriate to focus largely on U.S. actions and attitudes and on relations between the Cold War's two leading actors, the United States and the Soviet Union. It also makes sense to give substantial attention to the two large-scale but limited wars that grew out of the conflict, the Korean War and the Vietnam War, and to the most dangerous confrontation of the nuclear age thus far, the Cuban missile crisis. Above all, this book seeks to explain the Cold War's beginning in the mid-1940s, the alternating tendencies toward increased hostility and toward reduced tensions in U.S.-Soviet relations between the late 1940s and the mid-1980s, and the conflict's rapid and surprising ending in the late 1980s.

In my judgment, this short book is more successful in explaining how the Cold War began and changed over time than it is in analyzing what the Cold War was about—the goals, fears, and concerns on both sides that underlay the surface manifestations of the conflict. Five underlying factors—each of which could be the subject of a separate, longer book—come to mind immediately.

First, as suggested earlier, the United States and the U.S.S.R. had fundamentally different ideologies that affected virtually every aspect of their approaches to both domestic affairs and international relations. U.S. officials (and most voters) believed in individual freedoms protected by law, elected government, and regulated capitalism at home and the desirability of spreading similar forms of democracy and capitalism abroad. Soviet leaders, in contrast, rejected individual freedoms, elected government, and capitalism as outdated, "bourgeois," concepts both domestically and internationally, and sought instead the spread of communist beliefs and institutions. Writing in 1999, historian Frank Ninkovich captured the essence of the conflict: "The cold war was a historical struggle over which ideology or way of life would be able to form the basis of a global civilization."

Because foreign policies are based on perceived national interests as well as on ideologies, however, occasionally the two nations were able to work together to a considerable extent. Their alliance in

World War II and the period of détente in the early 1970s were the best examples.

Second, both U.S. and Soviet leaders had deep-seated concerns about national security throughout the Cold War. For Americans, these concerns largely began with the Japanese attack on Pearl Harbor on December 7, 1941, which prompted feelings of vulnerability that continued throughout the wartime and postwar years. The Cold War com petition—and especially Russia's testing of nuclear weapons beginning in 1949 followed by a nuclear arms race—helped to maintain these feelings throughout the conflict.

Beginning with Vladimir Lenin in 1917, Soviet leaders feared intervention by capitalist ("imperialist") nations to destroy the communist experiment in Russia. Small-scale interventions by Allied forces between 1918 and 1920 enhanced these fears, as did the tenet of Marxist-Leninist ideology that capitalist nations would try to end communism by military means. That belief appeared to come true on June 22, 1941, when Nazi Germany violated a 1939 nonaggression pact and attacked the Soviet Union. The all-out German effort to conquer Russia left lasting feelings of vulnerability and a determination to protect Russia's security in the future at all costs. As late as the early 1960s, Soviet leaders feared the possibility of a West Germany armed with a small quantity of atomic bombs almost as much as they feared the reality of a technologically superior America loaded with nuclear weapons and delivery systems.

Third, largely for reasons relating to ideology and security, America and Russia undertook continuing efforts during the Cold War to expand the number of allies each nation had and prevent losses to the other ideology, whether by choice or by conquest. Examples of the seriousness with which each side sought to avoid losing allies include the U.S. interventions in Korea and Vietnam and the Soviet interventions in Hungary and Afghanistan.

Fourth, U.S. and Soviet leaders repeatedly sought to avoid substantial fighting between the two nations' forces that easily could have led to World War III. In other words, whether the top leaders during periods of high tension were Harry Truman and Joseph Stalin, John Kennedy and Nikita Khrushchev, or Ronald Reagan and Yuri Andropov, there was a strong commitment on both sides to avoiding war between America and Russia. Memories of the devastation of World War II encouraged restraint, as did the fact that both sides possessed nuclear weapons by the early 1950s. Avoiding World War III was the greatest achievement of U.S. and Soviet leaders during the Cold War.

Fifth, because domestic politics and foreign policies are inextricably intertwined, the Cold War involved struggles for power and the exercise of power domestically as well as internationally. Scholars of the U.S.S.R. frequently argue that Stalin's determination to maintain total control over the Russian people contributed to his decision shortly after World War II to have the Soviet news media portray Western nations as implacably hostile. This alleged hostility, in turn, justified political repression and large-scale military spending at a time when most Russians wanted more consumer goods and greater individual freedom. Both during Stalin's time and later, disagreements over Soviet foreign policy were used to justify demotions and other shifts in power within the Soviet leadership.

In America, with congressional elections every two years and presidential elections every four, the struggle for power between Democrats and Republicans is virtually constant. Not surprisingly, the central foreign policy issue after 1945—U.S. relations with Russia and other communist nations—quickly became a staple of electoral politics throughout the nation and of partisan jockeying for advantage in Washington. In the late 1940s, prominent Republicans and Democrats also worked to end the influence of members of the Soviet-directed American Communist party and their supporters in government agencies, labor unions, and other areas of American life. Although the issue of "communists-in-government" largely disappeared by the mid-1950s, the question of which party or candidate could handle relations with Russia and other communist nations more effectively continued to be a major issue in elections well into the 1980s.

One simply cannot understand important U.S. Cold War policies—for example, why America did not establish diplomatic relations with communist China for thirty years after 1949, or why President John Kennedy believed that his only realistic choice was to demand the removal of the Soviet missiles from Cuba in 1962—without knowledge of the domestic political context in which these policies were made.

My primary goal in this book is to offer students and teachers a relatively brief, interpretive overview of the Cold War. I hope that this text reflects the four values that I admire most in the work of fellow scholars: readability; accuracy within the limits of current scholarship; willingness to make judgments, however tentative and open to subsequent revision; and fairness to all the individuals and governments involved.

Perhaps because the last value is the one that academics equipped with 20/20 hindsight and ideological agendas most often violate, I consider fairness the noblest virtue in writing contemporary history. In seeking to apply this virtue, one should seek to avoid self-righteous, vindictive criticisms of leaders who often were forced to make decisions in the midst of uncertainty and conflicting pressures. One should also bear in mind an observation by the eminent British historian, C. V. Wedgewood: "History is written backward but lived forward. Those who know the end of the story can never know what it was like at the time."

I wish to thank all those who have read and commented on the book, either for this or for previous incarnations: Aleine Austin, William Burr, Wolfgang Christian, Andrew J. Davidson, Robert A. Divine, Earl Edmondson, A. S. Eisenstadt, John Hope Franklin, John Lewis Gaddis, Maureen Hewitt, Lucy Herz, Wallace Irwin, Jr., Walter LaFeber, Patricia W. Levering, Arthur S. Link, Elizabeth Morgan, Thomas R. Maddux, Charles Neu, Louis Ortmeyer, David Patterson, Jack Perry, Harry Stegmaier, Jr., Samuel Walker, and Robert Williams. I am also grateful to my students at George Mason University, Western Maryland College (now McDaniel College), Earlham College, and, since 1986, Davidson College. They have helped me to keep learning about the past and caring about our common future.

This book is dedicated to two scholars who have helped me immeasurably over the past thirty-five years: John Lewis Gaddis, a professor at Yale University who is America's foremost authority on U.S.-Soviet relations; and the late Arthur S. Link, my graduate school adviser at Princeton University, who first sparked my interest in the role of domestic politics and public opinion in the making of U.S. foreign policy. Superb historians, their writings deserve careful reading and re-reading.

PROLOGUE

Uneasy Allies, 1941–1945

I got along fine with Marshal Stalin. He is a man who combines a tremendous, relentless determination with a stalwart good humor. I believe he is truly representative of the heart and soul of Russia, and I believe that we are going to get along very well with him and the Russian people—very well indeed.

President Franklin D. Roosevelt
Radio address to the American people
December 24, 1943

Of course, one of the most pressing questions in everybody's mind is what Russia intends to do about the political integrity of small states around her borders—Finland, Poland, the Baltic and Balkan states.

Wendell L. Willkie
Republican leader
The New York Times Magazine
January 2, 1944

In retrospect, the twenty months beginning with Nazi Germany's invasion of the Soviet Union* in June 1941 and ending with the capture of a huge German army at Stalingrad and a successful Soviet offensive against German forces in February 1943, formed a major turning point in twentieth-century history. In 1941 German dictator Adolf

*The terms "Soviet Union," "Russia," and "U.S.S.R." are used synonymously, all referring to the former Union of Soviet Socialist Republics (U.S.S.R.). Similarly, "United States" (abbreviated to "U.S.") and "America" refer to the United States of America, and "Britain" and "Great Britain" refer to the United Kingdom of Great Britain and Northern Ireland.

Hitler, a compulsive highstakes gambler in the often fatal game of world politics, made two moves that ultimately led to the destruction of German military power and his own death by suicide as his ruined and defeated nation was preparing to surrender in May 1945. The first of these moves was the massive German invasion of Russia, beginning on June 22, 1941. Not only was Hitler choosing to attack the nation with which he had signed a nonaggression pact less than two years earlier, but he was also taking on a populous nation to the east before he had defeated his chief enemy to the west, Great Britain. Hitler's second and even more inexplicable move was to take on a third potent enemy by declaring war on the United States on December 11, 1941, four days after Japan's attack on Pearl Harbor formally brought the United States into World War II.

In 1941 Hitler had thus unwittingly put together the Big Three—America, Britain, and Russia—as leaders of a twenty-five nation anti-Axis coalition known as the Grand Alliance. And in 1942 and 1943, that coalition turned the tide of battle away from the initially successful Axis nations and toward the Allies, who were superior in population, raw materials, and their ability to manufacture war materiel.

The Big Three's joint war against Germany was less than half over by February 1943, but the outcome no longer seemed in doubt—assuming that the Allies remained united in the war effort. And if they won, the two largest and most powerful nations on their side, America and Russia, stood to have far more influence in world affairs than either had ever had before.

Even in wartime, America—unlike Russia—was a relatively open society in which news media conveyed to the public the major issues in world affairs being discussed in the political capital (Washington) and in the media capital (New York), and in which conscientious pollsters surveyed and widely publicized the opinions of average citizens. One of those issues, whether the two emerging "superpowers" would be able to cooperate in fashioning a genuine and lasting peace after the war, was summed up in a question the Gallup pollsters frequently asked, "Do you think Russia can be trusted to cooperate with us when the war is over?" Never absent from public discussion, this ethnocentric yet pertinent question grew in strength and urgency as German armies retreated or were overwhelmed in 1943 and 1944, and it became a major theme in newspapers and in news magazines like *Time* and *Newsweek* by early 1945. A more pressing issue in 1942 and 1943, well known to President Franklin Roosevelt and other officials but little discussed publicly in Washington or in the media, was whether the Soviet leader, Joseph Stalin, might make a separate peace with Hitler, thus destroying the Grand Alliance before Germany was defeated.

These two issues were related: if the Allies fell apart during the war, they obviously would not be able to cooperate as victors afterward. Each of the two issues also showed a level of suspicion toward the Soviet Union that seldom appeared in official or media discussions of America's other key ally, Britain.

The tensions in U.S.-Soviet relations during World War II can be well illustrated by focusing on three questions that bear on the coming of the Cold War. First, why did U.S. officials fear during 1942 and 1943 that Stalin might make a separate peace with Hitler? Second, what were Stalin's and Roosevelt's goals for the postwar world, and how might they be evaluated? And third, how and why did the future of Poland become a contentious issue in Big Three relations in 1944 and 1945, one that in retrospect portended the eventual collapse of the Grand Alliance? Consideration of these questions will help explain why there was substantial concern—in Washington, in Moscow, and elsewhere—about whether U.S.-Soviet cooperation would continue in the postwar world.

U.S. leaders were well aware that Stalin had good reasons to consider trying to work out a separate peace with his former partner, Hitler. First, Russian troop losses—killed, wounded, captured, and missing—were horrendous, averaging well over 100,000 per week from mid-1941 through 1943 (all told, an estimated 27 million Russians died in the war, compared with about four hundred thousand Americans—a ratio of more than fifty to one). By the fall of 1942, most of the western half of the Soviet Union lay in ruins, and each day's fighting resulted in even more damage. Second, from his Marxist-Leninist viewpoint, Stalin distrusted all the large Western capitalist nations, not just Nazi Germany, believing that they all sought the destruction of the world's only major communist nation.

Recent history seemed to confirm his communist ideology. His two main allies, America and Britain, had sent troops to Russia in 1918–20, partly to help the conservative "whites" against the communist "reds" in the civil war that followed the Bolshevik Revolution of 1917. The U.S. had refused to recognize the Soviet government until 1933, and the British had acquiesced in excluding Czechoslovakia's eastern neighbor, Russia, from the infamous Munich conference of 1938, which effectively ceded Czechoslovakia to Hitler. Throughout the mid-to-late 1930s, in fact, the Western democracies had turned a deaf ear to Russia's pleas for a united stand against German expansion. Not without some reason, Stalin suspected that the British and French wanted Germany to attack his country and destroy its communist government.

When Germany attacked Russia in June 1941, Roosevelt and Winston Churchill, the British prime minister, offered Stalin support, but only because they considered Hitler a much greater threat. Proclaiming that he would do everything that he could to assist the Russians, Churchill, formerly an avid anti-Bolshevik, used his clever wit to explain his change of heart: "If Hitler invaded Hell, I would make at least a favorable reference to the devil in the House of Commons." Harry Truman, at the time a little-known senator from Missouri, expressed many Americans' distaste for both governments when he commented that, although he did not want to see Hitler win, the United States should help whichever nation was losing "and that way let [both of] them kill as many as possible. . . ."

During 1942 and 1943, Stalin came to believe that, despite soothing words to the contrary, his Western allies were doing something similar to what Truman had suggested. They were bleeding Russia, he thought, in two ways: first, by not delivering on time all of the supplies they promised the hard-pressed Russian forces; and second, by not opening a large-scale second front in Western Europe. By forcing Hitler to shift troops to the west, such a front could ease German military pressure on Russia, and perhaps shorten the war as well.

The absence of a second front in northwestern Europe in 1942 or 1943 was the third and perhaps the key reason why Stalin considered a separate peace. He desperately urged his allies to invade Europe: he sent Foreign Minister V. M. Molotov to Britain and America in May–

June 1942 to plead for a major second front to be opened that year and received an apparent public promise from Roosevelt to do so. But Churchill argued that opening a large-scale second front was impossible, both because of a shortage of equipment and supplies and because he did not want to risk heavy British losses. The Western allies thus launched a much smaller operation against German forces in North Africa than Soviet leaders would have liked. Again in 1943, the promised second front was postponed as British and U.S. forces fought relatively small numbers of German forces in Italy. Much more than Churchill, Roosevelt favored a second front, but he likewise did not wish to risk heavy losses—a luxury of choice that the embattled Stalin could only dream of having.

Upon learning in June 1943 that there would be no major second front until the next year, an angry Stalin wrote Roosevelt that the Soviet government's "confidence in its allies . . . is being subjected to severe stress." The Soviet leader cited the need to reduce "the enormous sacrifices of the Soviet armies, compared with which the sacrifices of the Anglo-American armies are insignificant." In 1943 Stalin recalled his pro-Western ambassadors from London and Washington and entered into secret peace negotiations with Germany. "The first cracks in the wartime alliance began over the issue of the second front," historian Robert Messer has concluded, "and formed the gap between promise and reality that widened steadily during 1942 and 1943."

Despite these and other tensions, relations between the Soviets and their Western allies improved in the fall of 1943, culminating in a generally positive meeting between Roosevelt, Churchill, and Stalin at Teheran, Iran, in November. At this meeting the two Western leaders made a firm commitment to Stalin to open a second front in France the following spring, and Stalin promised to enter the war against Japan within three months after Germany was defeated. Numerous other issues were discussed, but few concrete decisions were made. What stood out was a general spirit of cooperation, made easier by the fact that winning the war—an easier task than working out the details of the ensuing peace—would continue to have the highest priority for the foreseeable future. This emphasis at Teheran on not letting specific disagreements undermine the broader commitment to

Big Three cooperation would continue for the next fifteen months, until after the Yalta Conference of February 1945.

Most Americans, including President Roosevelt, wanted strongly to believe that America and Russia would be able to cooperate in shaping a lasting peace. Indeed, what seemed at the time to be the alternative—a third and even more devastating world war—was almost too horrible an idea to contemplate. Yet thoughtful Americans realized that the two nations had very different histories, ideologies, and postwar objectives, and that it would take highly skilled diplomacy—and perhaps some luck—to keep U.S.-Soviet relations from turning sour after Hitler's defeat.

By the time of the Teheran Conference, both Stalin and Roosevelt appeared to be committed to working out a peace settlement that would be acceptable to both nations. From Stalin's standpoint, this should have been fairly easy to do—except for the inherent untrustworthiness of the "imperialist" (capitalist) nations. The key, Stalin thought, was for the Big Three to make deals in which each nation's basic interests were protected. To Stalin, the Big Three, having won the war, should make the peace. The opinions of the people of the defeated Axis nations, or even of other small countries in Europe and Asia, were not important.

Stalin, the U.S.S.R.'s absolute dictator, knew just what he wanted for his country. He wanted to return the Soviet Union to Russia's 1914 borders: that is, he wanted back all the lands—including the Baltic states and eastern Poland—that had been seized from Russia during and after World War I. He wanted to help ensure that Germany would remain weak after the war, so that it could not prepare for a third horrible war against the U.S.S.R. He wanted reparations from Germany to assist in rebuilding the shattered Soviet economy. He wanted sufficient control over the nations between Russia and Germany—from Finland and Poland in the north to Romania and Bulgaria in the south—so that they could never again be allies of Germany or another Western power in a war against the U.S.S.R. And he wanted some relatively modest concessions in Asia in return for his promise to enter the war against Japan.

Perhaps above all, Stalin wanted his Western allies to accept his requests as appropriate and legitimate. Russia had made the lion's share of the sacrifices required to defeat Germany, and it deserved proper compensation. What he was asking for was not only earned, he believed, but necessary for Soviet security. In his view he was not asking for too much, partly because the "imperialist powers" would still control the rest of the world, including Western and Southern Europe, the oil-rich Middle East, Africa, Latin America, and much of Asia. In short, Stalin was pursuing what might be called a diplomacy of clarity, in which much of the world would be divided into well-defined spheres of influence, each under the ultimate control of one of the Big Three nations.

Stated in this simplified way, Stalin's postwar goals appear reasonable, indeed almost benign. Yet there were problems with Stalin's approach—and, equally, with Stalin himself as a leader—that concerned thoughtful Americans and Britons, including Roosevelt and Churchill. The biggest problem with the approach was that it almost certainly would destroy the possibility of self-determination—that is, freedom from external domination and freedom for internal democratic political processes—for the roughly 90 million people of Eastern Europe. These were values that Americans believed they were fighting for, values that were embodied in such important wartime documents as the Atlantic Charter of 1941 and the Declaration of the United Nations of 1942.

A second problem for America and Britain was whether Stalin's goals were as clear and as limited as they appeared to be at the time. Was it possible that, after absorbing Eastern Europe into his communist sphere of influence, he would encourage the communist parties that he controlled in other countries—France and Italy, for example—to try to take power? As a Marxist-Leninist, Stalin believed in the gradual but inevitable triumph of communism; that is, in what Soviet scholar Konstantin V. Pleshakov has called "revolutionism." In short, could a committed Marxist-Leninist's desire for revolution be limited to a well-defined sphere of influence?

A final problem involved Stalin himself. In the late 1920s and 1930s, Stalin had been responsible for the deaths of millions upon millions of Soviet citizens—either through deliberate starvation, mistreatment in the gulags (prison camps) in Siberia and elsewhere that his henchmen set up, or simply the execution of large numbers of his fellow citizens, including many of his most capable military officers and other officials. Several months after dividing Poland with Hitler in late 1939, Stalin ordered the execution by firing squad of at least fourteen thousand captured military officers and other Poles in the Katyn Forest in western Russia. During World War II few people except Stalin himself knew the details of all the atrocities he had ordered, but many Americans did know that he was a dictator who was likely to trample on basic human rights in any region he controlled.

In contrast to Stalin's emphasis on clarity centered on spheres of influence, Roosevelt's strategy for achieving U.S. aims in the postwar world might be called the diplomacy of ambiguity. Roosevelt's policy was ambiguous in that his public statements consistently emphasized the broad ideals he was seeking, whereas his private diplomacy with Stalin, Churchill, and other leaders reflected the frequent compromises of principle that he knew he had to make. These compromises were necessary because the U.S. had no realistic way to coerce its allies to take actions that would undercut their immediate interests and feed their fears of insecurity. In the long run, however, Roosevelt was confident that America's liberal ideals would prevail—as indeed they eventually did, in many respects, when the communist system collapsed in Russia and Eastern Europe in the late 1980s and early 1990s.

Roosevelt embodied the liberal ideals of his generation: international cooperation under farsighted U.S. leadership, both in newly crafted institutions (e.g., United Nations, International Monetary Fund) and in less formal ways; increasing freedom of trade and investment, in order to provide the widespread prosperity that would help to maintain social peace within nations and prevent future wars between them; the gradual spread of democratic institutions, made possible by increased levels of education and prosperity; an end to colonialism and other forms of spheres of influence as the world moved closer together economically and politically; and a decrease in the worldwide supply of armaments as nations gained confidence in their ability to resolve conflicts nonviolently. Roosevelt articulated these ideals eloquently in his speeches and messages to Congress and in his radio addresses to the American people during the war.

Although Roosevelt believed in these ideals, he also was a highly practical leader who appreciated the importance of power in world affairs. He knew, for example, that Russian power would predominate in Eastern Europe, just as Britain and America would hold the high cards in other places including Italy, where, despite Soviet protests, the Americans and the British effectively excluded the Russians from influence in shaping the peace after the Italians surrendered in 1943. At Teheran, Roosevelt shared with Stalin his thinking about the "Four Policemen" who would be responsible for maintaining order after the war. In his view, Russia would be the "policeman" for Eastern Europe; Britain for Western Europe; China for Asia; and the United States for the Americas and the Pacific, presumably including Japan. Only Roosevelt, the master of the politics and diplomacy of ambiguity, could seriously consider ideas like these and yet tell Congress in March 1945 that the results of the recently completed Yalta Conference "ought to spell the end of the system of . . . spheres of influence, the balances of power, and all the other expedients that have been tried for centuries—and have always failed. We propose to substitute for all these a universal organization [the United Nations] in which all peace-loving nations will finally have a chance to join."

Roosevelt believed that communism would gradually evolve in the direction of capitalism and democracy, while the capitalist countries would continue to move toward providing more government services, thus permitting an eventual convergence between the two systems. If Western leaders (notably Roosevelt himself) worked to establish warm personal relations with Stalin, if America and Britain did not team up against Russia diplomatically, if legitimate Russian security needs were met, and if the Western allies kept showing the Soviet dictator that they—unlike Hitler—sought peace and prosperity for all, Roosevelt believed that Russia gradually could become a comfortable member of the U.S.-led family of nations. In the meantime, the president hoped that Stalin would pursue moderate measures in Eastern Europe in order to smooth the transition to the postwar world.

In implementing his two-part strategy to (a) keep the Russians in the war and (b) pave the way for a lasting peace, Roosevelt played down communist ideology as a motivating factor in Soviet foreign policy and treated Stalin, like Churchill, as the leader of a great power with whom he could make deals. Indeed, about the only area in which he did not try to deal with Stalin involved the secret U.S.-British effort to develop the atomic bomb, code-named the "Manhattan Project." Roosevelt and Churchill sought to keep this information secret from the Russians—as well as from everyone else except those working directly on the project.

Scholars disagree about the wisdom of Roosevelt's approach to the peace. Some believe, for example, that the president voluntarily should have shared information about the atomic bomb project with Stalin—especially in 1944 when he learned that Stalin already knew about it through spies—in order to lessen the Soviet dictator's suspicion about possible Anglo-American collaboration against him. In regard to Eastern Europe, most historians contend that Roosevelt did about as well as he could have, considering that Russian armies were occupying that region in 1944 and 1945. But other scholars think that Roosevelt conceded too much, arguing that he should have adopted a firm policy toward Stalin no later than 1944, perhaps even changing U.S. and British military strategy in order to "save" parts of eastern Germany and Eastern Europe for the West. Whatever one may think about Roosevelt's strategy for the peace, however, his largely cooperative, optimistic approach helped to keep the Grand Alliance functioning fairly smoothly—except for the Polish issue—until his death on April 12, 1945.

Despite Roosevelt's generally conciliatory approach and his awareness of Soviet power in Eastern Europe, the issue of the future of Poland led to serious strains in the Grand Alliance, especially during the last ten months of the war in Europe (July 1944–May 1945). Like the title characters in Shakespeare's *MacBeth* and *King Lear*, Poland's modern history almost defines the word "tragedy." With Russia to its east and Germany to its west, Poland at times has been independent, and at other times it has been swallowed up by one or both of its powerful neighbors. For the twenty years between the world wars

Poland had been independent; in September 1939 it had been divided between its two conquering neighbors; and in June 1941 the Germans seized all of it as part of their invasion of Russia. By 1944 the Russians were pushing the Germans back through Poland, whose postwar independence was very much in doubt.

In retrospect, the odds in 1944 of a freely chosen government ruling Poland after the war were, to use baseball star Dizzy Dean's phrase to describe the chances of a weak-hitting pitcher getting on base in a key situation, "slim or none." From Stalin's viewpoint, the reasons for ensuring Soviet control of Poland's postwar government were many and compelling. First, in his view, Russia had to have secure routes through Poland in order to prevent a German military resurgence; therefore a government "friendly" to Russia had to hold power in Warsaw. Second, given the long history of enmity between Poles and Russians, he believed that any freely chosen Polish government would display hostility toward the U.S.S.R. Third, the leaders of the Polish government in exile, located in London during the war, had confirmed Stalin's contention of their inherent hostility by publicizing the Katyn Forest massacre and by refusing to agree to return the land Poland had taken from Russia after World War I. In short, Stalin saw no possibility of a compromise that would achieve his goal of a pro-Soviet Polish government and his allies' desire for Polish self-determination.

As Soviet troops progressively occupied Poland during 1944 and early 1945, Stalin left little doubt that he intended to dominate postwar Poland. Having broken relations with the Polish government-in-exile more than a year earlier, he set up the communist-dominated Polish Committee of Liberation at Lublin in eastern Poland in July 1944. And despite a plea from Roosevelt, Stalin recognized the Lublin committee as the legitimate Polish government in January 1945.

Roosevelt and Churchill had one more chance—the Big Three conference at Yalta in February 1945—to try to work out arrangements that might permit a greater degree of self-determination for the Poles. In several conversations with Stalin, the two Western leaders eloquently expressed their concern for Polish independence. Facing an upcoming election in which the British public might well hold him accountable for Poland's fate, Churchill was especially vocal about the issue. In a meeting on February 6, Churchill entreated Stalin to permit Poland to exercise its "sovereign independence and freedom":

> I want the Poles to have a home in Europe and to be free to live their own lives there. . . . This is what is dear to the hearts of the nation of Britain. This is what we went to war against Germany for—that Poland should be free and sovereign. Everyone here knows . . . that it nearly cost us our life as a nation.

After a brief intermission, Stalin replied with equal conviction:

> The Prime Minister has said that for Great Britain the question of Poland is a question of honor. For Russia it is not only a question of honor but of security. . . . During the last thirty years our German enemy has passed through this corridor twice.

Roosevelt achieved many of his goals at Yalta, including a voting formula in the new United Nations organization, Soviet recognition of Jiang Jieshi's (Chiang Kai-shek) anticommunist government in China, and a definite Soviet commitment to enter the war against Japan. But despite his and Churchill's efforts, little was achieved on the Polish issue except vague agreements to "reorganize" the Lublin committee and to hold "free and unfettered elections" at some unspecified time in the future. In short, the communist Lublin group, subservient to Stalin, almost certainly would dominate postwar Poland. Yet Roosevelt, ever the skillful politician, largely hid this unpleasant fact from Congress and the American public—and from his vice president, Harry Truman—during the last six weeks of his life.

"Mr. President," Chief of Staff William D. Leahy commented while returning to Washington, "[the agreement on Poland] is so elastic that the Russians can stretch it all the way from Yalta to Washington without technically breaking it." Roosevelt replied, "I know it, Bill—I know it. But it's the best I can do for Poland at this time."

Why did Roosevelt care about Poland's future? Why didn't he graciously concede to Stalin what he almost certainly was going to take anyway, and tell Congress and the public that American power, while great, still was limited? There were several reasons: (a) like most other U.S. officials at the time, he did not want to see Europe divided between closed spheres of influence; (b) like Churchill and most Americans, he thought that the Poles—and other East Europeans—had a moral right to at least partial self-determination; and (c) he was well aware that it would hurt his party tremendously if the 6 million Polish Americans, who tended to vote heavily Democratic, concluded that Roosevelt had accepted Soviet domination of postwar Poland. Indeed, Roosevelt had assured Polish-American leaders before the 1944 elections that he supported a free and independent Poland, and he could not afford to renege on that promise. As a communist and as a citizen of a country that had never had an elected government, Stalin did not understand that voters in Western democracies—or at least enough of them to swing elections—made up their own minds.

In the weeks after Yalta, Roosevelt continued to warn Stalin that Russia's unilateral actions in Poland threatened U.S.-Soviet relations. He wrote Stalin on March 31 that "a thinly disguised continuation of the present Warsaw government would be entirely unacceptable, and would cause our people to regard the Yalta agreement as a failure."

The Polish issue thus illustrates a broader point about the coming of the Cold War. As much as from any of the many specific wartime and postwar dilemmas and disagreements, the Cold War grew out of the contrasting national traditions, political ideologies, and approaches to foreign policy—the different assumptions and ways of looking at the world—that formed a vast chasm between Soviet and Western leaders even as they collaborated in the war against Nazi Germany. Had he lived, and had he sought continued collaboration with Stalin, even Roosevelt, with all his political dexterity in placating a variety of domestic and foreign constituencies, might well have failed to prevent a sharp downturn in U.S.–Soviet relations once the spotlight in the West had shifted from Hitler's ideas and practices to Stalin's, and once Stalin himself could focus on new enemies.

The issue of what Roosevelt might or might not have been able to accomplish in U.S.-Soviet relations, had he lived, is fascinating to students of history, partly because it is important not to view historical developments as predetermined. But might-have-beens are always speculative, and the more important truth of what did happen emerged soon enough: U.S.-Soviet relations deteriorated rapidly after the war ended in August 1945.

CHAPTER ONE

Downward Spiral During the Truman-Stalin Years, 1945–1953

The Cold War Begins, 1945–1946

Beginning with post-Yalta acrimony over the fate of Eastern Europe in March and April 1945, Soviet relations with America and Britain deteriorated gradually and fitfully during 1945, and then more sharply and steadily after the turn of the year. Occasionally productive negotiations between the two sides continued in the Council of Foreign Ministers from the fall of 1945 until Secretary of State James Byrnes resigned in early 1947. But there could be little doubt that Truman intended to pursue a tough anti-Soviet policy when he attended Winston Churchill's famous "iron curtain" speech in Fulton, Missouri, in March 1946, and especially when he publicly fired Secretary of Commerce Henry Wallace that September, after Wallace made a speech urging greater American cooperation with Russia. So sharply had the once favorable public attitudes toward the former ally dropped by then, that Truman could count on strong public and congressional support for his decision to fire the controversial liberal cabinet member.

Of the major issues in dispute, none was more bitter than that of Eastern Europe, which Stalin believed had been settled in his favor in negotiations before and during the Yalta Conference. As usual, Roosevelt's actions in regard to Soviet behavior in Eastern Europe after Yalta were ambiguous: he expressed concern to Stalin about Soviet heavy-handedness, but urged Churchill to "minimize" the issue. In contrast, the forthright Truman denounced Soviet actions in Poland in a meeting with Foreign Minister Molotov on April 23. A believer in Woodrow Wilson's ideal of national self-determination, Truman tried numerous tactics, including a proposal for the internationalization of the Danube River and hard bargaining over peace treaties for Rumania and Bulgaria, to weaken Russian influence in the region. Few U.S. officials agreed with Secretary of War Henry Stimson, who argued that if the U.S. wanted peace with Russia, it had to acknowledge Soviet dominance in Eastern Europe, just as the other powers had to accept the U.S. sphere of influence in Latin America.

Early in the postwar period, Stalin did not insist on completely subservient governments in all of the Eastern European nations—Hungary was relatively independent internally until 1947, and Czechoslovakia until 1948. But because he viewed Eastern Europe as vital to Russia's security, the Soviet leader was determined to prevent any nation in the region from developing close economic or military ties with the West. By the late 1940s, handpicked leaders were installed by means of political purges and show trials of dissidents, until most of Eastern Europe, including all six countries that would join the U.S.S.R. to form the Warsaw Pact, were fully subservient to Stalin.

Another frequently acrimonious issue involved policy toward defeated Germany. During the war, official U.S. thinking on this issue had been confused and contradictory, wavering between a desire to impose a harsh peace that would end once and for all the threat of German militarism, and a desire to rehabilitate Germany as the cornerstone of future European prosperity. Russia, having suffered the most at the hands of Germany, was determined to keep it as weak as possible, partially by forcing it to pay substantial reparations in order to help rebuild Soviet industry. The Soviet leaders' deep fears of a possible German revival contributed to their determination to maintain a sphere of influence in Eastern Europe.

At Yalta, Stalin got Roosevelt to agree, "as a basis for negotiations," that Germany would have to pay $20 billion in reparations, half of it to Russia. At the Potsdam Conference of the Big Three in

July 1945, Stalin pressed his demand for $10 billion in reparations, to be collected primarily in Germany's industrialized western zones. But Truman and Byrnes, convinced of the need to rebuild German industry and fearful that U.S. aid dollars in effect would be used to pay for reparations from the western occupation zones, refused to agree to a dollar figure on reparations for Russia and suggested that the Soviets could remove whatever equipment they could locate from their own zone in the east.

U.S. leaders did allow Russia a small percentage "of such industrial capital equipment as is unnecessary for the German peace economy," but this vague agreement meant little in practice. Russian leaders complained that Western leaders had repudiated the spirit of Yalta and shown insensitivity to their legitimate needs for recovery. The failure at Potsdam to develop a common policy on Germany contributed to the gradual evolution of two Germanys, one allied with the West and one with the U.S.S.R.

A third issue that produced tensions, especially in 1946 and 1947, related to the "Northern Tier" countries: Greece, Turkey, and Iran. This was a region of traditional Anglo-Russian rivalry, with America becoming increasingly involved as it assumed the role of the economically weakened Britain. Due to internal instability, increasing importance as a source of oil, and proximity to important trade routes in the Middle East, the Northern Tier countries offered an inviting target for great power machinations. Russia had long wanted a guaranteed outlet through the Dardanelles strait to the Mediterranean, and national minorities in the mountainous regions in eastern Turkey and northern Iran were susceptible to Soviet influence. Moreover, Stalin did not see why the West should claim exclusive rights to Iran's huge oil reserves. Finally, despite Stalin's acceptance of Britain's dominant position in Greece, the right-wing Greek government was engaged in a bitter guerrilla war against communist-led opponents supplied by Yugoslavia and other communist nations to the north.

In the view of some Western leftists, Stalin callously abandoned the Greek rebels in exchange for British concessions in Eastern Europe. While Greece was in fact an example of Stalin's emphasis on pursuing Russia's self-interest rather than always supporting communist-led revolutionary movements abroad, the rebels still were able to mount a strong campaign against the British-backed government.

The first public Cold War crisis occurred in March 1946 in regard to Iran. When the Iranian government refused to grant Russia an oil concession equal to that given Britain, the Soviets supported a revolt in northern Iran and refused to withdraw their troops, as they had previously agreed to do, on March 2. Byrnes, whom Truman privately and others publicly had labeled as "soft" on Russia, now moved forcefully to demonstrate his resolve. On March 5 he sent a message to Moscow demanding the removal of Soviet troops from Iran, informed the press of his strong stand even before receiving a reply, and encouraged Iran to take the issue to the U.N. Security Council. After hearing of alleged Russian troop movements, Byrnes angrily told an associate, "Now we'll give it to them with both barrels."

Even though the Soviets declared in late March that their army was leaving Iran, Byrnes refused to remove the issue from the agenda of the U.N. Security Council. A week later, Russia and Iran announced an agreement on Soviet troop withdrawal, coupled with oil concessions for Russia. After the Russian troops were withdrawn, Iran, with U.S. support, reneged on the oil agreement and settled back into the Western sphere of influence.

Fourth, economic issues other than those relating specifically to Germany and Iran separated Russia and the West. Needing to rebuild their economy and at the same time arguing that they could help to prevent unemployment in the U.S. after the war, the Soviets in January 1945 requested a $6 billion loan at low interest. The request stirred debate within the administration, but Russia received no answer at either Yalta or Potsdam. In August the Soviets requested a $1 billion loan from the Export-Import Bank, but the State Department stalled on the issue, finally telling the Russians in February 1946 that the loan request was "one of a number of outstanding economic questions" between the two nations. By then relations had cooled so markedly that the administration almost certainly could not have obtained congressional approval for a loan even if it had asked for one. Russia, for its part, chose not to join the two U.S.-dominated organizations designed to ensure postwar prosperity, the World Bank and the International Monetary Fund. Stalin thus had decided that there would not be one cooperative world economy, as Western leaders had hoped, but rather two competing ones.

A fifth issue that harmed U.S.-Soviet relations was social instability and the related rise of the political left throughout Europe in the early postwar years. The devastation caused by the war, combined with the leadership of communist and socialist parties in opposing right-wing dictators like Hitler and Spain's Francisco Franco, led to the growing influence of left-wing parties in much of Western and Southern Europe. Russia was not responsible for the social instability and contributed only modestly to the rise of the left, but U.S. leaders feared that the Soviets might benefit from these trends and that such key Western countries as France and Italy might end up with governments dominated by communists with close ties to Moscow.

Another important issue involved U.S.-Soviet rivalry in East Asia, especially in regard to Japan and China. At Yalta, Stalin had won territorial concessions from Japan—notably the Kurile Islands and the southern half of Sakhalin Island—but Russia never achieved an effective voice in the occupation of Japan. "I was determined that the Japanese occupation would not follow in the footsteps of our German experience," Truman recalled. "I did not want divided control or separate zones." Soviet leaders negotiated vigorously in the early postwar period to try to increase their influence on Japan's reconstruction, but to no avail. Although American unilateralism in postwar Japan angered Stalin, there was little, short of declaring war, that he could do about it.

Under the leadership of General Douglas MacArthur, America dominated Japan, transforming the former enemy into a close and increasingly prosperous ally. Over Soviet objections, the United States and fifty other nations signed a peace treaty with Japan in September 1951, and in a separate security treaty the U.S. ensured that its armed forces and weapons could continue to be deployed there. As Edwin O. Reischauer noted in 1950, "Our position there is not very different from that of Russia in the smaller countries of Eastern Europe, however dissimilar our motives may be."

To put it mildly, U.S. policy was not as successful in China. Truman and most other U.S. officials wanted China to continue to be

America's ally, but they recognized that Jiang Jieshi's Nationalist government was corrupt and might not be able to win the long-standing civil war with the communists, led by Mao Zedong (Mao Tse-tung). Partly for its own reasons and partly because of pressure from Republicans, the Truman administration briefly sent fifty thousand U.S. troops to North China in 1945 to assist Jiang's forces in keeping Japanese-held land from being occupied by the Chinese communists, and continued to send substantial military and economic aid to Jiang's government through 1948. At the same time, especially during General George C. Marshall's mission to China in 1946, U.S. leaders urged Jiang to negotiate a compromise settlement with Mao. Sporadic negotiations between the two sides failed, and by 1948 the communists clearly were winning the civil war.

Frustrated by America's "failure" in China, conservative critics blamed Roosevelt for "selling out" China at Yalta and demanded that Truman take stronger measures to try to prevent a Nationalist Chinese defeat, but Truman refused in 1948 and 1949 to send U.S. troops to China. While some Americans blamed Russia for Jiang's difficulties, Stalin had given only modest aid to Mao and indeed was ambivalent about whether he even wanted the Chinese communists to win the civil war. The reality was that the Chinese themselves—not America or Russia—would decide their nation's future.

The last major issue—clearly the most portentous one—was policy toward atomic energy. America and Britain had worked together closely during the war to develop the atomic bomb. As was noted earlier, Roosevelt decided not to tell the Soviets about the project. Truman mentioned the new weapon to Stalin in a brief conversation at Potsdam in July 1945—but only after the first bomb was tested in New Mexico.

Upon hearing the news of the successful blast at the Japanese city of Hiroshima on August 6, which killed roughly eighty thousand people, Truman remarked to an associate that "this is the greatest thing in history." In a radio address explaining the significance of what had happened, the president reported deceptively that "Hiroshima, an important Japanese Army base," had been destroyed. A few days after a second atomic bomb obliterated Nagasaki on August 9, the war in the Pacific came to an end, and America's use of atomic weapons appeared vindicated.

Truman's decision to drop atomic bombs on densely populated Japanese cities without explicit warning was controversial within the government and the scientific community at the time, and it has been debated vigorously by historians and political scientists ever since. Careful studies of the issue by Martin J. Sherwin and other scholars have concluded that Truman did not use the weapons primarily to intimidate Russia, as some writers had charged; rather the decision resulted more from the momentum of bureaucratic decision making on the subject and from the assumption that any weapon available should be used to convince the "fanatical Japs" that continuing the war was futile, thereby avoiding a costly invasion of Japan. By 1945, few high U.S. officials had moral scruples about bombing civilians.

Whatever the precise role of U.S.-Soviet relations in Truman's decision to use atomic weapons, Stalin was apprehensive about America's possession of them. Germany, with its technological superiority, had come close to defeating Russia earlier in the war, and now Russia, despite its great victory, faced even greater insecurity. In mid-August a concerned Stalin told a high-level meeting in the Kremlin: "A single demand of you, comrades: Provide us with atomic weapons in the shortest possible time. You know that Hiroshima has shaken the whole world. The equilibrium has been destroyed. Provide the bomb. It will remove a great danger from us."

As historians Vladimir O. Pechanov and C. Earl Edmondson have shown, the hardening of Soviet policy, evident at the Foreign Ministers' meeting in September and in other actions that fall, was related in part to the intense anxiety apparent in Moscow after Hiroshima and Nagasaki. After meeting with people close to the Soviet leadership, Averell Harriman, the U.S. ambassador in Moscow, wrote Secretary of State Byrnes in November that the sudden appearance of the bomb "must have revived their own feeling of insecurity." Harriman noted that "the Russian people have been aroused to feel that they must again face an antagonistic world. American imperialism is included as a threat to Russia."

Given the enormous complexity of the issues involved in atomic energy and the deepening Cold War atmosphere, it was highly unlikely that America and Russia would have been able to agree in 1946 on international control of atomic energy and hence have prevented an atomic arms race. Nevertheless, the Truman administration made an effort, however flawed, in that direction. A carefully drafted study, directed by Assistant Secretary of State Dean Acheson and Tennessee Valley Authority director David Lilienthal, was completed in March. Their report proposed that an international "Atomic Development Authority" be established, with control over all aspects of nuclear energy. On-site inspections would be necessary to make international control workable.

While this proposal was fair, at least from the U.S. viewpoint, the Soviets almost certainly would have rejected it because of Stalin's determination to build a nuclear arsenal for his nation to ensure military equality with America. But the U.S. negotiator, Bernard Baruch, never gave the Acheson-Lilienthal proposal a chance. Instead, he made changes in it that strongly favored the United States, and then told his Soviet counterparts they would have to accept his entire proposal or get nothing. Not surprisingly, the Russians rejected the proposal, denouncing it as a disguise for a permanent U.S. atomic monopoly. America, in turn, rejected Russia's one-sided proposal that existing stocks of nuclear weapons be destroyed. Both nations thus continued their substantial nuclear programs, leading in 1949 to the first successful Soviet test and, in the early 1950s, to the decision by each government to develop the vastly more destructive hydrogen bombs.

The nuclear arms race quickly became a central feature of the Cold War, distinguishing the U.S.-Soviet rivalry from other great power conflicts in the past. Nuclear weapons both set limits to the struggle—that is, helped to keep it cold—and also intensified it in many ways, not the least of which was the fear in each country that the other might try to obliterate it in a surprise attack. Even at those times in which there were relatively few other major issues in dispute, the threat of nuclear destruction loomed like a thunderhead over U.S.-Soviet relations.

These seven major issues—and other lesser ones, such as the status of Korea—tended to separate Russia from America and Britain early in the postwar period. All of these issues posed genuine and difficult dilemmas for both sides; they were not merely pretexts for animosity. They all grew out of World War II and out of Germany's conquests in Europe and Japan's in Asia; they thus had their origins well before Truman replaced Roosevelt in April 1945 and Clement Attlee replaced Churchill as Britain's prime minister that July, and should not be viewed primarily as the consequence of inexperienced leadership. Given the intractability of the issues and the intensity of emotions on both sides as early as 1946, the leaders of Russia and the West deserve credit for maintaining at least the semblance of peace in Europe for more than a generation after World War II. Their behavior in Asia had more tragic consequences.

Although numerous images harmful to U.S.-Soviet relations flourished in the late 1940s, perhaps the most important ones were, on the U.S. side, the Munich analogy and the myth of American virtue and, on the Russian side, the myth of inevitable capitalist-imperialist hostility, contributing to an obsessive fear of Russia's own weakness, and the view that only the Soviets could ensure their own security. Within a year after the war there began to develop what have been called mirror-image official viewpoints: Russia (or, as seen from Moscow, America), with its threats and growing armaments, was pushing the world toward war.

The Munich Conference of 1938, at which the British and French caved in to Hitler's demand for western Czechoslovakia in the hope of maintaining peace, was a powerful symbol to many Americans of the dangers of appeasing an unscrupulous dictator. Ernest R. May and other historians have noted how deeply this analogy affected the thinking of leading American policymakers after the war, and how many tended to view Stalin as another Hitter bent on world domination. This was also the thinking of literally thousands of editorialists, radio commentators, politicians, business and labor leaders, clergy, and others who influenced popular opinion on foreign policy issues.

Stalin often was ruthless in defense of what he perceived to be Soviet interests in the areas he controlled. But, as his pullback from Iran in 1946 should have suggested, he was basically cautious and did not initiate war, as Hitler did. "The image of a Stalinist Russia poised and yearning to attack the West, and deterred only by our possession of atomic weapons," Kennan observed a decade later, "was largely a creation of the Western imagination." The Munich analogy, in short, not only clouded U.S. perceptions of world affairs, it also infuriated the Russians, who viewed comparison with the hated Nazis as an almost unspeakable obscenity.

The other vital image in understanding American attitudes and behavior was the myth of unusual virtue and superiority to other nations, what historian T. H. Von Laue has called "unconscious ethnocentric arrogance." This was simply the view, reinforced strongly by the nation's involvement in World War II, that America was the hope of the world both in its wondrous internal institutions and in its selfless commitment to world peace, justice, and prosperity. A public opinion survey in the summer of 1946 found that only 15 percent of all Americans were satisfied with the current state of international relations, and that most of the rest blamed Britain and, especially, Russia for their discontent. "Their own country, on the other hand, seemed to them to be trying steadfastly to achieve justice and harmony," the public opinion analysts concluded. "It was, if anything, too generous with its material goods, and too lenient toward those governments which place obstacles in the road toward these goals."

As Stalin allegedly was following in Hitler's footsteps, so Truman, many Americans thought, was bringing to fruition the noble ideals of Woodrow Wilson and Franklin Roosevelt. Even those Americans who did not like Truman's policies still envisaged their nation as the world's virtuous leader. Critics as diverse as Commerce Secretary Wallace and conservative Senator Robert Taft (Rep., Ohio), for example, agreed with Truman that America had a unique and noble destiny. This proposition, while accepted with reservations by many West Europeans grateful for American assistance against the Nazis and in postwar recovery, obviously was not considered self-evident in Moscow.

In increasingly virulent official statements in leading newspapers like *Pravda* (Truth) and elsewhere, the Russians also trumpeted the superiority of their system and its eventual triumph over decadent capitalism. At the same time, they insisted that the West was preparing to attack the Soviets in order to destroy their way of life. This second image more accurately reflected their feelings of insecurity, their technological inferiority in the military and other sectors, and their growing isolation in world affairs. Their isolation, in turn, was intensified by their own vitriolic propaganda, their frequent rudeness and deviousness in diplomatic gatherings, their brutal suppression of dissent in Eastern Europe, and their highly publicized spying in the West. While these measures may have been necessary in their view to ensure their security, they may well have lessened Russia's actual security by inspiring alliances against it. As both nations were to discover (but not necessarily to learn) several times during the Cold War, an obsession with security may actually decrease it and lead to the brink of war.

Finally, what role did domestic politics play in the shift toward Cold War in 1945 and 1946? Because of Stalin's virtually complete control, Russia did not have domestic politics in the Western sense. But there was a strong public desire for greater freedom and for more consumer goods now that Nazi Germany had been defeated. Today's liberated Russian historians acknowledge that there existed considerable public sentiment for improved relations with the West, including increased trade. None of these desires were to be realized, however: Stalin called for further sacrifices to deter possible Western threats and unleashed his secret police to clamp down on the independent thought and expression that had been permitted, within limits, to improve morale during the war.

In America, jockeying for political advantage never stops, even in wartime. With the popular Roosevelt dead and the war over, Republicans saw an opportunity to gain control of Congress in the 1946 elections and to take the presidency two years later. On domestic issues, they could run against the federal government and labor unions, both of which had become more powerful during the Roosevelt years. They could also run against the open influence of the Moscow-controlled American Communist party in labor unions and against its largely secret infiltration of other institutions, including the federal government. On foreign policy issues, the Republicans could denounce Truman's "weakness" in dealing with Russia—unless the administration clearly stood up to the U.S.S.R.

While there were limits to what Truman could do to deflect the Republican challenge on domestic issues, he could stand up to the Soviets—a policy shift urged on him in the fall of 1945 by his White House Chief of Staff, Admiral William Leahy, and by the two leading senators on the Foreign Relations Committee, Democrat Tom Connally of Texas and Republican Arthur Vandenberg of Michigan. Vandenberg, whose state contained a large number of Polish Americans plus even more anticommunist Republicans, was adamant that Russia should be opposed firmly on all fronts.

Truman never revealed just what effect domestic politics had on his decision by early January 1946 to stop "babying the Soviets." But he was very much aware of growing congressional criticism of Byrnes's continuing efforts to make deals with them and by congressional efforts, now that the war was over, to assert authority on particular foreign policy issues. While Byrnes, after a tongue-lashing by Truman in January 1946, was allowed to continue to negotiate with Russia, he was instructed to emphasize a strong anti-Soviet stand in his public statements. In this case, Truman almost certainly was affected by strong pressures from Congress to take a harder line toward the U.S.S.R.

It is true that, as the Cold War developed, the administration's options in U.S.-Soviet relations were limited by the almost universal anti-Russian sentiment that its own anti-Soviet statements and policies had helped to solidify. But both the public and the press had numerous sources other than the administration on policy toward Russia, and these were largely hostile to Moscow by March 1946. In the midterm election that fall, Americans of East European descent, angry about communist gains in their former homelands, deserted the Democrats in droves to help the Republicans gain control of both houses of Congress for the first time since 1928. Especially after this election, it was only natural that the beleaguered administration would embrace the widespread and growing anti-Soviet sentiment in the nation and try to turn it to its own political advantage.

Containment and Countercontainment, 1947–1949

The events that signaled the enunciation of a definite U.S. policy of "containment" of communism occurred in rapid-fire succession in a crisis-laden atmosphere from February through July of 1947. The spark that set off the chain reaction inside the government was the British message to the State Department, delivered on February 21, that, because of internal economic difficulties, Britain would have to stop giving military and economic aid to Greece and Turkey as of

March 31. Top officials—already concerned about Western Europe's economic problems, exacerbated by severe winter weather—quickly agreed that America would need to assume Britain's role in order to prevent the spread of Soviet influence in the region. The problem was to convince an economy-minded, Republican-controlled Congress to make prompt and substantial commitments to these countries.

In a meeting with congressional leaders at the White House on February 27, Truman, newly installed Secretary of State George Marshall, and other officials presented their case. When Marshall's low-key presentation failed to sway the congressmen, Undersecretary of State Dean Acheson asked to speak. The influence of the democracies in world affairs had been declining ever since the end of the war, Acheson declared, while Russia had been expanding its influence. If Greece or Turkey now fell under its sway, Asia, Africa, and the Middle East would be open to Soviet penetration. Moreover, Soviet ideology was implacably hostile to the West, and the division of the world was more profound than at any time since the ancient rivalry between Rome and Carthage. Failure to act thus would create a grave threat to American security. "Mr. President," a shaken Senator Vandenberg said when Acheson had finished, "if you will say that to the Congress and the country, I will support you and I believe that most of its members will do the same."

On March 12, before a joint session of Congress and a nationwide radio audience, Truman did just that. The president did refer to the situation in Greece and Turkey, and he did ask for $400 million in aid for the two nations. But in the best-known part of the speech he sweepingly divided the world in two and, in what became known as the Truman Doctrine, pledged American assistance to the "free peoples":

> At the present moment in world history nearly every nation must choose between alternative ways of life. The choice is too often not a free one.
>
> One way of life is based upon the will of the majority, and is distinguished by free institutions, representative government, free elections, guarantees of individual liberty, freedom of speech and religion, and freedom from political oppression.

> The second way of life is based upon the will of a minority forcibly imposed upon the majority. It relies upon terror and oppression, a controlled press and radio, fixed elections, and the suppression of political freedoms.
>
> I believe that it must be the policy of the United States to support free peoples who are resisting attempted subjugation by armed minorities or by outside pressures.

As Henry Wallace and some other commentators pointed out afterward, the governments America would be supporting in Greece and Turkey were a far cry from the ideal represented in Truman's speech. Even some within the administration, such as Kennan, considered the apparent commitments in the speech too imprecise and far-reaching. But Truman's approval rating in public opinion polls increased from 49 percent in January to 60 percent in late March, and the percentage of Americans who viewed foreign policy issues as the most important facing the nation shot up from 22 percent in December to 54 percent in March. Despite grumbling from some in Congress who believed that they had no choice but to approve the aid measure now that the president had staked U.S. prestige on it, the Senate approved the expenditure by a vote of 67 to 23 in late April, and the House concurred in early May by 287 to 107, with solid Republican as well as Democratic majorities in favor. With the Cold War in full swing for the following fifteen years, both Democratic and Republican presidents could count on strong congressional support, especially when military spending was involved.

In a commencement address at Harvard University on June 5, Secretary of State Marshall made a general offer of economic aid to Europe in order to facilitate "the revival of a working economy in the world so as to permit the emergence of political and social conditions in which free institutions can exist." This offer led to the development of the Marshall Plan and the eventual expenditure of more than $12 billion in economic aid, which proved invaluable in restoring the economies of Western Europe and earned the enduring gratitude of millions of citizens of the nations involved. Not entirely altruistic, the Marshall Plan led to large orders for goods in America and to greatly increased U.S. trade and investment in Europe. Unwilling to accept the strings inevitably attached by American oversight of the program, Russia declined to participate, and forced its satellites to do likewise.

The final highlight of this period of intense activism in U.S. foreign relations was the appearance, in the July issue of the prestigious journal *Foreign Affairs*, of an article entitled "The Sources of Soviet Conduct" and written by "X" (soon identified as Kennan). In an administration short on experienced and knowledgeable students of Soviet behavior, the articulate, scholarly Kennan emerged as the leading U.S. government expert on Russia. Called home from Russia in 1946 and installed by May 1947 as head of the State Department's Policy Planning Staff, Kennan provided theoretical underpinnings for American policy in the early postwar period.

Given the Cold War atmosphere, it is not surprising that most of his colleagues paid more attention to his scathing indictments of the Soviet system and its alleged tendency toward expansionism than they did to his calls for restraint and balance in American policy. The "X" article, which first used the word "containment" to describe U.S. policy toward Russia and which was the most famous of Kennan's writings, focused on the evils of Soviet communism and urged "a long-term, patient but firm and vigilant containment of Russian expansive tendencies" to be achieved, in part, by the "application of counter-force at a series of constantly shifting geographical and political points."

In his memoirs, published in 1967, Kennan regretted his "failure to make clear that what I was talking about . . . was not the containment by military means of a military threat, but the political containment of a political threat." Regardless of what Kennan may have wished he had included, the "X" article as written clearly contributed to the deepening hostility toward Russia in 1947 and 1948.

Apart from the often self-righteous rhetoric, what did containment mean in practice between 1947 and 1949? Contrary to the warlike language of Truman's speech to Congress, before 1950 it did not mean a global anticommunist crusade, but rather a more limited one in which distinctions between vital and peripheral interests were made. While recognizing the tendency of even the most carefully conceived policy to bend with events, five overarching trends seem clear:

1. Major economic and military commitments abroad, centered in Europe and more limited elsewhere than they would become after

early 1950. Within Europe, the greatest emphasis was given to increasing the strength of the western zones in Germany, which in May 1949 became the Federal Republic of Germany.

2. The limiting of defense spending to what Truman believed the nation could afford (about $12–14 billion per year), leading to an emphasis in military planning on nuclear weapons—still a U.S. monopoly—to deter possible Soviet attacks.
3. Open support for any communist nation willing to break with Moscow (e.g., Tito's Yugoslavia), and covert support (e.g., through activities of the Central Intelligence Agency, established in July 1947) to opponents of Stalin in Eastern Europe.
4. An unwillingness to send massive U.S. aid to forestall a communist victory in the civil war in China, despite pleas from right-wing Republicans and others to "save Jiang."
5. An unwillingness to explore seriously with Russia possible areas of compromise in regard to major European issues (e.g., Germany).

While most of these themes of U.S. strategic thinking in the late 1940s are fairly self-explanatory, the last one requires elucidation. Because high U.S. officials normally did not test seriously the occasional Soviet offers of negotiations on major issues between 1947 and 1953, it is difficult to judge the Russian leaders' sincerity. In the spring of 1947, for example, Stalin gave a friendly interview to Governor Harold Stassen of Minnesota and, in the Council of Foreign Ministers meeting in Moscow, had Molotov suggest renewed bargaining on Germany. But Western leaders were suspicious of Soviet intentions—a suspicion enhanced by Foreign Minister Molotov's frigid personality and his persistent rejection of U.S. proposals—and Marshall reported upon returning to Washington that no progress had been made on major issues.

After the failure of the Moscow talks, there was little serious negotiating on major East-West issues during the remainder of the Truman-Stalin years. Although Soviet officials deserve their share of the blame for tensions during these years, it is also true that Marshall and his successor, Acheson, interested as they were in denouncing Soviet behavior and in creating "situations of strength" prior to serious negotiations, contributed to the ominous breakdown of East-West diplomacy after 1947. "There is only one language they understand, force," Truman remarked to an associate in 1949. As historian Alonzo L. Hamby has noted, "The president and his subordinates celebrated American superiority, engaged in self-righteous stubbornness toward the Soviet Union, and clothed even their most constructive proposals in the garments of American mission and destiny."

In the late 1940s Stalin demonstrated that hard-nosed containment was a game two could play. Denouncing the Truman Doctrine and Marshall Plan as a capitalist offensive against his regime, the Soviet dictator took steps which, from his viewpoint, contained the West. The noncommunist, elected Hungarian leader, Ferenc Nagy, was removed from office in May 1947; the Cominform—which included the French and Italian communist parties as well as those of Russia and six East European ones—was established in September 1947 to tighten Moscow's control over the international communist movement; and, in a move that shocked Western opinion, Soviet collaborators overthrew the elected Czechoslovak government in February 1948. Czech leaders had made the mistake of agreeing to accept aid under the Marshall Plan, a move quickly squelched by Moscow but which nevertheless had proved their "unreliability." Both the mysterious death in early March of Czech Foreign Minister Jan Masaryk, a friend of the West, and the widely doubted explanation that he had committed suicide by jumping out of a window, symbolized for many the brutality of Stalinism.

The Berlin crisis of 1948–49 provided another excellent example of the reciprocal nature of containment. Just as the Marshall Plan appears to have played a part in precipitating the events in Czechoslovakia, so Allied steps toward organizing a separate West German state and introducing a new currency for West Germany apparently led the Soviets to impose, in late June 1948, a complete blockade of all surface routes through eastern Germany to West Berlin, which since the war had remained an enclave under the three Western powers' control inside East Germany. An outpost of relative economic prosperity and political freedom more than one hundred miles inside the Soviet sphere, West Berlin was, as Nikita Khrushchev later put it, a "bone in the throat" of Russia. Fearing above all else a strong and rearmed West Germany, Stalin apparently believed that the blockade would force the West to negotiate with Russia a settlement of the German issue as a whole.

If that was indeed Stalin's reasoning, he made a serious miscalculation, for by this time Truman obviously was not going to accommodate Russia, especially not under duress during an uphill presidential campaign. The president responded with a massive and continuing airlift of supplies to the more than 2 million West Berliners and the Allied personnel stationed there. Although tensions frequently ran high, neither side wanted war: Stalin kept channels for negotiation open, and Truman did not force the issue of Western surface access rights to Berlin. After negotiations in Moscow failed during the summer, the tendency in Washington was to forget about negotiating with Russia and step up planning for a formal Western military alliance, established in April 1949 as the North Atlantic Treaty Organization (NATO), and for a West German state, led by the staunchly anticommunist Konrad Adenauer.

By November 1948 Kennan was concerned about the West's "general preoccupation with military affairs, to the detriment of economic recovery and of the necessity for seeking a peaceful solution to Europe's difficulties." In retrospect, this concern seems largely justified. But it must be added that Stalin's moves were themselves contributing to the increased militarization of Western policy that the Soviet leader so greatly feared. And it also should be pointed out that, after Czechoslovakia and Berlin, the Truman administration clearly was acting in accord with public sentiment. The respected Survey Research Center of the University of Michigan reported in October 1948 an "almost unanimous belief that Russia is an aggressive, expansion-minded nation," and noted an "overwhelming demand for firmness and increased 'toughness' in relations with Russia. . . ."

Their blockade having failed either to isolate Berlin or to change Western policy elsewhere in Germany, the Soviets signaled in early 1949 their interest in ending this dangerous stalemate. With normal diplomatic channels disrupted, Stalin on January 30 used his reply to a question by journalist Kingsbury Smith to suggest the possibility of fruitful negotiations. With America then taking the initiative, secret discussions took place in February and March between the Deputy U.S. Representative to the UN Security Council, Philip C. Jessup, and his Soviet counterpart, Jacob Malik. After significant Soviet concessions, on May 5 an announcement was made that the blockade would be lifted on May 12 and that a Council of Foreign Ministers meeting to focus on German issues would convene in Paris on May 23. Although the United Nations had failed in the years since 1945 to live up to the hopes of its founders, it nevertheless proved its worth as the locus for delicate and important international negotiations.

When Secretary of State Acheson returned to Washington after the completion of the Council of Foreign Ministers meeting, he was, according to *Time*'s lead story in its issue of July 4, 1949, "pleased but not complacent." According to Acheson, since 1947 "the position of the West has grown greatly in strength, and that . . . of the Soviet Union in regard to the struggle for the soul of Europe has changed from the offensive to the defensive." In his statement concerning the meeting, Truman emphasized that Britain, France, and the United States had shown great unity in dealing with Russia.

From their viewpoint, Truman and Acheson had reason to be pleased with overall developments in Europe since those hectic days when the Truman Doctrine was being formulated early in 1947. Buoyed by substantial U.S. support, the Greek government gradually had defeated the insurgency, and both Greece and Turkey had become members of the Western alliance. Austria, although still occupied by Russian as well as Western troops, clearly was tilting toward the West. The Marshall Plan had strengthened the economies of most West European nations, including France and Italy, whose Communist parties had failed in their bid for power. Compared with eastern Germany, the western zones already were an economic and political showcase, and Berlin had become a symbol of the West's determination to stand up to the Russians.

Even in Eastern Europe, Yugoslavia's Tito had broken with Stalin in 1948, and he was showing definite signs of being able to maintain his independent course, in part because of U.S. economic aid. Covert CIA activities were underway on a substantial scale in Eastern Europe, and Radio Free Europe and Radio Liberty were beaming the West's propaganda behind the "iron curtain." More seriously, political repression and economic difficulties were sapping the vitality of East European nations. In a Europe caught between containment and countercontainment, the West was more than holding its own.

Significantly, the *Time* article, which had begun by praising Acheson's work in Europe, ended by denouncing the administration's policy in Asia. After reporting that twenty-one senators had criticized "the bankrupt U.S. policy toward China," the influential magazine concluded: "Time, and the Russian tide, were working against the Western nations in Asia. What had to be done had to be done fast." Much to the dismay of *Time* and of many Americans, the communists finally won the Chinese civil war that fall, and Jiang fled to the island of Taiwan. And to the surprise and dismay of administration officials, Russia exploded its first atomic bomb that September. Like some earlier shooting wars, the Cold War was getting nastier and less manageable with each passing month.

The Most Dangerous Phase, 1950–1952

Of all the years between the end of World War II and the end of the communist system in Eastern Europe in 1989, 1950 stands out as the most fateful in terms of America's stance in the Cold War. Before the year ended, the U.S. had more than tripled its defense budget, was openly aiding Jiang on Taiwan and the French in Indochina, was fighting North Korean and Chinese troops in Korea, had committed itself to the rearmament of West Germany and the stationing of more than four divisions of its own troops in Western Europe, was moving rapidly to develop the hydrogen bomb, and was negotiating for new military bases in Spain and elsewhere.

In testimony about NATO on April 27, 1949, Acheson had assured concerned senators that "the disarmament and demilitarization of Germany must be complete and absolute," that America did not plan to send a large number of troops to defend Europe, that the administration was not contemplating security agreements with nations outside the North Atlantic region, and that membership in NATO did not imply acceptance of European colonialism in Africa and Asia. Partly as the result of opportunities and dangers created by the Korean War, the administration by the end of 1950 reneged on all of these assurances.

The early 1950s were the most dangerous phase of the Cold War not because of the Korean War in itself, but rather because of what the Korean War confirmed: namely, that both sides, prisoners by now of the Cold War tendencies to miscalculate and to think the worst of the other's intentions, were prone to tragic errors of policy. It also was highly dangerous because, in the wake of the communist victory in China in October 1949, neither America nor Russia had a clearly formulated policy in Asia, as events quickly confirmed. Whereas both sides' vital interests in Europe had been largely delineated by the summer of 1949, neither side was able, even in the early 1950s, to develop a coherent, workable strategy toward Asia. If ever there was an experience that demonstrates the dangers of blocking the channels of effective communication and proceeding on the basis of ideology, dubious assumptions, and domestic pressures, this period was such a time.

Many of the errors of U.S. policy during the last years of the Truman administration appear, at least in general terms, in National Security Council Paper Number 68, one of the most significant documents of the Cold War. Prepared under the leadership of Paul Nitze, Kennan's hawkish replacement as head of the Policy Planning Staff, the secret NSC-68 called for a U.S.-led offensive against Soviet influence in the world. Viewing communism as monolithic, the policy report called for a firm response to communist aggression anywhere and in whatever form it might appear. It also suggested that America should work to remove Russian power from Eastern Europe, a policy proposal that soon came to be known as "rollback" or "liberation."

"The assault on free institutions is world-wide now, and in the context of the present polarization of power a defeat of free institutions anywhere is a defeat everywhere," the report noted ominously. Responding to the explosion of the first Soviet atomic bomb, NSC-68 argued that "[t]he Soviet Union is developing the military capacity to support its design for world domination" and asserted that it might be able to launch a powerful attack against the West by 1954. To meet the communist threat, the report urged a vast increase in U.S. defense spending, stepped-up covert activities, and other actions to increase the nation's power and that of its allies.

Although NSC-68 was completed in April 1950, Truman did not approve it until September, three months after the outbreak of war in Korea. By then its hard-line conclusions appeared highly plausible, especially to those who viewed the Korean War as just one step in the Kremlin's "design for world domination." Most historians today view

NSC-68 as alarmist in its description of Soviet intentions and mistaken in its assumption of a monolithic communist bloc. NSC-68 also exaggerated the Soviet military threat to the West.

Even before the Korean War, the administration was moving away from Kennan's original emphasis on containment of Russia to the NSC-68 emphasis on opposing communism wherever it might appear, even if it was associated with an indigenous revolutionary movement against a repressive or colonial government. In so doing, U.S. officials were making two errors of policy, one in regard to China and the other in regard to Vietnam. In China the administration was moving toward the decision, cemented in stone by the Korean War, to continue to treat Jiang's regime on Taiwan as the sole government of China, even after it had lost control of every Chinese province except Taiwan, and to have no relations with Mao's government on the mainland, which actually ruled the overwhelming majority of Chinese.

Refusing to establish diplomatic ties with China largely because its government was communist was inconsistent: America maintained diplomatic relations with the most powerful communist nation, Russia, and with its satellite nations in Eastern Europe. But the decision with regard to China was understandable in the tense conditions of late 1949 and early 1950. Because Truman disliked China's new regime and did not want to show any signs of weakness in standing up to communism, he believed that recognition should come only when the new Chinese leaders demonstrated that they wanted good relations with the U.S. Yet China's new leader, Mao, was moving in the opposite direction: seeking improved relations with Stalin and proclaiming his commitment to the communist cause, he went to Moscow in the winter of 1949–50 to seek friendship with, and aid from, Russia. The Chinese also arrested an American official and seized buildings that had housed the U.S. consulate in Beijing (Peking). Mao's unfriendly actions and anti-American rhetoric made it clear that, in order to recognize his government, U.S. leaders would have to decide that it was in their own long-term interest to do so. Instead, the administration mirrored the hostility, with Truman by 1951 referring to the Chinese government as "that cutthroat organization" and "a bunch of murderers" whom he would never recognize.

Whereas in its China policy the key issue was whether the administration could accept the communist victory in the civil war and gradually encourage China's traditional nationalistic rivalry with Russia, in its policy toward Vietnam the dilemma was whether to support French colonialism or Asian nationalism. Because America historically had stood for self-determination and because Roosevelt generally had opposed the reinstatement of European colonialism in Asia after World War II, it might appear that this would have been an easy choice in favor of supporting the Vietnamese. In the eyes of administration leaders, it definitely was not. Vietnam's drive for independence from France was led by Ho Chi Minh, a communist trained in Moscow in the 1920s, whereas France played a pivotal role in Acheson's plans for a united, militarily strong Western Europe. Moreover, U.S. officials feared the possible expansion of Mao's influence in Asia and believed that a capitalist Southeast Asia—an underdeveloped area that could provide markets and serve as a source of raw materials—was needed to ensure economic growth in Western Europe and Japan.

On a visit to Paris in May 1950, therefore, Acheson acceded to France's long-standing request for military and economic aid in Indochina. "The United States Government," Acheson declared in his fateful announcement that marked the first step in the ever-increasing U.S. involvement in Vietnam during the 1950s and 1960s, "convinced that neither national independence nor democratic evolution exist in any area dominated by Soviet imperialism, considers the situation such as to warrant its according economic aid and military equipment to the Associated States [French-sponsored puppet governments in Indochina] and to France."

Even more than in its China policy, the administration was permitting its obsession with the evils of communism to cloud its thinking. Although he was a communist, Ho was also a nationalist determined not to become subservient to Moscow or Beijing. "It is better to sniff French dung for a while than eat China's all our life," he once observed in a comment reflecting Vietnam's traditional hatred of Chinese domination. The administration's error lay not in failing to support Ho, which hardly could have been expected in the anticommunist atmosphere of the late 1940s and early 1950s, but in attaching itself to French colonialism, which was highly unpopular throughout

Asia. As historian George C. Herring has concluded, "Regardless of his ideology, Ho by 1950 had captured the standard of Vietnamese nationalism, and by supporting France . . . the United States was attaching itself to a losing cause."

In fairness to Truman and his advisers, it should be noted that the decision to aid the French in Vietnam did not appear to be momentous at the time, and that the decision to continue to support Jiang evolved only gradually, more slowly than many domestic critics of the administration would have liked. Indeed, the "loss" of China unleashed an often vicious barrage of criticism against the administration for its alleged foreign policy failures. The bipartisanship that had dominated foreign policy decisions in Congress from the passage of the aid to Greece and Turkey in 1947 through the acceptance of U.S. participation in NATO in the summer of 1949 was at a low ebb. The Democrats were losing the Cold War, critics like Congressman Richard Nixon (Rep., Calif.) and Senator Kenneth Wherry (Rep., Nebr.) charged. The administration was doing too much in Europe and too little in Asia, Senator Robert Taft (Rep., Ohio) insisted, and it was spending far too much money for the meager results it had been achieving. Such charges apparently were having an impact: America was falling behind in the Cold War, a plurality of respondents told the pollsters, and Russia was winning.

For better or worse, accusations by leaders of the opposition party that the administration in office was losing the Cold War were a recurring feature of American political rhetoric from 1949 through 1980. What was different in this highly dangerous phase of the Cold War was that, in addition, Senator Joseph McCarthy (Rep., Wis.) and others were charging that high U.S. officials were traitors to their country, that at least some of the major foreign policy developments of the late 1940s resulted from disloyalty to America.

This reckless attack, which others started well before McCarthy discovered the publicity to be gained from it, was given credence by the arrest and conviction of several people on charges of spying on the U.S. atomic energy program, and especially by the charge in 1948 that Alger Hiss, an official in the State Department under Roosevelt, had been a Soviet spy during the 1930s—a charge that documents released from Soviet archives in the 1990s proved to be accurate. The charges and countercharges relating to the Hiss case made headlines throughout 1949, and on January 21, 1950, Hiss was convicted of perjury in connection with testimony before the House Un-American Activities Committee. On February 9, McCarthy made the first of his sensational, never-substantiated charges that there were large numbers of communists in the State Department.

The sharp attacks on Truman's foreign policy and on the loyalty of high officials (including Acheson and Secretary of Defense Marshall) helped to keep the administration on the defensive during the remainder of Truman's term. Seeing political gain, responsible Republican leaders refused to criticize McCarthy and the others who were trafficking in innuendo and fear, and the president's sharp criticisms of McCarthy tended to be dismissed as self-serving. The anti-communist hysteria and the denunciation of the nation's leaders placed Truman in a no-win situation: no matter how strongly he opposed Stalin, Mao, Ho, and the other "communist devils," he could never do enough to satisfy his critics.

The vocal right-wing critics of the administration were especially vehement in their denunciations of Acheson, whose resignation or firing was demanded repeatedly after the communist victory in China, and again after the outbreak of the Korean War. In his National Press Club address in January 1950, Acheson had reiterated the administration's position that the American "defensive perimeter" ran from Alaska to Japan and then south to the Ryukyu Islands and the Philippines. Those friends of the West living on the mainland of Asia would need to depend first upon their own efforts and then "upon the commitments of the entire civilized world under the Charter of the United Nations." After Russian-backed communist North Korea began its invasion of U.S.-backed, capitalist South Korea on June 25, Acheson's critics were quick to blame him for the attack on the grounds that he had given North Korea the green light by not including South Korea within America's line of defense. Acheson, a lawyer before becoming a statesman, sought to defend himself by citing his reference to UN commitments and by noting that America had taken the lead, through the UN, in coming to South Korea's defense.

Why did the North Koreans attack? The main reason was the desire of the North Korean government, led by Kim Il Sung, to unify

Korea under its leadership. The U.S.-Soviet decision to divide Korea temporarily at the 38th parallel at the end of World War II was purely arbitrary, and both the North Koreans and the South Koreans, under Syngman Rhee, wanted to unite the country. Indeed, their troops had skirmished repeatedly during the late 1940s in the area near the 38th parallel.

By early 1950, Kim had decided that he wanted to try to conquer South Korea and sought support from Stalin and Mao. Fresh from his own victory in China, Mao encouraged Kim's plans; but Stalin hesitated, fearing U.S. intervention to save Rhee. Finally, after about fifty telegrams and a visit from Kim, Stalin gave his consent in April—but only if Mao also approved. "If you should get kicked in the teeth, I shall not lift a finger," Stalin told Kim. "You have to ask Mao for all the help." When Kim visited Beijing in May to ask for China's support, Mao also was reluctant at first, citing the danger of U.S. intervention. Partly because Kim portrayed Stalin as more optimistic about the chances for success than in fact he was, Mao eventually approved Kim's plan.

Stalin had put Mao in a tough spot. If he said yes, he might well have to send Chinese soldiers to fight the Americans in Korea, thus putting aside his highest priority: defeating Jiang Jieshi and establishing his own rule on Taiwan. If he said no, he would appear to be going against the wishes of the leader of the communist movement, Stalin, as well as upsetting Kim and raising doubts about his commitment to leading the revolutionary movement in Asia. A personal motive also may have influenced Mao: if Chinese troops did end up fighting U.S. forces in Korea, the proud, ambitious leader would get credit among other communists for his courage in "fighting imperialism."

Records of Stalin's meetings with Kim suggest that the Soviet leader approved the invasion—and provided Soviet advisers to plan it and military equipment to make it possible—for several reasons. He believed that Mao's victory in China and the Soviet atomic bomb had improved the "international environment." He also told Kim that "information coming from the United States" suggested that America would not send troops to defend Rhee.

Although Stalin had spies in Washington who had access to secret U.S. documents suggesting that America would not defend South

Korea, he did not need spies to know that the U.S. had withdrawn its forces from South Korea in mid-1949 and placed that nation outside its defense perimeter early in 1950. In retrospect, both of these U.S. moves look like first-class blunders, especially considering that 33,000 Americans and an estimated 2 million Koreans and Chinese died in the conflict.

And why did the Truman administration respond so decisively to a situation that might well have been viewed as a civil war between Koreans? The main reason was Truman's belief that America's credibility as the leader of the noncommunist world was being tested. "If this was allowed to go unchallenged it would mean a third world war, just as similar incidents had brought on the second world war," Truman later remembered thinking as he rushed back to Washington to plan the U.S. response. "It was also clear to me that the foundations and the principles of the United Nations were at stake unless this unprovoked attack on South Korea could be stopped."

Truman, who vividly recalled the 1930s and was sensitive to the attacks on the administration for its "weakness" in Asia, never hesitated to act forcefully in this situation. Indeed, if any communist leaders genuinely thought that he would do otherwise, they were sadly misinformed about both the president and the political climate in which he operated. Truman received strong support for military action from his cabinet, leaders of both parties in Congress, the press, and public opinion polls. He also received a lucky break when, due to Russia's continued boycott of the UN Security Council for its failure to seat Mao's government, the administration was able to conduct its military operations against North Korea under UN auspices.

Just as the Soviets and Chinese would have been pleased to have Korea united under Kim, so leading U.S. officials, refusing to recognize the North Korean government, had long desired the unification of the country according to Western principles. Thus, the administration did not hold for long to its original public objective in the Korean War—driving the North Koreans out of South Korea and restoring the 38th parallel as the boundary between the two sides. Instead, under pressure from the U.S. commander, General Douglas MacArthur, and some officials in Washington, by September the administration had decided to try to destroy the North Korean army and unite the penin-

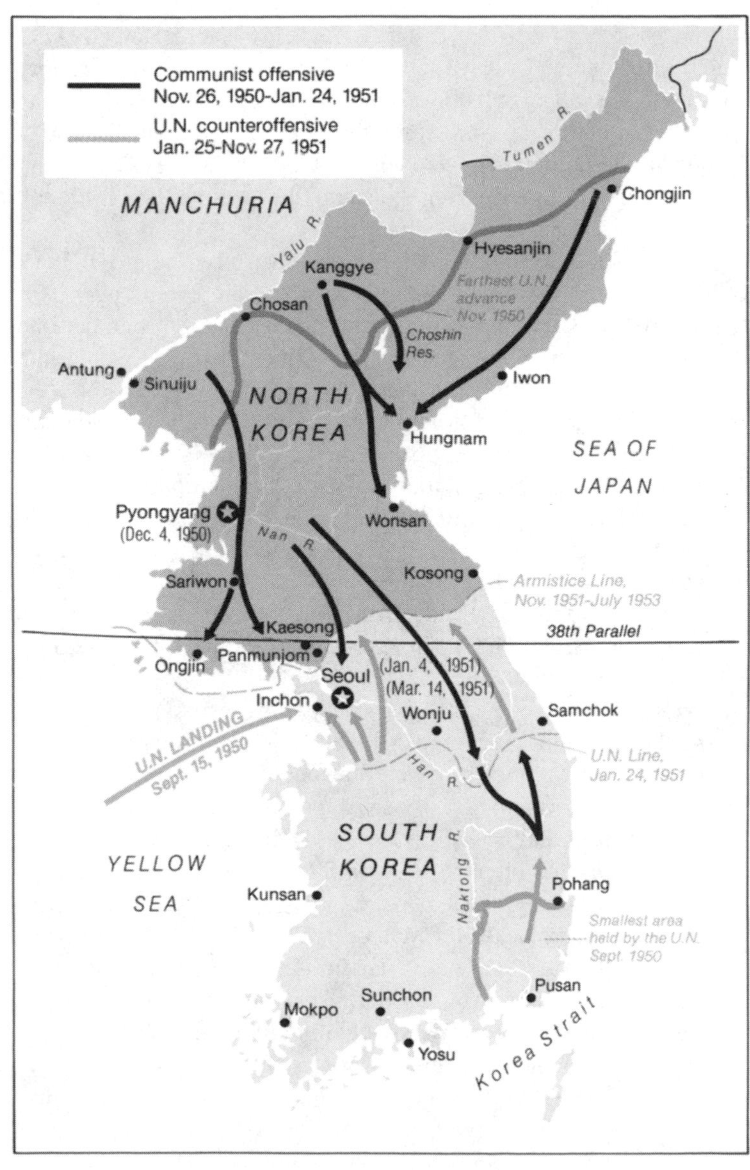
Communist offensive
Nov. 26, 1950-Jan. 24, 1951
U.N. counteroffensive
Jan. 25-Nov. 27, 1951
MANCHURIA
Tumen R.
Yalu R.
Chongjin
Hyesanjin
Kanggye
Farthest U.N. advance Nov. 1950
Chosan
Choshin Res.
Antung
Sinuiju
Iwon
NORTH KOREA
Hungnam
SEA OF JAPAN
Pyongyang
(Dec. 4, 1950)
Wonsan
Nan R.
Kosong
Sariwon
Armistice Line, Nov. 1951-July 1953
Kaesong
38th Parallel
Ongjin
Panmunjom
Seoul
(Jan. 4, 1951)
(Mar. 14, 1951)
Inchon
Wonju
Samchok
U.N. LANDING
Sept. 15, 1950
Han R.
U.N. Line, Jan. 24, 1951
SOUTH KOREA
YELLOW SEA
Naktong R.
Pohang
Kunsan
Smallest area held by the U.N. Sept. 1950
Pusan
Sunchon
Mokpo
Yosu
Korea Strait

sula under South Korean leadership. Areas held by North Korean forces were hit repeatedly by devastating U.S. bombing raids and artillery and naval fire, all of which resulted in heavy military and civilian casualties in both parts of Korea. After a bold amphibious landing at Inchon in mid-September, which turned the North Koreans' flank and forced them to withdraw from the south, the situation began to look favorable for America and its allies.

Whereas the North Koreans and Soviets had miscalculated in June, by early autumn it was the Americans who were overplaying their hand. Ignoring suggestions for a ceasefire at the 38th parallel and disregarding repeated warnings by the Chinese that they would join the fighting if the Americans came too close to their territory, the primarily American UN forces invaded North Korea late in September and October and bombed bridges on the Yalu River between North Korea and China. Contemptuous of the Chinese communists and friendly to Jiang, MacArthur assured Truman on October 15 that, in his opinion, the Chinese would not risk becoming involved in the Korean conflict. When large numbers of Chinese soldiers crossed the Yalu River and then attacked effectively, the Americans, who had seemed close to total victory in Korea, were forced to fall back rapidly toward the 38th parallel.

Working with newly available documents, several scholars have shown that the Chinese became involved in the war primarily because of pressure from Stalin, who urged Mao on October 1 to send "volunteers" because "the situation of our Korean friends is getting desperate." A week later Stalin promised to supply the Chinese with air cover for their troops and other types of military assistance. In addition, Mao and other Chinese leaders feared that U.S. control of all of Korea would lead to attacks on China designed ultimately to overthrow their government. As Mao stated in a Politburo meeting on August 4: "If the U.S. imperialists won the war, they would become more arrogant and would threaten us. We should not fail to assist the Koreans."

As Marxist-Leninists, Chinese leaders believed that the "imperialists" would not be satisfied until they had destroyed every communist government; thus they felt they had to intervene to deter further American "aggression" in Asia. Ironically, the original U.S. goal also had been defensive: to prevent the further spread of communism. "In retrospect," historian Shu Guang Zhang has noted, "we can see that neither state had the aggressive intentions that the other so consistently attributed to it."

After the large-scale Chinese intervention, MacArthur asked for permission to carry out massive air strikes against China, but officials in Washington, wishing to avoid a wider and more dangerous war, denied his request and ordered him to concentrate on stabilizing the UN position near the 38th parallel. When, in the spring of 1951, MacArthur publicly implied that Truman was an appeaser and disobeyed orders by crossing the 38th parallel again, the president, backed strongly by the joint chiefs of staff, fired him on April 11. Still viewing Russia as enemy number one and the defense of Western Europe as the top priority, General Omar Bradley, the chairman of the joint chiefs, told Congress that an all-out war in Asia would be "the wrong war, at the wrong place, at the wrong time, and with the wrong enemy." In a relatively brief period the administration had gone from containment to liberation and then back to containment.

With the outspoken MacArthur gradually fading from public view and the front in Korea stabilized by late spring, U.S. officials in Washington and East Asia, in Acheson's words, "found themselves united on political objectives, strategy, and tactics for the first time since the war had started." In other words, the administration was ready to try to negotiate a settlement. Following the pattern of the Berlin negotiations of 1949, Kennan met secretly with Malik twice in early June and learned that the Soviets wanted to end the hostilities. After Malik publicly affirmed Russia's interest in a peaceful solution on June 23, the administration moved rapidly to make contact with the Chinese and North Korean commanders, and formal negotiations began on July 10. Although an armistice agreement was not signed until July 1953 (partly due to Stalin's actual reluctance to negotiate seriously and Truman's refusal to return Chinese and North Korean prisoners of war against their will), the overall intensity of the fighting subsided.

In the absence of a peace agreement, Truman's popularity, which had taken a nose dive after Chinese intervention dashed hopes for an early victory, never again reached its level of July 1950. Republicans, smelling victory in 1952, jumped on inconsistencies in U.S. policy in Asia and played on the popular feeling that all America was getting from its involvement in Korea was casualties, inflation, and higher taxes. In a Gallup poll in October 1951, 56 percent responded that Korea was a "useless war." Yet the public strongly approved the keystones of America's Cold War stance: hostility toward Russia and mainland China, large defense expenditures, production of hydrogen bombs, rearmament of Germany, a strong American military presence in Europe, U.S. bases in Japan, and support for Jiang. Truman might not have been able to win an election for dogcatcher in 1951 and 1952, but his vision of America as the assertive leader of the "Free World"—the vision of NSC-68—was more solidly embedded in public thinking than ever before.

The depth to which U.S.-Soviet relations had dropped was illustrated by Kennan's experience in 1952 as ambassador to Russia. Kennan was sent to Moscow without instructions from his own government. Accordingly, he did not seek an appointment with Stalin, for, "being effectively without instructions, I had nothing to say to him." At the same time, Kennan was shocked by the "viciousness and intensity" of the anti-American propaganda that spewed forth daily from the Russian news media. The U.S. embassy was bugged, and he felt like a prisoner in his official residence. Although he knew that Soviet charges against America were greatly exaggerated, he did believe that U.S. military activities in Europe and the Mediterranean were at times unnecessarily provocative: "I began to ask myself whether . . . we had not contributed, and were not continuing to contribute—by the overmilitarization of our policies and statements—to a belief in Moscow that it was war we were after."

While traveling through Germany that September, Kennan carelessly stated that living under police-state conditions in Moscow reminded him of living in Berlin in the early 1940s. Infuriated by Kennan's comparison of Russia and Nazi Germany, the Soviet government refused to let him reenter the country, thus ending his brief tour as ambassador. In doing this, ironically, it closed the door on one of the very few high-level U.S. officials of that era who could see both sides in the Cold War.

Conclusion

An analogy from nature that is often applied to the study of history is that of the forest and the trees. Some historians, it is said, "can't see the forest for the trees"—that is, they are unable to perceive the overall significance of events because they are so busy looking at details. Others, who can't see the trees for the forest, make generalizations readily but often ignore specific facts that might force them to modify their broad conclusions.

At the level of the "trees," there is much to praise—and a good deal to criticize—in the behavior of America, Russia, and their various allies. The U.S., for example, can be praised for its leadership, through the Marshall Plan, in the revitalization of Western Europe. This leadership helped the nations in the region achieve both prosperity and lasting democracy. America also deserves praise for taking the lead in setting up—and funding—the international institutions that have contributed to widespread prosperity (the International Monetary Fund, the World Bank, and several others), peacemaking, human rights, and a heightened concern for the less fortunate throughout the world. The Russians can be praised for carefully avoiding the use of their military forces in large-scale combat against Americans not only in Europe but also when their ally, North Korea, faced imminent defeat during the Korean War.

Among other things, one can criticize the harshness with which Stalin's henchmen operated in Eastern Europe, or America's break with its earlier commitment to anticolonialism when it openly supported the French in Indochina beginning in 1950. Stalin's and Mao's approval of Kim Il Sung's plan to invade South Korea had truly tragic consequences. Not only was there horrendous loss of life and destruction of property, but U.S. officials for years afterward concluded that communist leaders would use any available means to expand the territory they controlled. America's success in a limited war in Korea led many officials in the 1960s to think that the U.S. could win a limited war in Vietnam as well. One also can regret the rigidity and self-righteousness that infected both the U.S. and Soviet governments between 1945 and 1953—a noxious fever that recurred frequently during the thirty-five years after Truman and Stalin left the stage.

At the level of the "forest," an effort to be even-handed in reaching conclusions can easily obscure deeper truths. The deepest truth about the Cold War is that it was, as Truman said in his famous speech in March 1947, a struggle between "two ways of life," one based on the goal (however imperfectly realized at times) of individual liberty and democracy, and the other on the persistent reality of "terror and oppression." According to Vaclav Havel, a Czech dissident who became president of his country after it broke free from Russia in 1989, Soviet-style communism was "a genuinely totalitarian system" that "permeated every aspect of life and deformed everything it touched, including all the natural ways people had evolved of living together."

Viewed in this light, U.S. policymakers were wise to oppose the spread of totalitarian communism and to hope that this fundamentally flawed form of social organization, once contained, would eventually die out and be replaced by political and economic institutions that permitted the free flowering of human potential, in all its richness and diversity. That Truman and his successors made mistakes in implementing their anticommunist policies, especially in Asia, cannot be doubted. But the overall direction of their policy—committing U.S. leadership and resources to stem the tide of communism and to encourage freedom, democracy, and economic growth throughout the noncommunist world—was admirable indeed.

CHAPTER TWO

The Institutionalized Cold War, 1953–1962

In retrospect, the decade between the coming to power of new leaders in both America and Russia in early 1953 and the Cuban missile crisis in late 1962 has several unifying themes. One is an increased desire for improved relations among the highest-ranking leaders on both sides—notably Premier Nikita S. Khrushchev and President Dwight D. Eisenhower—who were, however, limited by their own Cold War assumptions, their mutual reluctance to make the substantive concessions required to reach agreement on important issues, and the continued hardline stance of many of their own advisers and of others with influence in their societies. A second theme is expanded official and nonofficial contacts between the two sides, contributing to an overall decline in tensions to a level below that of the last Truman-Stalin years. A third theme is the recurrence of some issues that had been important in the early years of the Cold War, such as the still unresolved German question and problems created by the nuclear arms race. During these years America maintained a huge advantage over Russia in nuclear striking power, which meant that U.S. leaders could take tough stands, confident that Soviet leaders would back down during crises. A fourth theme is the spreading of the Cold War to nations previously untouched by direct U.S.-Soviet competition—Laos, Egypt, the Congo, Cuba, and others—all of which, from the American viewpoint, were within the Western sphere of influence. Many of these developing nations were emerging from European colonial rule, and therefore lacked experience in self-government. Their political instability, their need for economic assistance, and their potential strategic value in the East-West competition all made them targets for idealistic and self-serving involvement by the two superpowers.

Despite some modest improvements in relations, therefore, the combination of potentially catastrophic issues and Cold War methods of operation resulted in frequent periods of tension reminiscent of the late 1940s and early 1950s. Having become institutionalized during the Korean War, with large military, intelligence, foreign-aid, and propaganda bureaucracies and industries on both sides dedicated to waging it, the Cold War looked by the late 1950s as if it might last forever.

On the communist side, this decade belonged largely to Khrushchev and, to a much lesser degree, to Mao. After a period of collective leadership following Stalin's death, Khrushchev emerged by 1955 as the top Soviet leader, though he was still much more subject to constraints and pressures from others in the Kremlin than Stalin had been. Having risen from his peasant birth to a high position under Stalin, Khrushchev possessed qualities that Stalin had lacked: affability, an enjoyment of mingling with people and of making speeches, an interest in traveling abroad and meeting foreign leaders, and a concern about the popularity of his government both at home and abroad. Khrushchev could be rude and threatening, as when he angrily took off his shoe and beat it on the table at the United Nations in 1960, but Westerners who dealt with him felt that they were dealing with a genuine, approachable human being.

As the Russian scholars Vladislav Zubok and Constantine Pleshakov have noted, a "basic contradiction" underlay Khrushchev's approach to East-West relations. The Soviet premier wanted both improved relations with the West and the right to support communist revolutionaries in developing nations. A committed Marxist-Leninist, Khrushchev believed that the U.S.S.R. had the duty to support the "inevitable" triumph of communism worldwide. Seeing Khrushchev's policies in the Third World as expansionist and threatening, U.S. leaders were determined to oppose them.

A more militant Marxist-Leninist than Khrushchev, Mao shocked Soviet leaders by insisting that Russia should be willing to risk nuclear war to spread communism. Kept out of the UN and other international forums largely by the United States, China broadcast diatribes against Western imperialism and threatened Jiang Jieshi's government on Taiwan. Although some U.S. leaders and intelligence analysts were aware by the mid-to-late 1950s of tensions in Sino-Soviet relations, most politicians and commentators, committed to the concept of a unified Sino-Soviet bloc, tended to discount this rift until it became unmistakable in the early 1960s.

On the U.S. side, the moderate Eisenhower and his publicly hardline, privately cautious secretary of state, John Foster Dulles, contributed the most to policymaking during the 1950s, and President John F. Kennedy had the greatest influence in 1961 and 1962. In the wake of the Vietnam War and Watergate, Eisenhower's historical reputation grew considerably, and he is now frequently viewed as a president more interested in lessening Cold War tensions than waging an unremitting struggle against international communism. While there is considerable validity in this interpretation, some scholars carry it too far. Eisenhower often was quite cautious in his response to Soviet initiatives on Cold War issues, and he pursued a vigorous policy of containing Russian and Chinese influence in the Third World. Although it is now known that Eisenhower maintained personal control of policy on major issues, it often appeared at the time that he had delegated his authority to the articulate Dulles and his equally hardline brother, CIA director Allen Dulles.

One major revisionist point that has gained acceptance is the president's and the secretary of state's awareness of strains in Sino-Soviet relations. Their efforts to isolate China were designed at least partly to increase Mao's reliance upon Russia, thus increasing tensions between the two communist giants. Eisenhower's and Dulles's public statements frequently included phrases like "international communism" and Russia's "puppet regime" in China. In fact, the top U.S. leaders were much better informed than these public remarks would suggest, and their diplomacy often reflected a sophisticated strategy designed to divide Russia and China.

Just as there has been some tendency to underestimate Eisenhower's commitment to the Cold War, Kennedy's commitment frequently has been overstated. Although the young, activist president supported U.S. involvement in anticommunist guerrilla wars and greatly increased defense spending at a time when America already had a substantial strategic advantage, he was willing to seek improved relations with Russia and even with China. Moreover, the major issues he faced in his first two years in office—Laos, Vietnam, Berlin, Cuba, the role of the CIA, arms control, and others—were bequeathed to him, in ominous form, by the Eisenhower administration. This point is made not to exonerate Kennedy of all errors, but rather to note the pronounced continuities between Eisenhower's last years and Kennedy's first two, which together form the second dangerous phase in the Cold War.

The Cold War at Home

Before proceeding to discuss in more detail the diplomacy of the 1950s and early 1960s, I think it appropriate to focus briefly on the domestic context of the Cold War in the United States, the atmosphere which would have made it difficult to shift policy toward Russia and China abruptly even if it had been possible diplomatically to do so. In focusing on America, I am not suggesting that there were no domestic influences on policymaking in Russia and China. On the contrary, "vigilance against imperialism" served as an important justification for limiting freedom of expression and enforcing sacrifices in Eastern Europe and North Korea as well as in the two major communist nations. It also seems clear that important elements of the national security establishment in Moscow—like their counterparts in Washington—came to have a stake in continued hostility, and that political leaders in Moscow and Beijing—as in Washington—used attacks on the "correctness" of rivals' views on foreign policy as a means of wresting power from them. Moreover, the Soviets had several serious accidents in their nuclear-weapons and biological-warfare programs, resulting in numerous deaths and substantial damage to the environment. But while the effects of the Cold War may have been equally profound in some communist countries, they were more visible in America's largely open society, with its tradition of free expression, profitable defense industries, and elections to reward or punish politicians in power.

One other caveat is required at this point: what follows is not intended primarily as an indictment of Cold War America, but rather as an effort to provide information about some of the effects of the Cold War on the nation's life. The excesses that I describe generally were byproducts of the American people's attempt to adjust to the nation's bewildering new role of superpower; they were not, on the whole, sinister schemes concocted by malicious officials or private groups. The threat of nuclear war was frightening. The "burdens of world leadership" were substantial. Domestic communism was a threat to democratic institutions, though not to the degree that many Americans thought it was in the 1940s and 1950s. But as some people also realized at the time, excessive anticommunism also was a threat to the nation's institutions and values, and it is this theme that I shall develop here.

Beginning in the late 1940s and continuing until the mid-1960s, staunch anticommunism was a staple of American public life. Although the practical message of McCarthyism was that those who did not demonstrate an unswerving commitment to anticommunism risked losing their jobs, most Americans needed no such stimulus to convince them that Russia and China should be opposed vigorously. The Cold War consensus on this point included political parties, labor unions, and business groups; mass circulation magazines and daily newspapers; ethnic and religious groups; veterans and professional organizations; and liberal and conservative interest groups. The American Bar Association's Standing Committee on Education Against Communism, one of the numerous committees established throughout the society to alert the public to the Red threat, warned as late as 1964 that "to mistake the illusion of peace for genuine peace would be a profoundly dangerous, perhaps fatal mistake," and that because "the clash between our two systems is . . . irreconcilable, then our victory will not be achieved until freedom and justice prevail everywhere in the world."

Liberals like Democratic Senator Hubert Humphrey and conservatives like Republican Senator Barry Goldwater disagreed on the best means of opposing communism, but they both strongly supported anticommunism as the central thrust of U.S. foreign policy, and both consistently voted for generous appropriations for the Defense Department, the intelligence agencies, and America's allies abroad.

Humphrey, the Senate's leading liberal, warned in 1955, a time of relative thaw, that "we should not be deluded by Communist strategy. We know its objective." "A tolerable peace . . . ," Goldwater wrote in 1960, "must follow victory over communism."

The news media also were preoccupied with this issue. The three news magazines—*Time, Newsweek,* and *U.S. News and World Report*—all took a tough Cold War stance, as did the most widely circulated magazine, *Reader's Digest*. Respected reporters like Theodore White and Charles Mohr left Time-Life Publications after their stories were repeatedly altered to reflect publisher Henry Luce's hard-line anticommunist, pro-Jiang viewpoint. Only slightly more conciliatory were the two most influential newspapers in Washington, the *New York Times* and the *Washington Post*. Both the newspaper with the largest circulation, the *New York Daily News*, and the largest chain, the Hearst papers, were virulently anticommunist. Widely circulated columnists like David Lawrence, Joseph Alsop, and William S. White all adamantly opposed the Russian and Chinese governments and warned repeatedly that America was falling behind in the Cold War.

The obsession with communism filtered down to the nation's youth. Boy Scouts were taught that communists were the enemy; parochial school students learned that communism was inherently evil because it was "godless"; and public school students had to memorize the "evils" of communism to pass civics tests. Congress pointedly added the phrase "under God" to the Pledge of Allegiance, recited daily in schoolrooms across the country. When fear of atomic attack ran high in the late 1950s and early 1960s, civil-defense programs were introduced into the schools. In one ludicrous but not atypical example, students at a public high school in Baltimore were taught to get down on their knees and put their heads on the seats of their desks whenever the teacher blew a whistle—as if that would somehow protect them during a nuclear attack. From the late 1940s through the early 1970s, men graduating from high school could expect to be drafted into the army and sent to serve in places like Germany, Turkey, Korea, and ultimately Vietnam. To pay these and other costs, more than 11 percent of the entire Gross National Product was devoted to defense spending in some "peacetime" years.

To be sure, some liberals opposed the drift of American policy. An occasional magazine like the *Progressive* and a few groups like the Friends [Quaker] Committee on National Legislation called for improved relations with Russia and recognition of mainland China. A well-organized segment of the scientific community opposed the atmospheric testing of nuclear weapons, and several liberal groups developed around this issue in the late 1950s. But overall, critics of America's Cold War stance, frequently denounced as "soft on communism," attracted meager support from the general public or from politicians. And for every liberal who actively sought a relaxation of Cold War tensions, there was a staunch conservative who demanded "victory" in the Cold War against communism.

By the mid-1950s, the bedrock of support for a strongly anticommunist foreign policy came from conservatives of both parties (mostly Democratic in the South, mostly Republican in the North and West); from ethnic groups of East European descent (concentrated in large northern cities like Buffalo, Cleveland, and Chicago); from fundamentalist Protestants and conservative Catholics; from labor unions like the AFL-CIO and their political supporters like Senator Paul Douglas (Dem., Ill.); and from people connected with the military, especially officers charged with the task of combating communism all over the globe, contractors dependent on military procurements for much of their livelihood, and veterans proud of their service in previous wars and determined that the nation's defenses should remain strong. Public opinion studies found that men, who occupied virtually all of the leadership positions in American society at the time, consistently took a more hardline position on Cold War issues than did women. The strength of anticommunist feeling was such that, to my knowledge, not a single senator publicly advocated a fundamental shift in policy toward Russia or recognition of mainland China between 1953 and 1962.

Analysis of the anticommunist impulse frequently focused on the influence of defense industries and the military in setting national priorities. In his farewell address on January 17, 1961, Eisenhower noted that, since World War II, America had created "a permanent armaments industry of vast proportions," that the "defense establishment" of the government had 3.5 million employees, and that defense spending exceeded the net profits of all American corporations. "In the councils of Government, we must guard against the acquisition of unwarranted influence, whether sought or unsought, by the military-industrial complex," the president warned. "The potential for the disastrous rise of misplaced power exists and will persist." Eisenhower said that the nation "must also be alert to the danger that public policy could itself become the captive of a scientific-technological elite."

Although Eisenhower's warning became a standard feature of liberal and New Left rhetoric in the 1960s, its validity has remained difficult to assess. At what point, for example, does influence become unwarranted? Is the close relationship between Defense Department officials, contractors, promilitary magazines like *Aviation Week*, defense-industry lobbyists, and members of Congress compatible with the national interest, or does it fuel needless and dangerous arms competition? And even if many large corporations, labor unions, universities, and research institutions profit substantially from defense contracts, do the benefits they provide to the nation outweigh the costs? These issues involve value judgments as well as facts, but there can be no denying Eisenhower's comment that "the very structure of our society" had been affected by the militarization of American life during and after World War II.

The Cold War had other important consequences for American institutions and values, some known at the time and others revealed later. One consequence well known at the time was the purging of officials who were accused of disagreeing with policy on sensitive issues. Respected experts on China like John Stewart Service and John Paton Davies were fired from the State Department in the early 1950s for predicting earlier that Jiang probably would lose the civil war in China. J. Robert Oppenheimer, one of the nation's most distinguished atomic scientists, had his security clearance removed, partly due to his opposition to developing the hydrogen bomb. The message quickly spread through a demoralized State Department and other agencies that clear thinking and independent analysis might well lead to the unemployment lines.

Little known at the time was the fact that the FBI, the CIA, and the Defense Department, in addition to or as a byproduct of their normal functions, were secretly abusing the civil liberties and threatening the health of numerous Americans and Canadians. The FBI, for example, conducted continuing surveillance against civil rights leader Martin Luther King, Jr., on the premise, never substantiated, that "Communist influence" dominated his movement. Contrary to its charter, the CIA also conducted extensive surveillance of individuals within the United States, including members of Congress. Seeking to learn to control behavior, the CIA conducted experiments with hallucinogenic drugs on unsuspecting Americans, at least one of whom committed suicide while unknowingly under the influence of LSD. Experimenting in bacteriological warfare, the navy in 1950 blanketed San Francisco for six days with a bacteria known as serratia (which, it was discovered later, could cause a fatal pneumonia). And the army in 1953 conducted chemical warfare tests over St. Louis, Minneapolis, and Winnipeg, Canada, dropping cadmium sulfide and zinc in aerosol clouds.

The most serious threat to the health of Americans at the height of the Cold War involved nuclear testing, which took place above ground in Nevada and in the Pacific between 1945 and 1963. During that time, an estimated 250,000 servicemen were exposed to testing at fairly close range, and thousands of civilians in Utah also were exposed to radiation from the tests. An epidemiologist for the state of Utah, Dr. Joseph Lyon, testified in April 1979 that children growing up in his state's fallout areas in the 1950s suffered 2.5 times as much leukemia as children living there before and after the tests. The tests continued even though Atomic Energy Commission (AEC) officials were aware by 1953 of the high levels of radiation hitting some Utah communities, including St. George, a town AEC chairman Lewis L. Strauss described as one "they apparently always plaster." "In school they showed a film called 'A is for Atom, B is for Bomb,'" one Utah resident recalled. "Most of us who grew up in that period added 'C is for Cancer, D is for Death.'"

Less carefully studied have been the effects of the testing on the servicemen who were ordered to lie in trenches as close as thirty-five hundred yards from the spot where atomic weapons larger than those dropped on Hiroshima and Nagasaki were being detonated. During the AEC's "Operation Teapot" series of tests in 1955 and at other times, the army was interested in learning if soldiers could survive on the nuclear battlefield; accordingly, thousands of GIs were exposed to large doses of radiation (often leading to nose bleeding and other symptoms) during the blast, and then they were ordered to march over radioactive terrain to "take" an objective closer to ground zero. Many servicemen were hospitalized as a result of this experience, and some who thereafter contracted leukemia or fathered children with severe deformities became bitter about being used as "guinea pigs" during their military service.

Another disturbing effect of the Cold War on American life was the compromising of respected private institutions to further the anticommunist crusade. The *New York Times* withheld news (such as the secret preparations for the Bay of Pigs invasion) potentially embarrassing to the government; CBS regularly passed on information gained in news gathering directly to the CIA; professors at leading American universities helped to recruit foreign students for the CIA and were paid to make trips abroad to gather intelligence; the AFL-CIO worked closely with American officials in undermining governments in Latin America; and missionaries, doctors, and corporate officials worked as secret agents for the CIA. When in the late 1970s Catholic officials looked into the qualifications for sainthood of the famous American medical missionary who had served in Laos in the late 1950s, Dr. Tom Dooley, they found that he had been closely involved with the CIA's counterinsurgency work there. Although most Americans did not realize the extent of CIA involvement abroad during the 1950s and early 1960s, many in the affected nations did, thus lending some credibility to Russian and Chinese charges that most Americans abroad were CIA agents.

In sum, the America that the Cold War helped to create was so convinced of its responsibility to lead the "Free World" against communism that it made preparations for war the chief priority of the federal government, fired dedicated State Department officials, risked the lives of its own citizens in chemical— and nuclear—weapons testing, and involved itself in trying to direct the internal affairs of scores of nations around the globe. Although Americans did not know everything the CIA was doing, the attentive public, members of Congress, journalists, and of course leaders of the administration knew that the CIA, under the president's direction, was involved in overthrowing the nationalistic government of Iran and restoring the Shah to power in 1953, overthrowing the procommunist government of Guatemala in 1954, and in trying to overthrow the communist government of Cuba in 1961. Most people did not know about serious CIA plotting in places like Laos, Indonesia, Syria, the Congo, and British Guiana, but most probably would have acquiesced as they did in the other three situations. And yet Americans almost certainly would have been infuriated to the point of demanding war if a foreign government had been discovered trying to overthrow their nation's government or assassinate its leaders. "From today's perspective," CIA official Richard Bissell recalled in 1996, "many episodes [of covert action in the 1950s and 1960s] might be considered distasteful, but during the Eisenhower and Kennedy years the Soviet danger seemed real and all actions were aimed at thwarting it."

Reflecting the Cold War mentality, a secret government panel reported in 1954 that America "must learn to subvert, sabotage, and destroy our enemies by more clever, more sophisticated and more effective methods than those used against us." The danger, always easier to grasp in retrospect, was that the nation might prove even more successful in subverting its own institutions and values.

A Modest Improvement in East-West Relations, 1953–1955

For approximately three years after the death of Stalin in March 1953—and the end of the Korean War that July—there occurred a limited but nonetheless significant improvement in East-West relations. The change occurred mainly in Soviet relations with the West, for America refused to recognize mainland China, which Dulles described as "fanatically hostile to us and demonstrably aggressive and treacherous." Eisenhower agreed that Mao's government was "beyond the pale"; indeed, his administration's major policy initiative in Asia was to "unleash" Jiang Jieshi's exile government, supplied with U.S. arms, to conduct raids against the mainland and, later, against North Vietnam. Hostile to Taiwan and to the United States both in word and in deed, Mao provoked serious crises in regard to the offshore islands of Quemoy and Matsu in 1954–55 and again in 1958.

So hostile was Dulles's attitude toward communist China that, when Foreign Minister Zhou Enlai offered to shake hands with him at the Geneva Conference on Indochina in 1954, Dulles turned his back on him and walked away. The next year Zhou proposed at the Bandung Conference of nonaligned nations that America and China begin negotiations on outstanding issues. The administration initially declined, but soon meetings at the ambassadorial level were occurring in Geneva and Warsaw. Despite these contacts between 1955 and 1967, U.S. officials continued to insist that Jiang Jieshi was China's legitimate leader and, despite a 1957 invitation from Beijing to American journalists, refused to allow journalists or other Americans to visit the mainland.

Fortunately, U.S.-Soviet relations were considerably more positive, even though the vast majority of U.S. officials and the public continued to believe that Russia was a mortal enemy. It could be argued, at the risk of giving Soviet leaders too much credit, that improvements in U.S.-Soviet relations occurred despite Dulles's opposition and Eisenhower's hesitation—in other words, that Russia's repeated diplomatic initiatives and occasional concessions created a momentum for achieving modest agreements that even the skeptical secretary of state could not withstand. Taking office on a platform criticizing containment and calling for a determined policy of "liberation" of Eastern Europe and China from Soviet rule, the new Republican administration found itself negotiating with Russia while, at the same time, continuing Truman's policy of building alliances against it.

The Eisenhower administration, Adam Ulam has observed, "was well suited to counteract Soviet misbehavior, to isolate and contain a Russia of the Stalinist model. But it was ill suited to deal with intermittent Soviet misbehavior combined with appeals for friendship and eulogies of coexistence." Nevertheless, the new leaders on both sides were able to lessen tensions somewhat, and that in itself was a rare achievement during the fifteen years between 1947 and 1962.

The new administration's basic objective was to wage the Cold War more vigorously, more coherently, and more economically than its predecessor had done. The vigor and coherence were to come from the effort to ring Russia and China with a series of alliances, all led by the United States, while simultaneously encouraging dissension and revolt within the communist bloc and generally discouraging nonalignment and neutralism outside it. Using the promise of aid and the fear of communism as lures, America was able to sign up several nations for the Southeast Asia Treaty Organization (SEATO), founded in 1954, and several others for the Baghdad Pact (later the Central Treaty Organization, or CENTO), designed to protect the Middle East. In theory, America now had reliable allies from Norway and Great Britain (members of NATO) in the west, to the Philippines and Australia (members of SEATO) in the east.

The financial savings were to come from replacing expensive limited wars like Korea with low-cost CIA operations and from the administration's "New Look" defense strategy, which was designed to lessen reliance on conventional forces in favor of nuclear weapons and the bombers and missiles capable of delivering them. This approach, Dulles declared, would allow the West "to retaliate, instantly, by means and at places of our own choosing," thus keeping the communists off balance. By spending less on expensive ground forces, the nation could achieve, in the parlance of the time, "more bang for a buck."

Although critics at home and in Western Europe feared that this approach might lead to nuclear war at the slightest provocation, Dulles remained vague as to precisely what means America would use in particular situations, and Eisenhower, as is now well known, kept a cool finger on the nuclear trigger. Concerned about the economic consequences of large defense budgets and deficit spending, the president limited military spending to roughly $40 billion per year, below what Democratic critics by the late 1950s considered necessary. One consequence of the administration's economy campaign, together with its desire not to "lose" any more nations to communism, was its emphasis on relatively inexpensive covert operations, which peaked during the 1950s and early 1960s.

In Europe, the administration showed affinity for West Germany's conservative, anticommunist government led by Konrad Adenauer, who adamantly opposed any negotiations with the Soviets on Germany that might involve compromises in the Western position. Determined that West Germany be rearmed, Dulles pressured the anxious French to choose between participation by German soldiers in a common European army or German membership in NATO. The French Assembly reluctantly approved the latter on December 24, 1954, and West Germany joined NATO the following year. When Moscow responded by creating a formal military alliance of its own in 1955, the Warsaw Treaty Organization, the military division of Europe became formal.

In Asia, Dulles and some other high officials in the spring of 1954 flirted with the idea of using atomic bombs against Ho Chi Minh's forces in order to forestall a communist victory in Indochina, but Eisenhower and congressional leaders demurred. At a news conference on April 6, the president, citing the strategic and economic importance of Southeast Asia, did endorse the so-called "domino theory," the view that the fall of one nation in a region to communism would lead to rapid communist victories in the rest of that region's nations, and he also let Dulles travel to London to try to persuade Prime Minister Churchill of the necessity of intervention in Vietnam to save the French. Churchill and his foreign minister, Anthony Eden, remained unpersuaded, and on May 7 the beleaguered French garrison at Dien Bien Phu surrendered to the North Vietnamese.

When the Geneva Conference that summer awarded Ho Chi Minh only the northern half of Vietnam, pending unifying elections in 1956, Dulles was angry that the communist-led independence movement had won anything. Pledging generous public aid and private CIA assistance, the United States quickly helped to establish the strongly anticommunist Ngo Dinh Diem as the new ruler in the southern half of Vietnam and supported him in his refusal to cooperate in holding the elections in 1956. America also worked to disrupt the Hanoi government by urging Catholics to leave North Vietnam and by sponsoring secret raids from South Vietnam and Taiwan. In Iran, Guatemala, and now South Vietnam, American money and power seemed nearly invincible.

The new Soviet leaders respected U.S. economic and military might, and they also wanted a better relationship with America than had existed during Stalin's last years. During the spring and summer of 1953 the new premier, Georgi Malenkov, repeatedly called for improved relations with the West; the Soviet press published much less anti-U.S. propaganda; and *Pravda* even published the full text of Eisenhower's speech of April 16 calling for settlement of outstanding disputes and steps toward disarmament. The Soviets were helpful in concluding the armistice in Korea in July, and they renewed Stalin's intriguing offer of 1952 to negotiate the creation of a unified, neutral Germany. Sensing the improved atmosphere, Churchill on May 11 called for a summit conference of world leaders, but U.S. officials, notably Dulles, were cool to the idea.

The U.S. ambassador in Moscow, Charles Bohlen, later regretted that he did not urge Eisenhower to accept the proposal for a summit in 1953, for "there might have been opportunities for an adjustment of some of the outstanding questions, particularly regarding Germany." The cautious, anticommunist president developed a "stock answer" to questions from reporters about a possible summit meeting: "I would not go to a Summit because of friendly words and plausible promises by the men of the Kremlin; actual deeds giving some indication of a Communist readiness to negotiate constructively will have to be produced before I would agree to such a meeting."

Could there have been substantial progress in resolving such key East-West issues as Germany and arms control in 1953 or 1954? One cannot be sure, for Churchill's proposal to start serious negotiations quickly was not implemented. But there clearly would have been enormous obstacles to overcome. Dulles and other State Department analysts, with their Cold War mindset, refused to believe that any significant changes had taken place in the Soviet approach to world affairs. Many Americans, having been sold on the unmitigated evil of communism and on the necessity of sacrifices to wage the Cold War, would have been reluctant to support a sudden shift in policy, especially with McCarthy still claiming that conciliatory leaders were traitors. Allied leaders like Adenauer also would have opposed a sudden shift in U.S. policy.

The Soviets, for their part, were involved in 1953 and 1954 in a serious struggle for power in the Kremlin that was hardly conducive to effective negotiations. Research in Soviet archives opened in the early 1990s suggests that debate within the top Soviet leadership in the summer of 1953 resulted in victory for those who wanted to maintain a separate East German state, and defeat for those who had wanted to ease Cold War tensions by permitting the creation of a neutral united Germany. In short, domestic constraints and the burdens of alliance systems would have made it hard for either side to have made the large concessions necessary for a substantial shift toward détente. Nevertheless, one can fault U.S. leaders for not exploring more fully the possibility of mutually acceptable agreements with Russia before additional alliance building virtually froze the situation in Germany.

The conditions necessary for top-level U.S.-Soviet talks finally existed in 1955. With Khrushchev having emerged as the chief Soviet leader and negotiator, with Dulles having achieved his goal of West German participation in NATO, and with Russia showing "constructiveness" by negotiating with the West a peace treaty for Austria in the spring of 1955, the stage was set for the summit meeting in Geneva that July, the first such meeting since Potsdam exactly a decade before. The Russians were represented by Premier Nikolai Bulganin and by Communist party leader Khrushchev, who held the real power; the Americans were represented by Eisenhower and Secretary of State Dulles, who had urged the president not to go but who at least was there to ensure that he did not give anything away. British and French leaders also were present, but obviously in secondary roles. Eisenhower had "no illusions" about the summit's likelihood of success, and he and Dulles assured Congress that "Geneva was not going to be another Yalta." Khrushchev, who had little experience in world affairs, remembered being worried about whether the Soviet leaders could "represent our country competently" and "keep the other side from intimidating us." Thus, neither leader was expecting that the conference would accomplish much.

Not surprisingly, their modest expectations were fulfilled. Taking place in an atmosphere more conducive to press coverage and posturing than to serious negotiations, the leaders' statements repeatedly exposed the gulf separating the two sides. Each side professed to desire the unification of Germany, but only on its own terms. The British and Russians traded proposals for demilitarizing Central Europe, but they were mutually unacceptable. To counter Soviet disarmament proposals made earlier in the year, Eisenhower presented an "open skies" proposal in which America and Russia would exchange maps of their military installations and permit aerial inspection in order to lessen fear of secret military buildups and the possibility of surprise attacks. The Soviets, who traditionally feared espionage and sought to conceal their military weakness, rejected this proposal. "We knew the Soviets wouldn't accept it," Eisenhower admitted later. As at Potsdam, the major specific agreement at Geneva was to refer all areas of discord to subsequent meetings of the Council of Foreign Ministers.

Despite the predictable disagreement on major issues, the Geneva summit was valuable because it introduced the leaders of the two sides to each other. Eisenhower and Khrushchev knew very little about each other prior to Geneva; the president, for example, did not realize until well into the conference that Khrushchev was "the real boss" in the Soviet delegation. Informal social gatherings often proved to be more useful in breaking down barriers than did the formal meetings in which leaders tended to read from prepared texts. Once at dinner Eisenhower expressed his concern that hydrogen bombs could "easily and unwittingly destroy the entire Northern Hemisphere." "War has failed," he told the Soviets with his usual unaffected sincerity, "The only way to save the world is through diplomacy." His listeners nodded vigorously in approval. Khrushchev had included General Georgi Zhukov in the Soviet delegation because he hoped that Zhukov's friendship with Eisenhower during World War II might "serve as the basis for conversations that would lead to an easing of tension between our countries." But, Khrushchev noted colorfully in his memoirs, "that vicious cur Dulles was always prowling around Eisenhower, snapping at him if he got out of line."

More than anything else, the Geneva summit proved to the world that Soviet and Western leaders could sit down and discuss the issues that divided them, even shaking hands and issuing a civilized communique at the end of the meetings. The summit thus dealt a serious blow to the assumption, common in both countries in earlier years, that all-out war between the two sides was inevitable. As Eisenhower noted in his memoirs:

> . . . in spite of what happened thereafter, the cordial atmosphere of the talks, dubbed the "Spirit of Geneva," never faded entirely. Indeed, the way was opened for some increase in intercourse between East and West—there began, between the United States and Russia, exchanges of trade exhibitions, scientists, musicians, and other performers; visits

> were made by Mikoyan and Kozlov to the United States, and returned, by Vice President Nixon and my brother Milton, to the Soviet Union and Poland. These were small beginnings, but they could not have transpired in the atmosphere prevailing before Geneva.

Cultural, economic, and scientific exchanges between Russia and America, moribund since the late 1940s, were renewed in 1955 and continued to expand on a fairly regular basis during the next two decades. Soviet pianist Emil Gilels and violinist David Oistrakh made a big hit with U.S. audiences in the fall of 1955, and a largely black American company performing the musical *Porgy and Bess* proved a tremendous attraction in Moscow and Leningrad that winter. After additional successful exchanges on an ad hoc basis, America and Russia signed a formal exchange agreement on January 28, 1958.

Bob Loftus, an American who was involved in arranging a tour for forty Russian home builders in the United States in 1955 and who toured Russia with a group of American home builders in 1956, recalled that one of the Russians told him before leaving America, "We just don't believe that people who are spending so much wealth on their homes and their families are preparing for war against my country, as we have been told so many times." When Loftus attended a performance in the Kiev Opera House the next year, the man's teenage daughter whispered in his ear: "You must live in a wonderful country. My father has told us all about it."

Although cultural exchanges were not always this successful, one should never underestimate the importance of unofficial contacts in improving the general atmosphere in which U.S.-Soviet relations were conducted after 1955. They often were especially meaningful to Russians, who generally had far fewer opportunities than Americans for travel and for contact with the outside world. Equally significant to Russians concerned that Westerners viewed them as inferior, the exchanges symbolized a spirit of equality between their country and America. While the exchanges and the eventual development of U.S.-Soviet trade did not guarantee good relations, they served as something of a safety net to inhibit a drop in U.S.-Soviet relations to the level of 1950–1952. Exchanges of all types may be viewed, therefore, as a concrete, enduring manifestation of the "spirit of Geneva."

The Second Dangerous Phase, 1956–1962

U.S.-Soviet relations during the late 1950s and early 1960s seemed to support the maxim (reaffirmed in the late 1970s) that if relationships between the two superpowers did not continue to improve, they declined; in other words, superpower relationships did not remain fairly stable, as they frequently did between a great power and a lesser one. While improved official and informal relationships increased the chances for constructive bilateral communication, this period demonstrated that they did not in themselves overcome long-standing patterns of conflicting interests and mutual distrust. To prevent the worsening of relations, positive breakthroughs needed to occur on at least one key issue, in this case perhaps Berlin or nuclear testing. The failure of both sides to reverse the downward slide in U.S.-Soviet relations in the late 1950s thus contributed to the frenzied, warlike atmosphere of the early 1960s.

Zbigniew Brzezinski has called the period of the late 1950s and early 1960s in East-West relations a time of "premature Soviet globalism." He noted that "Soviet international activity acquired for the first time a distinctly global range." But such globalism was premature, he argued, because Russia did not yet have the military or economic power to sustain far-flung interests. Under pressure domestically and from within the Eastern bloc to make tangible progress on East-West issues, especially Berlin, Khrushchev exaggerated Soviet strength and threatened the West in the hope that his diplomatic initiatives could succeed. Not surprisingly, his apparent animosity—combined with rhetorical and material support for "wars of national liberation" in developing nations—triggered the hostility and uncompromising resolve in the West that the events of 1953–1955 had only slightly moderated.

It would be inaccurate to blame Soviet actions alone for the tensions that culminated in the Cuban missile crisis of 1962. For if Russia was pursuing a somewhat unpredictable policy of premature globalism, America was embarked on a full-fledged policy of mature globalism, involving the nation's determination, in President Kennedy's famous words, "that we shall pay any price, bear any burden, meet any hardship, support any friend, oppose any foe to assure the survival and the success of liberty." A 1978 Brookings Institution study of U.S. armed intervention abroad between 1946 and 1975 confirmed the historical accuracy of Kennedy's vow: military interventions short of war peaked between 1956 and 1965, with an average of twelve incidents occurring annually during that period. If extensive covert activities, military and economic aid packages, and other types of official and unofficial actions directed against "communism" are added in, there can be little doubt that America's Cold War interventionism was reaching its peak.

While U.S. interventionism of the 1950s and 1960s sometimes had tragic consequences, it must be noted that this was not always the case, and that, moreover, U.S. officials often were idealistic in assisting in "nation-building" in the Third World. "The key point is that this massive U.S. intervention, both overt and covert, was aimed politically at building what our people thought of as more just and progressive societies," Wallace Irwin, Jr., a State Department official, recalled. "We weren't just against the Reds; we were for democracy and we believed ourselves to have a missionary duty to export it."

Using both pressure and persuasion, U.S. officials sometimes lessened corruption in developing nations, helped these nations modernize their fiscal and monetary systems, and insisted successfully that elections be held and reforms be carried out. In short, while military interventions like the Bay of Pigs in Cuba and the Vietnam War are justly remembered, the efforts of numerous officials and private groups to improve conditions in the Third World—while simultaneously combating communism—should not be forgotten.

The year 1956 was a difficult one in world affairs for both Russia and America. In a passionate, secret, four-hour speech to the Twentieth Party Congress on February 24, Khrushchev denounced Stalin for domestic crimes and mistakes in foreign policy, endorsed "peaceful coexistence" and steps to end the arms race, and indicated that the Kremlin would relax its tight control in Russia and recognize diversity in the international communist movement. The CIA quickly obtained copies of the speech, made it public in the West, and distributed it throughout Eastern Europe.

Partly due to the speech and partly due to the long buildup of pressures for *de-Stalinization* (less government oppression, more personal freedom) in Eastern Europe, demands for change spread rapidly. By summer Poland was in turmoil, and the Soviets faced a serious challenge to their authority there. The Polish Communist party was split between old-line Stalinists, who wanted to use force to repress the demands for change, and those who demanded greater independence from Moscow and believed that concessions needed to be made in order to win greater popular support. Wishing to avoid military intervention, in October the Soviets finally agreed that a Polish communist leader associated with the second viewpoint, Wladyslaw Gomulka, would be permitted to take power. "There is more than one road to socialism," an exultant Gomulka declared on October 20. He warned the Kremlin that the Polish people would "defend themselves with all means; they will not be pushed off the road of democratization." Although Poland continued to be communist and remained in the Russian bloc, these developments weakened Soviet influence there and set an example that other satellite nations emulated.

Events in Hungary in the fall of 1956 were more tragic. Emboldened by the successful defiance of Soviet rule in Warsaw, students took to the streets in Budapest on October 23 to demand that a popular reform communist, Imre Nagy, be permitted to overhaul Hungary's Stalinist political system. As the turmoil spread, the Soviets agreed to the change, and by October 28 they even agreed to remove their tanks from around Budapest. Responding to the demands of students and workers, Nagy announced that Hungary planned to leave the Warsaw Pact and permit the creation of opposition parties.

To the Soviets, the "counterrevolution" in Hungary was going much too far. With the support of hardline communist leaders in other East European countries, Khrushchev ordered Soviet forces to crush the rebellion. The poorly armed students and workers fighting Soviet tanks on the streets of Budapest in early November won tremendous sympathy in the West, but the Russians quickly restored order and eventually executed Nagy and imposed a regime much harsher than Gomulka's or Tito's. Kept secret at the time, it was reported in 1991 that 669 Soviet soldiers were killed and roughly 1,500 were wounded in the fighting in Hungary. Like the U.S. casualties in Korea, these Soviet losses resulted from a superpower's determination to keep its sphere of influence intact.

Russia's actions in Hungary provided the U.S. media with fresh material for their favorite ongoing story, the horrors of communism, while the Russian press emphasized their nation's vigilance in guarding the Eastern bloc against Western imperialism. The Russian press did not explain why the revolt in Hungary had taken place, and the American press generally was not interested in Russia's reasons for suppressing it. The communications gap between the two sides, a basic feature of the Cold War, continued to flourish.

While the Eastern bloc in 1956 was dealing with pressures for de-Stalinization and freedom from Soviet rule, the Western alliance was feeling the strains of decolonization and defiance of U.S. leadership. In late October, only days before the Soviets moved on Budapest, Israel, France, and Great Britain launched coordinated attacks against Egypt, a former British protectorate. The Anglo-French aim was to repossess the Suez Canal and, apparently, to overthrow Egyptian President Gamal Abdel Nasser. Furious that he had not been informed in advance and disapproving of an action reminiscent of nineteenth-century colonialism, Eisenhower went on television and announced that America could not accept "one code of international conduct for those who oppose us and another for our friends."

Fearing increased Russian influence in the Middle East, the Eisenhower administration took strong and successful diplomatic action at the UN and elsewhere to force the removal of the foreign forces from Egypt. Meanwhile the Soviets made strong threats against Britain and France, and even proposed to Eisenhower that America and Russia conduct a joint military intervention to restore peace in the Middle East. Faced with hostile world opinion and pressure from the two superpowers, Britain and France halted their attack and removed their troops by December, and Israel, under intense U.S. pressure, followed suit by the following March.

Despite their understandable anger at the time of the Suez crisis, U.S. officials bore considerable responsibility for precipitating it. Nasser, whose neutralism in the East-West struggle angered Dulles, had made a deal in September 1955 with Russia to exchange Egyptian cotton for Czechoslovakian weapons. Seeking to limit Soviet

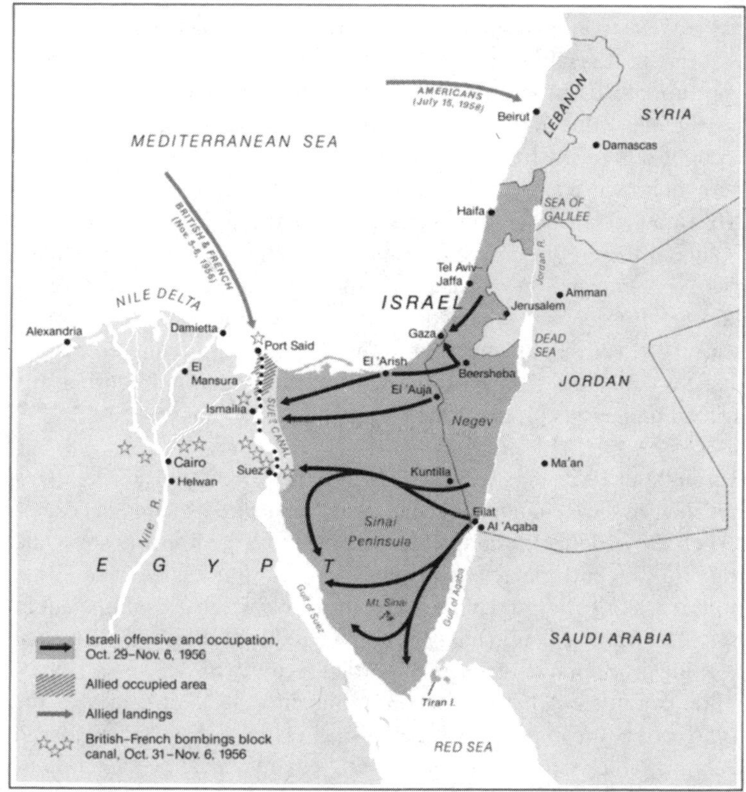

influence, Dulles promised to help Egypt build a large dam at Aswan on the upper Nile to provide electricity and water for irrigation, but then, in July 1956, reneged on the pledge when Nasser carried through with the Czech arms deal. In response, Nasser nationalized the Suez Canal, removing it from British control. Infuriated by the seizure and tired of following Dulles's advice (in this case, not to use force against Egypt), the British, French, and Israelis decided to strike. The inept U.S. hand in the whole affair left some bitterness among officials in London and Paris, bitterness that harmed NATO and that still rankled when America asked for help in Vietnam a decade later.

Finally, the Suez crisis damaged U.S.-Soviet relations, despite their common opposition to the attack. Wishing to minimize the harm to the Western alliance and to maintain America's special relationship with Israel, Eisenhower in his public statements repeatedly made it appear that Russia was the real culprit. And the Soviets, in their public statements and diplomatic notes, engaged in denunciations, threats, and appeals to international morality that were wholly inconsistent with their own actions at that very moment in Hungary. When in early November Khrushchev threatened a nuclear attack on England and France if they refused to leave Egypt, Eisenhower placed the Strategic Air Command on full alert and told an aide that he was ready, if Western Europe was attacked, to hit Russia "with everything in the bucket." Such threats and counterthreats, backed by unprecedented nuclear capabilities on both sides, were not uncommon during this second dangerous phase of the Cold War.

Throughout 1955 and 1956 a strong plurality of Gallup's respondents had viewed the Republicans as the party "best able to maintain peace." In February 1956, for example, 36 percent chose the Republicans while only 18 percent selected the Democrats; the remainder were either undecided or believed that the two parties were equally competent in this area. Many election analysts considered Eisenhower's success in keeping the nation at peace an important factor in his lead over Democratic candidate Adlai Stevenson going into the final weeks of the 1956 campaign; in their view, the crises in Hungary and Egypt turned a comfortable victory into a landslide, as many undecided voters concluded that they should support the experienced president in a time of crisis. In May 1957, after the two crises had ended, the public chose Republicans as "best able to maintain peace" by an impressive 45 to 19 percent. Remarkably, however, by July 1960 Democrats led Republicans 41 to 25 percent on the question of the party best able to "increase respect" for America in the world.

What had happened to erode the Republicans' position and, in effect, to make a Democratic victory in 1960 more likely? The answer, of course, is plenty, more than could be discussed in detail here. There were, as mentioned earlier, tensions with mainland China in the Taiwan straits region, and difficulties in such places as Lebanon, Laos, Berlin, Cuba, and the Congo ("Zaire" since 1972). A nation with global responsibilities had to accept wide-ranging difficulties and expenses, spokesmen for the State Department and the so-called foreign policy establishment in New York kept reminding the public. But more than anything else, the concerns of these years that gradually eroded the Republican position resulted from frightening advances in military technology and in potential military capabilities. Incorrect without necessarily being insincere, Democrats, disgruntled military officers, and journalists could use these developments to claim that America was falling dangerously behind Russia in the arms race and to call for large new defense expenditures.

When Eisenhower rejected these demands as unnecessary for the nation's defense and potentially harmful to its economy, the more hardline Democrats, such as Senators Stuart Symington of Missouri and Henry Jackson of Washington, suggested that the president was flirting with disaster. "Though by early 1959 we knew the Soviet Union still led us in certain areas of missile research and production . . . ," Eisenhower noted in his memoirs, "we also knew that our total defense capabilities—including manned bombers, emerging long-range ballistic missiles, and nuclear weapons of all kinds—had a superiority overwhelming enough to deter the Soviet leaders from aggression." Fearing Russia and lacking the knowledge to evaluate complex defense issues, the general public, as in the late 1940s and again in the late 1970s, tended to be susceptible to warnings about America's "weakness."

The public's susceptibility to "missile gap" charges began on October 4, 1957, when Russia stunned Western opinion by launching the first man-made satellite, *Sputnik I*. Russia might have a larger army, Europeans and Americans had believed, but surely the United States, which had first developed atomic weapons and numerous other scientific marvels, was years ahead in technology. In one stroke the Russians had demonstrated that this was not necessarily the case, and predictably Khrushchev boasted about it. A summary of *Sputnik*'s implications—more useful in illustrating the widely shared perception that America now was on the defensive than in explaining what actually had happened—appeared shortly thereafter in the *New York Times:*

> *Militarily*, the launching of *Sputnik* means that Russia is ahead of the U.S. in rocket development. That lends substance to the Soviet claim of

> having at least a prototype of the "ultimate weapon"—the intercontinental ballistic missile [ICBM].
>
> *Politically*, the satellite gave the Russians an opportunity to proclaim the Soviet Union a first-class power whose views must carry weight in every capital. . . . They are already moving to undermine Western alliances by suggesting that the U.S. and Russia deal directly with each other on such questions as control of arms and spheres of influence. . . .
>
> *Psychologically*, Moscow used the satellite as ground for assertions of scientific preeminence and military power, as proof that communism is the wave of the future. The impact of those assertions on other nations, particularly the uncommitted, could be formidable.

American analysts understandably assumed that the Soviets would press their temporary advantage in high-powered rocket boosters and quickly develop a large ICBM force capable of raining nuclear weapons on American cities. Instead, the Soviets decided to deploy only a few of the expensive liquid-fuel missiles in the next few years, thus waiting until cheaper solid-fuel missiles became feasible in the mid-1960s. But they did deploy large numbers of intermediate-range ballistic missiles (IRBMs), thus enabling Khrushchev to threaten West Europeans with destruction if his demands were not met. Under pressure from the Chinese to show toughness in dealing with the "imperialists" and from East Germany to resolve the Berlin issue, Khrushchev embarked in 1958 on a series of gambling, dramatic initiatives designed to break the East-West stalemate and achieve tangible gains for Russia.

Khrushchev's difficulties with regard to East Germany and Berlin—especially the relative affluence of West Berlin and the departure since 1949 of approximately 3 million East Germans through West Berlin to the greater freedom and opportunity of West Germany—caused serious strains for the German Democratic Republic, the East German communist state headed by Walter Ulbricht. From the Soviet viewpoint, the situation was at least as bad as it had been when Stalin had tried to force a resolution of the issue a decade before. Unless Khrushchev could convince or coerce the West to stabilize the situation through such steps as establishing diplomatic relations with Ulbricht's regime, the situation for the Soviets apparently could only get worse. But West German politicians of all major parties agreed during these years that formal recognition of East Germany—in effect, abandoning forever the dream of German reunification "in freedom"—was politically unthinkable; and Washington gave its unqualified backing to the West German position. Moreover, Khrushchev was worried about the growing West German military strength as well as NATO plans to provide nuclear delivery systems to West Germany.

Having failed at Geneva and elsewhere to convince Western leaders to negotiate to ease Russia's problems in Germany, Khrushchev in 1958 began to try to coerce them to do so. On November 10 he announced that the West would have six months in which to negotiate with the Soviets concerning its rights in Berlin. If serious negotiations had not begun by then, he warned that Russia would sign a separate peace treaty with East Germany, and that thereafter the West would have to deal directly with Ulbricht's government. Responding to this diplomacy by ultimatum, hawks in Congress urged a sharp buildup in American military strength, but Eisenhower refused, commenting after one National Security Council meeting that "in this gamble, we are not going to be betting white chips, building up the pot gradually and fearfully. Khrushchev should know that when we decide to act, our whole stack will be in the pot."

If Eisenhower did not increase defense expenditures, neither did he negotiate under duress. Instead, he calmly denied that a crisis existed. Asked by a reporter in March 1959 whether he would "use nuclear war . . . to defend free Berlin," the president replied: "Well, I don't know how you could free anything with nuclear weapons." Characteristically, Khrushchev alternated between making conciliatory statements and threatening West European leaders with nuclear destruction if they refused to negotiate. But when the Allies agreed to negotiate he let the deadline pass without signing the treaty with East Germany, and he accepted Eisenhower's invitation to visit the United States in September 1959.

Khrushchev's thirteen-day visit—the first ever by a top Soviet leader—was one vast media event. As the stocky, outspoken premier visited Washington, New York, and other cities and rural areas in the West and Midwest, finally returning to Washington for talks at nearby Camp David, the press and television followed his every word and action. When Secretary of the Treasury Douglas Dillon asked him a hostile question about the meaning of peaceful coexistence, Khrushchev responded, "Mr. Dillon, if you don't understand what peaceful coexistence between two systems is, I'm sorry. The time will come when you'll have to learn." In New York he responded to a group of businessmen extolling capitalism with the comment, "Every duck praises its marsh." After seeing a dance routine in Hollywood, he remarked that "humanity's face is more beautiful than its backside." According to a Gallup poll at the time, 52 percent considered Khrushchev's visit a "good thing," 19 percent thought it was a "bad thing," and 29 percent were neutral or undecided.

In his cordial meetings with Eisenhower at Camp David, Khrushchev agreed to abandon his ultimatum on Berlin when Eisenhower acknowledged that the military occupation of the city could not last forever. In addition to Berlin, the two leaders spent considerable time discussing Eisenhower's greatest concern of his last years in office, the need to end the arms race. "You know, we really should come to some sort of an agreement in order to stop this fruitless, really wasteful rivalry," Eisenhower commented. "That's one of our dreams . . . ," Khrushchev responded. "But how can we agree? On what basis?" Although no major arms control agreements were reached before Eisenhower left office, in 1958 the two governments had begun negotiations to ban atmospheric nuclear testing. Significantly, both sides observed a moratorium on such testing for nearly three years, until the international climate worsened in 1961.

The hopes of Khrushchev and Eisenhower to make substantial improvements in East-West relations, already strained by Chinese criticisms of coexistence and by French and West German reluctance to move too fast, came crashing to earth in May 1960. As with *Sputnik* two and one-half years before, military technology played a major role. Since 1956 the CIA, under the president's direction, had been using high-flying, lightweight U-2 aircraft to conduct surveillance of Soviet military installations. The Soviets knew about these flights and, Khrushchev recalled, "were more infuriated and disgusted every time a violation [of Soviet air space] occurred." To the Soviets, the flights were not only an insult to their sovereignty, but also a painful reminder of their inferiority to the West in most areas of military technology. The Russian leaders thus were elated when, after being hit by a Soviet antiaircraft missile, a U-2 crashed to the ground in central Russia in May and its pilot, Francis Gary Powers, who had bailed out, was captured.

The ensuing events offer a classic illustration of the triumph of national pride over conciliation in a time of unexpected tension. The administration first tried the cover story that a weather plane might have strayed accidentally over Soviet territory. Then, when Khrushchev produced Powers, the wrecked plane, and details of the U-2's mission, Eisenhower finally admitted the overflight. Wishing to maintain reasonably good relations between the two countries, Khrushchev carefully avoided blaming the president. But Eisenhower took full responsibility for the flight and, while saying that the U-2 missions would now stop, refused to apologize for Powers's flight. It had been necessary, he maintained, because of Russia's military secrecy. Although the administration mishandled the U-2 incident, it must be noted in fairness that the flights had provided the intelligence information that had enabled Eisenhower to resist the demands for higher defense expenditures.

Now it was Khrushchev's turn to defend his nation's pride. At the four-power summit meeting in Paris on May 16, the Soviet premier, in a bitter speech, accused America of aggression, demanded an apology for the U-2 missions as a condition for continuing the meetings, and withdrew his invitation for Eisenhower to visit Russia. When Eisenhower in a calm response refused to meet Khrushchev's demands, the Soviet delegation walked out, thus ending the summit before any substantive discussions had taken place. Because of the reactions on both sides to the U-2 incident, therefore, the president's sincere effort to improve U.S-Soviet relations collapsed eight months before he left office.

In his memoirs Khrushchev claimed credit for helping Senator Kennedy defeat Vice-President Nixon in the election that fall. Wishing to help Kennedy, Soviet leaders made the decision, Khrushchev revealed, to turn down the Eisenhower administration's request to release Powers before the election. Moreover, if the summit had been successful and if Eisenhower had visited Russia, the Republicans could have stood in 1960 as the party that had lessened East-West tensions.

Instead, due to the heightened Cold War tensions that continued throughout the year, Kennedy was able to keep Nixon on the defensive on foreign affairs in the campaign, insisting repeatedly that Eisenhower and Nixon had not done enough to defeat international communism. Although the election of 1960 is remembered primarily for its series of debates between the two relatively youthful and skilled campaigners, it might equally be remembered as a high-water mark of harsh Cold War rhetoric by both parties.

Whether Khrushchev's hostility to the West in 1960 actually helped Kennedy is not clear, for the young senator won the presidency by the thinnest of margins at a time when there were far more registered Democrats than Republicans. What is apparent in retrospect is that Khrushchev's hardline approach affected the new administration's policy toward Russia, and that he ultimately had the most to lose from the continuing deterioration of U.S.-Soviet relations after May 1960.

As they had during Eisenhower's last years as president, Cold War issues dominated public discourse during Kennedy's first two. In addition to unresolved problems relating to Berlin and to the frightening technology of the arms race, the Democratic administration that took office in January 1961 faced immediate competition with Russia in the Congo, Laos, and Cuba. It also faced a Republican party that, shorn of Eisenhower's calming leadership, demanded that Kennedy take an uncompromising stand toward international communism.

As there had been partisan pressure to take a stronger stand on China and Russia during the first dangerous phase of the Cold War, so there was heavy partisan pressure to take a bellicose position on Cuba and other Cold War issues in the early 1960s. On Cuba, for example, leading Democrats denounced the incumbent Republicans during 1960 for "doing nothing" about Premier Fidel Castro, and leading Republicans leveled precisely the same charge against the incumbent Democrats in 1961 and 1962. The result was a political atmosphere that was in some ways even more hardline toward any evidence of communist activity abroad than it had been a decade before.

During his first two months in office, Kennedy gave more personal attention to the situation in Laos than to any other single issue. U.S. policy in the late 1950s in this small, landlocked nation in Southeast Asia had contributed substantially to the problems that Kennedy now faced. Fearing the involvement of local communists in the Laotian government, the Eisenhower administration in 1959 had helped to overthrow the neutralist government of Souvanna Phouma and install a pro-Western one. But this new government had proved less viable than the previous one, thus allowing the Pathet Lao, a communist-led coalition, to gain both support and additional territory. Moreover, shortly after Kennedy took office the Soviets airlifted military supplies to the Pathet Lao.

Applying the usual Cold War double standard, U.S. officials professed to be horrified by this evidence of Soviet activity in Laos, a country in which the CIA had been doing most of the supplying of arms and manipulating of officials. Accordingly, Kennedy went on television on March 15 to warn the Russians that America might go to war in Laos if the pro-Western government's position continued to deteriorate. Neither Kennedy nor Khrushchev wanted war in this obscure nation, however, and negotiations to neutralize Laos began later that spring.

U.S. officials estimated that, in the absence of direct U.S. military intervention, the communists gradually would take control in Laos. In order to forestall a similar fate in neighboring South Vietnam, the administration moved in the spring and summer of 1961 to increase military aid to Diem's government and, beginning in early 1962, to send several thousand military "advisers" to South Vietnam. It is probably helpful to Eisenhower's historical reputation that he left office when he did, for the time bomb that his administration had planted in South Vietnam was getting ready to explode by the early 1960s. Diem's autocratic government was becoming increasingly unpopular, as large public demonstrations and repeated self-immolations by protesting, anti-Diem, Buddhist monks in 1963 confirmed. Diem's unpopularity, in turn, played into the hands of the communist Viet Cong guerrillas, who began in 1960 to operate openly, with support from North Vietnam, and succeeded in building a strong infrastructure in South Vietnam's rural areas.

Fearing sharp criticism from conservatives if he "lost" South Vietnam the way Truman had "lost" China, Kennedy gradually increased U.S. military personnel in South Vietnam to 16,500 while at the same time urging Diem to make reforms designed to win popular support. Although generally wishing to avoid publicity about the war in Vietnam, the administration did not seek to hide the fact that its new emphasis in military training on counterinsurgency (a fancy name for antiguerrilla warfare) was being tested there. Also being tested—and found wanting—in both the Eisenhower and the Kennedy-Johnson years was the theory of "nation-building," which was carried out increasingly behind barbed wire in "strategic hamlets." In addition to difficulties inherent in applying American ideas to Vietnamese circumstances, this program failed because of relentless Viet Cong attacks and because of the South Vietnamese government's ineffective effort to implement it.

Except for occasional questioning of policy toward Diem in liberal magazines, there was little domestic criticism of Kennedy's approach until the summer of 1963. Even then the criticism was directed mainly against U.S. support of Diem, not against the Cold War premises underlying the U.S. military involvement in South Vietnam. When Diem was overthrown with American approval on November 1, 1963, leading officials and journalists welcomed the development as strengthening the U.S. position in Southeast Asia. And when Kennedy was assassinated in Dallas three weeks later, the new president, Lyndon Johnson, and other top U.S. officials believed that America's prestige and honor were at stake in the continuing war in Vietnam. The U.S. "commitment" in Vietnam had taken on a life of its own.

In 1961 and 1962, communist Cuba was an incomparably larger public issue than either Laos or Vietnam. It was a hundred times closer to American soil (roughly ninety miles versus nine thousand); it had traditionally been within the U.S. sphere of influence; it had a leader whom the American news media depicted as a devil; it had exiles who settled in the United States and stirred popular opinion against Castro; and it had much more public support from Khrushchev than did the Pathet Lao or the Viet Cong.

When Castro had come to power through revolution in January 1959, many Americans had welcomed the change from the brutal, unpopular Batista regime. But relations between Cuba and the nation many Latin Americans had long considered the "colossus of the North" declined gradually in 1959 and more rapidly after Russia signed a trade agreement with Cuba the following February and Castro announced that his sympathies were with the socialist camp. Before the revolution, U.S. businesses had owned well over half of several key sectors of the Cuban economy, much of which Castro sought to bring under his government's control. What U.S. officials overlooked in their rush to denounce Castro's policies was that it would have been virtually impossible for Castro to implement significant social change in Cuba while fully compensating U.S. economic interests there. What critics of U.S. policy often ignored was that Castro not only was establishing a harsh dictatorship, but he also was aiding and encouraging communist revolutionaries in other Latin American nations.

By the time Kennedy took office the CIA, emboldened by its easy victory in Guatemala six years earlier, had developed a plan to train Cuban exiles to invade the island and precipitate the overthrow of Castro's government. Kennedy had insisted during the campaign that the government should be doing more to topple Castro, and now he could turn his words into actions. Although somewhat skeptical, Kennedy approved the continuation of planning for the mission and, in early April, approved the invasion itself. But he put the CIA on notice that U.S. involvement would remain limited, that he was making no promises to have U.S. troops bail out the fourteen hundred exiles should they encounter difficulties.

Unfortunately, CIA operatives failed to explain fully to the exiles the limited nature of the U.S. commitment, thus contributing to the bitterness in the exile community when the operation quickly failed and most of the invaders were killed or captured. Widely criticized by world leaders and by common citizens in Latin America, Western Europe, and elsewhere, the Bay of Pigs invasion remains a prime example of superpower arrogance and foolishness in a period of high international tensions.

Khrushchev soon demonstrated that he could be as foolhardy in his own way as Kennedy had been in his. At a summit meeting with the president at Vienna in early June, the Soviet leader was as blunt and blustering to Kennedy as he had been to Eisenhower the year before. Although Khrushchev did agree to help find a peaceful solution in Laos, he insisted that Russia retained the right to aid liberation struggles in the Third World. More ominously, he re-imposed his deadline on resolving the German issue, and declared that Berlin must become a "free city" without Allied military forces. This time, Khrushchev insisted, he was not bluffing: the decision to sign a separate treaty with East Germany if the deadline passed was irrevocable. "What I said might have sounded like a threat to Kennedy," Khrushchev admitted later.

Upon his return to Washington, Kennedy gave a somber televised report on his trip but declined to mention the ultimatum. Khrushchev, who was under tremendous pressure from East Germany and from his Kremlin colleagues to resolve the Berlin issue, publicized his threat concerning Berlin in mid-June.

Like Eisenhower during the preceding Berlin crisis, Kennedy soon was subjected to demands from hardliners within the government, from the opposition party in Congress, and from much of the press to demonstrate Western determination. Unlike his experienced predecessor, Kennedy acceded to these demands, and in a television address on July 25 asked Congress for $3.2 billion to supplement the regular defense budget, for authority to call up the reserves, and for a stepped-up civil defense program.

As was its practice during the Cold War, Congress moved quickly to approve all the military measures Kennedy requested. Leaving no doubt of his "toughness," Kennedy soon called up several reserve units for a one-year tour of duty and sponsored programs that urged the public to build fallout shelters for use in the event of nuclear war with Russia. Dismayed that America was proceeding with a rapid arms buildup at a time when it already had substantial nuclear superiority, Khrushchev insisted that the West was overreacting to his demands.

Fortunately for East-West relations if not for the residents of Berlin, Khrushchev and Ulbricht found their own way of stopping the hemorrhage of East Germans to the West, and thus of making the presence of free West Berlin in their midst more tolerable for the East German government. In the early morning of August 13, East German security forces began sealing off all roads between East and West Berlin, and within days a heavily guarded concrete-block wall separated the two halves of the city. The Western powers protested this move but, again recognizing the post–World War II division of Europe, did nothing effective to counter it. Like the Soviets' crushing of the Hungarian rebellion, the building of the Berlin Wall provided the West with valuable propaganda, for who would want to live in a country that refused to let its disaffected citizens leave?

Although Westerners denounced this Russian move at the time, it actually helped to defuse the Berlin crisis and, by stabilizing the situation within East Germany, paved the way for the subsequent easing of tensions in the area. But these consequences are much easier to grasp in retrospect than they were at the time, for U.S. officials had to continue to deal with persistent Soviet harassment of Western troop transports and military aircraft coming into Berlin. Khrushchev again let his deadline for the peace treaty with East Germany pass, but he was determined to keep reminding the Western powers that the situation in Berlin would remain abnormal until they established working relationships with the Ulbricht regime. So powerful a symbol of Cold War tensions was Berlin that, while the administration feverishly prepared its response during the Cuban missile crisis the next fall, many reporters assumed that the crisis atmosphere apparent in Washington probably involved Berlin.

In discussing the earlier dangerous phase of the Cold War, I emphasized the breakdown of effective communications between the two sides and the tendency to view the other side's actions in the worst possible light. Although there was much more diplomatic contact during the second dangerous phase, the same trends were apparent. Whatever the immediate issue—Laos, Berlin, nuclear testing—those in Washington and Moscow with a fervent Cold War perspective tended to respond to events in highly predictable ways. In Washington and in the American press, for example, Russia's resumption of nuclear testing late in the summer of 1961 frequently was viewed as a vicious attempt to intimidate the West into abandoning its position on Berlin. While this interpretation was plausible, the equally plausible explanation that the Soviets were trying to improve their inferior nuclear technology in the context of the Kennedy administration's rapid expansion of the U.S. missile force was largely discounted. But when America resumed atmospheric nuclear testing the following spring,

U.S. officials and most newspapers considered the move entirely justified. The issue of nuclear fallout, trumpeted during Russia's testing, now was played down or ignored entirely.

The unwillingness or inability to think clearly about how the other side might interpret one's own actions led to the Cuban missile crisis of October 1962, the climax of the Cold War. U.S. policy toward Cuba between 1960 and 1962 had violated every canon of international law and civilized bilateral behavior. America had sponsored an invasion, which had included bombing raids, against another sovereign state; it had trained and supplied exiles from that nation who, with the knowledge and support of the U.S. government, then conducted repeated raids against Cuba; it had engaged in frequent efforts to assassinate Castro; and it had canceled all trade with Cuba, virtually forcing some of the countries in Latin America that received U.S. aid to do likewise. Moreover, after the Bay of Pigs, Kennedy made several public statements reaffirming U.S. determination to overthrow the Cuban government. America had done all this and more to oppose a government that did not seriously threaten U.S. security, but which, like the United States, did reserve the right to try to influence developments in other Latin American nations. The Castro government's other major crime was that, partly in response to this unremitting U.S. hostility, it had allied itself ever more closely to the Soviet Union.

Recognizing that Cuba lay within the traditional U.S. sphere of influence, Soviet leaders had accepted an important role there only gradually with some reluctance. A relatively poor country with no valuable raw materials, Cuba did not offer the prospect of economic gain. Moreover, any Soviet military assistance might well be lost when, as expected, the "imperialists" to the north crushed Castro's revolution the same way the Soviets had eliminated Nagy's in Hungary. But Khrushchev, a committed communist, was inclined to assist a nation that, in his view, was choosing the communist path and thus was furthering the historic transformation of the world from capitalism to communism. He believed that he had every right under international law to assist another nation in defending itself from attack. If Castro succeeded with Soviet help, the premier could point to Cuba as an example of his effective leadership. Khrushchev also feared that, if Castro ever considered Soviet support insufficient, the Cuban leader might switch his loyalty to China, now Russia's bitter rival for leadership in the international communist movement.

Castro long had taken the U.S. threat to destroy his government seriously, and after the Bay of Pigs he successfully urged the Soviets to step up shipments of defensive weapons that could be used to raise the military losses America would have to accept if it tried to invade Cuba and overthrow its government. Although Republicans complained that Kennedy was "weak" in his dealings with Castro, U.S. officials argued throughout 1961 and 1962 that Cuba had the right to receive "defensive" weapons such as antiaircraft guns and fighter planes—as long as it did not export Soviet weapons to any other nation in the hemisphere. Under strong pressure from Republicans and Cuban exiles, in early September 1962 Kennedy warned that "very grave issues" would arise if the Soviets began to supply Cuba with offensive weapons such as ground-to-ground missiles. Since such missiles were at that very moment being introduced secretly into Cuba, the stage was set for confrontation when a U-2 flight over the western portion of the island discovered them on October 14.

Painfully aware of the poor planning and wishful thinking that had preceded his decision to authorize the invasion at the Bay of Pigs the year before, Kennedy set up a special committee of top officials, the ExComm (short for Executive Committee of the National Security Council), to debate the issue of how to respond to the Soviet move. This group, which included former Secretary of State Dean Acheson, spent a week debating U.S. options that ranged from invading Cuba or bombing the missile sites to proceeding through regular diplomatic channels to call for the missiles' removal or even doing nothing. The Joint Chiefs of Staff and some others, including Acheson, favored immediate military action to remove the missiles; others—led by Defense Secretary Robert McNamara and the president's closest confidant, Attorney General Robert Kennedy—supported a naval blockade followed, if necessary, by military action. The idea of trying to resolve the issue through private diplomatic approaches to the Soviets, perhaps by offering to trade the removal of Soviet missiles from Cuba for the withdrawal of U.S. missiles from Turkey, received little support. A key ExComm member was Llewellyn Thompson, a Soviet expert who had gotten to know Khrushchev and his colleagues well while serving as the U.S. ambassador in Moscow from 1957 to 1962. Thompson repeatedly gave sage advice about how the Soviet leaders were likely to react to the various U.S. actions that were being discussed; he helped to move the group away from urging immediate military strikes against Cuba.

Recently released audio tapes of meetings in the White House suggest that, among the many officials who offered ideas about how to react to the missiles, Kennedy himself was one of the most perceptive. Early in the deliberations, he noted that U.S. air strikes might be necessary to end the threat posed by the missiles. He soon became convinced, however, that U.S. military action carried grave risks and that other ways to remove the missiles should be tried first. By Thursday, October 18, Kennedy had concluded that "we should begin by blockading [the] Soviets against the shipment of additional offensive capacity, [and] that we could tighten the blockade as the situation requires."

On the evening of Monday, October 22, Kennedy dramatically went on national television to reveal the existence of the missiles, to announce the establishment of a U.S. naval "quarantine" (blockade) of Cuba to prevent the arrival of any additional offensive weapons, and to demand that Khrushchev remove the missiles immediately or face the gravest consequences. During six tense days filled with military maneuvers, public confrontations, secret diplomacy at the UN and in Washington, and statements of support from Allied leaders and of opposition from communist ones, the fate of the world—or at least much of the northern hemisphere—hung in the balance. Believing it genuinely possible that the Soviets might act impulsively or that a war might begin by accident, several U.S. officials feared that they and their loved ones might be dead before the end of the week. Soviet leaders wanted a peaceful outcome, but they also wished to avoid the humiliation of yielding to Kennedy's demands. Having witnessed the horrors of the German invasion during World War II, Khrushchev recalled that "the smell of burning" was again in the air.

The situation in and around Cuba was extremely tense. A huge U.S. military buildup in southern Florida and in the seas around Cuba convinced Castro that the U.S. was preparing to invade the island and topple his government. U.S. reconnaissance flights over Cuba were stepped up, including low-level flights over the missile sites. Cuban/ Soviet troops frequently fired at these planes, and on October 27 a Soviet antiaircraft battery shot down a U.S. plane and killed its pilot, despite instructions from Moscow to avoid provoking the Americans. Khrushchev was shaken by this development and feared that any misstep might might start a major war. The Soviet leader also was disturbed when Castro sent him a telegram that urged "the immediate launching of a nuclear strike on the United States" if the U.S. attacked Cuba. "You see how far things can go," Khrushchev told his advisers after reading Castro's message. "We've got to get those missiles out of there before a real fire starts."

Just how far things could have gone was confirmed in a startling revelation in 1992: Soviet commanders assisting in the defense of Cuba had battlefield nuclear weapons with roughly half the destructive force of the bombs dropped on Hiroshima and Nagasaki, and they might well have used them without consulting Moscow in the event of a U.S. invasion of Cuba—an option Kennedy was actively considering at the time the crisis was resolved. If America had invaded Cuba, Robert McNamara commented upon learning this new information, "there was a 99 percent probability that nuclear war would have been initiated."

Fortunately, diplomacy—what political scientist Alexander L. George calls "coercive diplomacy" because it was backed by the unmistakable threat of force—triumphed. After exchanges of messages and several days of quiet diplomacy in Washington, Robert Kennedy and Soviet Ambassador Anatoly Dobrynin discussed what appeared to be a final U.S. offer for peace on Saturday evening, October 27—an offer that led to what historian Barton Bernstein has called a "victory with compromise." At the meeting the president's brother made it clear to Dobrynin—and through him, to Khrushchev—that U.S. military action against Cuba was likely to occur very soon if the Soviets rejected the offer. The victory for America was the Soviet agreement to remove all of its missiles and long-range bombers from Cuba—a decision that infuriated Castro, especially because the Soviets did not even tell him about the deal before it was announced publicly on October 28. The compromise involved a public but vague U.S. promise not to invade Cuba and a private assurance to Dobrynin that the outmoded U.S. missiles in Turkey would be removed. To the relief of people all over the world, the Cuban missile crisis was over.

Why did the Soviets send the missiles to Cuba in the first place? The sinister reason that frequently appeared in the American press at the time—that Khrushchev must have been planning a surprise attack against the U.S. or Latin America—is not convincing, both because he could have attacked from Russia and, more important, because he had no desire to subject his country to the devastation of nuclear war. Much more credible is the explanation, corroborated by other Soviet sources, that Khrushchev gave in his memoirs: "The Americans had surrounded our country with military bases and threatened us with nuclear weapons, and now they would learn just what it feels like to have enemy missiles pointed at you." The Soviet ambassador to Cuba at the time, Aleksandr Alekseyev, was summoned to Moscow in May 1962 to be briefed on Khrushchev's plan. The Soviet leader was obsessed by his country's strategic inferiority, Alekseyev recalled, and "was looking for any way to talk to the Americans equally."

In the Soviet view, greater equality in nuclear arms would lessen the possibility that America might be tempted to strike first, destroy the Soviet nuclear capability, and suffer relatively little damage in return. And the fastest way to gain greater equality was to introduce medium-range missiles (of which the Soviets had ample supplies) into Cuba, which to the Soviets was the same as Americans having missiles in Western Europe and in Turkey.

A second reason was Khrushchev's belief that the missiles would prevent a U.S. invasion of Cuba to overthrow Castro, a move that Soviet and Cuban leaders considered quite likely in the atmosphere of continued hostility after the Bay of Pigs. A third reason was Khrushchev's hope—a classic example of wishful thinking—that Kennedy would accept the presence of the missiles in Cuba, so long as the Soviets kept their deployment secret until after the November elections. Finally, Khrushchev apparently believed that success in this venture not only would benefit him domestically, but that it also would demonstrate to the skeptical Chinese that the Soviets were the courageous leaders of the world communist movement.

And why did Kennedy pursue the course that he did? After all, in theory he could have accepted the presence of the missiles, which would not have prevented America from being able to destroy Russia in case of nuclear attack. In practice he believed that, given the strong public and congressional sentiment against both Russia and Cuba, he might well have been impeached if he had permitted the missiles to remain. Moreover, operational missiles in Cuba would have undermined the effectiveness of America's early warning systems, and they would have more than doubled the number of missiles the Russians could launch against U.S. targets. Granted that the missiles had to be removed, at least for political reasons and possibly also to maintain respect for U.S. leadership in world affairs, why did Kennedy not tell Soviet leaders privately that removal of the missiles had to begin by a certain date, and that the process had to be completed no later than another date?

This and other options that might have allowed Khrushchev to save face were rejected for a variety of reasons. Especially after the Bay of Pigs, Kennedy harbored an almost obsessive hatred of Castro, and he deeply resented the way Khrushchev had treated him at the Vienna summit. He also was angry that Soviet leaders had assured him repeatedly that no offensive weapons would be introduced into Cuba. Last and probably most important, as presidential aide Theodore Sorenson noted, Kennedy issued a public ultimatum partly to retain the diplomatic initiative in this delicate situation in which the missiles were rapidly becoming operational and in which Soviet officials already had shown considerable duplicity. By issuing a public ultimatum and instituting a blockade, Kennedy was making it clear to Russia's leaders that it was now impossible, personally and politically, for him to back down. In other words, this was not the time for more wishful thinking on Khrushchev's part.

Finally, why did Khrushchev agree to Kennedy's demand to remove the missiles? For one thing, Kennedy's approach (unlike the more hawkish bombing proposal) ruled out the killing of Russian soldiers and technicians, at least in the early stages of the crisis, and thus avoided putting Khrushchev under pressure to avenge the shedding of Russian blood. For another, the apparent proximity of nuclear war affected Khrushchev personally, as when he wrote movingly to Kennedy on October 26 that Russians "are normal people. . . [who] want to live and do not want to destroy your country." Khrushchev also appears to have had genuine respect for Kennedy as an honorable person who wanted peace and one who had the ability to recognize legitimate Soviet interests. "When he gave us public assurances that the U.S. would not organize an invasion of Cuba . . . ," Khrushchev recalled, "we trusted him."

By making the gross miscalculation that America would accept the presence of Soviet missiles in Cuba, Khrushchev flirted with the destruction not only of the missiles and the Russian technicians installing them, but also of Castro's government. And by blockading Cuba and by insisting publicly that Russia remove the missiles under the threat of force, Kennedy ran the risk that the Soviets, for reasons of national pride, would feel compelled to go to war rather than suffer a bitter humiliation. The Soviets also might have gone to war to defend their understanding of legitimate international behavior. As they pointed out at the time, it is an accepted principle in world affairs that one nation may assist another in providing for its defense. Indeed, the U.S. had built its containment policy after World War II on just this principle.

In view of the potential for catastrophe inherent in this situation, it is a tribute to both the Soviet and U.S. leaders that they showed sufficient restraint to reject the option of immediate military action, to negotiate in good faith in tense circumstances, and finally to pull their nations back from the brink of nuclear war. The prospect of all-out nuclear war, which never before had been so immediate and intense, contributed an important element of restraint on both sides. When it became clear within weeks after this sobering experience that both nations were seeking an improved atmosphere, the second dangerous phase of the Cold War was over.

Conclusion

Like the first phase of the Cold War, the second phase from 1953 through 1962 was marked by a huge gap on both sides between the repeatedly expressed desire for world peace and the reality of actions that contributed to East-West tensions. How could America, for example, insist on its commitment to world peace and at the same time refuse to let the actual government of the world's most populous nation occupy its country's seat in the United Nations? How could Russia convince other nations that it respected their independence movements while it was using force to suppress such developments in Eastern Europe? And how could either side, committed to perfecting its nuclear arsenal and (particularly for America) strengthening its military installations and covert operations bases around the globe, convince the other that its intentions were peaceful and defensive?

By the late 1950s and early 1960s, each superpower was running the real danger of becoming overcommitted, of assuming "responsibilities" that it could not fulfill. Russia was able to limit its involvement in places like Laos and the Congo, but it clearly overreached by placing missiles in Cuba. Similarly, America might get away with its covert activities in places like British Guiana and Indonesia, but skeptics were asking as early as 1962 whether U.S. troops would be any more successful in Vietnam than the French had been a decade earlier. By becoming deeply involved in a nation so close to America, Russia was asking for trouble; and by making commitments in an area of the world in which it had no vital interests, acting as if Vietnam were in Western Europe, America also was courting disaster.

These two key decisions—introducing Soviet missiles into Cuba and U.S. military "advisers" into Vietnam—were made at a time of great tension in East-West relations and must be viewed in that context. These fateful decisions also were made in the context of heavy domestic pressure on both Khrushchev and Kennedy to achieve some kind of victory in the Cold War. Like other miscalculations in the first dangerous phase, these actions at the height of the second dangerous phase of the Cold War reaffirm the conclusion that leaders of the opposing superpowers were especially prone to serious errors of policy at times in which their bilateral relations already had deteriorated sharply. Whether the leaders were Truman and Stalin or Kennedy and Khrushchev, the combination of hostility abroad and criticism at home could lead to policies in places like Korea, Vietnam, and Cuba that each superpower would come to regret.

But despite the frightening momentum of the Cold War and the double standard for judging international behavior prevalent in both Washington and Moscow, events after 1953 demonstrated that U.S.-

Soviet relations could be conducted at a more civilized level than they had been earlier. The several summit meetings between 1955 and 1961 allowed leaders to get to know each other and to learn which issues each side considered most urgent, and the negotiations on matters ranging from the important issue of arms control to the minor one of airline service between New York and Moscow paved the way for more substantial agreements beginning in 1963. The speed and openness with which negotiations were conducted during the week of the Cuban missile crisis suggests the value of the improvement in communications that occurred during the decade after Stalin's death.

In addition to defusing the Cuban crisis, leaders on both sides deserve credit for correctly gauging the other's view of its vital interests and thus avoiding war over such potentially explosive issues as Hungary, Suez, and Berlin. Cold War rhetoric and some actions notwithstanding, from 1953 forward top leaders in both countries generally were more interested in stabilizing U.S.-Soviet relations than they were in reaching out for clearcut victories over the other side. This was the reality upon which the two nations would build in the years following the brush with disaster in the fall of 1962.

The Cold War at Midpassage, 1957–1973

A PHOTO ESSAY

Overleaf: President Dwight D. Eisenhower (right) meets Premier H. S. Sudrawardy of Pakistan (a Third World ally) at the White House in July 1957. LC-U9-915-8.

Above: Vice-President Richard Nixon (far right) confers with Soviet Premier Nikita Khrushchev in Moscow in July 1959. LC-U9-2807-31. Opposite: Crowds line the streets during Premier Nikita Khrushchev's visit to Des Moines, Iowa, in September 1959. LC-U9-3113.

All photos courtesy of the Library of Congress.

THE ONLY
GOOD
COMMUNIST IS A
DEAD ONE

Above: A Soviet nuclear test, with tank maneuvers in foreground, in the late 1950s or early 1960s. LC-U9-10463. Opposite top: Downtown St. George, Utah, a community that frequently received high levels of raidiation from nuclear tests in Nevada during the the 1950s. LC-U9-907-0-2. Bottom: Unidentified woman examining model of a nuclear fallout shelter in September 1961. LC-U9-6743-6.

STANDARD
DESERET NEWS
MOUNTAIN WEST'S first NEWSPAPER

WASTE

The Cold War at Midpassage, 1957–1973

Opposite top: Section of the Berlin Wall, built in August 1961 to keep East Germans from escaping to the West. LC-U9-16223-23A/24. Bottom: U.S. and Soviet diplomats shake hands after signing the nuclear test ban treaty in Washington in August 1963. LC-U9-10240-23. Above: President John Kennedy (right) confers with Soviet Foreign Minister Andrei Gromyko in October 1963. LC-U9-10633-15.

Above: North Vietnam's Ho Chi Minh (left) seeks support from China's Mao Zedong in Beijing in November 1964. LC-U9-12776-4. Opposite top: National Security Adviser McGeorge Bundy (left) and General William Westmoreland (center) meet with U.S. forces in South Vietnam in February 1965. LC-U9-13316-17. Bottom: Soviet long-range missiles are paraded through Red Square in Moscow in May 1965. LC-14204-3.

Above: A large demonstration against the Vietnam War in Washington in October 1967. LC-U9-18187. Opposite top: President Lyndon Johnson discusses Vietnam policy with Secretary of State Dean Rusk (left) and Secretary of Defense Robert McNamara (right) in July 1965. LC-U9-14278-8A. Bottom: J. William Fulbright (left) and Wayne Morse, leading Senate critics of Johnson's Vietnam policy, confer in May 1966. LC-U9-15887.

Top: Reflecting the improvement in Sino-American relations, President Richard Nixon meets Chinese ping pong players in Washington in April 1972. LC-U9-25779A-10. Bottom: Secretary of State Henry Kissinger (center) and Defense Minister Melvin Laird (right) meet with Soviet Foreign Minister Andrei Gromyko (left) at the height of U.S.-Soviet détente in June 1973. LC-U9-27907-14A.

CHAPTER THREE

The Shift Toward Relative Détente, 1963–1972

During the forty years between the end of World War II and 1985, the decade between the resolution of the Cuban missile crisis in October 1962 and President Nixon's overwhelming reelection in November 1972 marks the only ten-year period during the Cold War in which U.S.-Soviet relations showed relatively steady improvement. In addition, Sino-American relations, which throughout the 1950s and 1960s symbolized the gulf separating the "Free World" from the "Communist bloc," improved dramatically in the early 1970s. When Nixon triumphantly visited both Beijing and Moscow in the first half of 1972 and pledged America to improved relations with both countries, and when Soviet officials subsequently visited Washington and toasted détente, the term "cold war" seemed applicable only to an earlier era.

At least as important as particular leaders like Nixon and Russia's Leonid Brezhnev in bringing about the relative détente of these years were international and domestic trends that established conditions conducive to improved East-West relations. There was the bitter Sino-Soviet split, fully public by the end of 1962, which made it in the interest of both countries to seek better relations with America in order to lessen their number of enemies. From the U.S. perspective, former CIA official Douglas S. Blaufarb has noted, the open split within the communist movement was the "most momentous" change in the international environment, making it possible for even hardline U.S. officials to put less emphasis on counterinsurgency by the late 1960s. "Before this development," Blaufarb observed, "the power balance appeared to depend upon containing the threat of monolithic Communism and preventing it from spreading further." There also was an important split within the Western alliance involving France's veto of Britain's bid to join the Common Market in January 1963, its recognition of mainland China a year later, and its growing independence from NATO in military policy. Other West European nations also moved toward expanded political and economic dealings with Russia, China, and East European nations, and the U.S. faced the choice of getting on the bus or being left behind.

Both the Sino-Soviet and the Franco-American rifts provided clear evidence of the importance of nationalism, of the refusal of nations in either bloc to defer obediently to the wishes of either superpower. And following Khrushchev's removal from power in October 1964, there was an emphasis in the Kremlin on less "adventurism" in foreign policy and on purchasing Western technology to improve the sluggish Soviet economy, both of which were welcomed by U.S. leaders.

Conditions within the U.S. also favored East-West détente. By 1963 the American public generally was tired of the bellicose Cold War rhetoric, as both public opinion polls and the response to diplomatic initiatives and conciliatory speeches demonstrated. By the late 1960s a large portion of both the public and the foreign policy establishment was sick of the seemingly endless Vietnam War, and most Americans had begun to question the Cold War clichés that trumpeted the virtue of ceaseless struggle against communism.

In addition to Vietnam and Lyndon Johnson's widely criticized intervention in the Dominican Republic in 1965 to prevent "another Cuba," pressing domestic problems such as race relations, inflation, and militant dissent among disaffected young people shifted attention away from superpower relations, and liberals insisted that the nation "reorder its priorities." Moreover, the policy of isolating China was steadily losing ground in both U.S. and international opinion, and many within the business community believed that restrictions on trade with Russia and Eastern Europe were untenable at a time when America was no longer as dominant in the international economy as it had been in the 1940s and 1950s. Despite continuing suspicion of Russia and China, therefore, most Americans supported concrete steps toward improving East-West relations. The stage was set for a highly constructive period in great power diplomacy.

An Improved Atmosphere in 1963

The last year of Kennedy's presidency was a watershed in U.S.-Soviet relations. In addition to the "Treaty Banning Nuclear Weapons Tests in the Atmosphere, in Outer Space and Under Water" signed in Moscow in August 1963, the two nations made a number of lesser agreements, including the installation of a "hot line" between the White House and the Kremlin to facilitate communications in times of crisis. In a move that served as a precedent for subsequent large-scale business deals, Kennedy in October 1963 approved the sale, through private channels, of $250 million of surplus American wheat to Russia. In a letter to Congress justifying his action, the president emphasized the practical point that "such sales will strengthen farm prices in the United States and bring added income and employment to American shipping, longshoremen and railroad workers as well as grain traders and farmers." Noting the improved atmosphere, a reporter covering U.S.-Soviet relations observed on October 3 that "the discussion has now been brought down from the realm of ideology to the familiar precincts of traditional diplomacy."

Although advocates of nuclear disarmament would have preferred an agreement banning underground testing as well, the test ban treaty still was a significant first step toward bringing the nuclear arms race under at least modest control. The signers eventually included more than one hundred nations, including the three major nuclear powers at the time—America, Britain, and Russia—but not France and China, both in the early stages of developing their nuclear capabilities. Atmospheric testing by the two superpowers had increased Cold War tensions and caused environmental damage from the mid-1940s through the early 1960s, and these in themselves were sufficient reasons to applaud the treaty. But its larger significance was that it demonstrated, after years of failure and disappointment, that the two sides were capable of achieving specific agreements in the emotion-charged area of defense policy. By undercutting the argument of hardliners on both sides that the only choice was to arm to the teeth and prepare for Armageddon, the successful negotiations made it possible to think in terms of additional agreements to bring some predictability to the arms race.

A key marker along the road to signing the treaty was a speech Kennedy gave at American University on June 10, 1963. In a tone far more conciliatory than is found in his major addresses of 1961 and 1962, the president told the graduating seniors that "both the United States and its allies, and the Soviet Union and its allies, have a mutually deep interest in a just and genuine peace and in halting the arms race." He urged Americans to "reexamine our attitude toward the cold war"; the time had come "not to see only a distorted and desperate view of the other side, not to see conflict as inevitable, accommodation as impossible, and communication as nothing more than an exchange of threats."

Kennedy reminded his listeners of Soviet sacrifices in World War II, of Russia's numerous achievements, and of the fact that the two nations had never been at war; yet "we are both caught up in a vicious and dangerous cycle in which suspicion on one side breeds suspicion on the other, and new weapons breed counterweapons." Promising that America "will never start a war," Kennedy urged Soviet leaders to work with him to break this cycle, and he outlined specific steps the United States was taking to facilitate the completion of a test ban treaty.

Kennedy's speech and his appointment of the respected Averell Harriman to head the nation's negotiating team were taken in Moscow as signs of U.S. seriousness in seeking a test ban treaty. The speech was reprinted in full in Soviet newspapers; some Russians, as tired of the Cold War as were many Americans, carried clippings of the speech in their wallets for months as a symbol of the improved East-West atmosphere. The president continued his largely conciliatory approach to the Soviets until his assassination that November. At the UN on September 29, for example, he applauded the "pause in the Cold War," urged "further agreements" to slow the arms race, and insisted that "the badge of responsibility in the modern world is a willingness to seek peaceful solutions." Although Kennedy balanced his speeches with reminders that "basic differences" in outlook still remained, his approach was more conducive to improved relations than it had been in previous years.

Khrushchev, for his part, was eager to improve relations with the West at a time of intense Sino-Soviet hostility. The Russians needed a positive achievement to balance the humiliation in Cuba the previous fall, and they also needed concrete agreements with the West to demonstrate to other communist parties that their policy of peaceful coexistence was more beneficial than Beijing's outspoken insistence on hostility toward the capitalist nations. Far behind the West in nuclear missiles and bombers, the Russians needed time to move toward equality in strategic weapons before risking another confrontation with the United States. As Soviet Deputy Foreign Minister Vassily Kuznetsov bitterly warned U.S. diplomat John McCloy shortly after the missile crisis, "You Americans will never be able to do this to us again." Most important, the Russians needed agreements with the West in order to ensure that they would be able to meet the challenge from China. Indeed, negotiations in Moscow between Russia and China broke off—without any progress toward resolving outstanding issues—on July 21, just four days before Soviet, British, and U.S. negotiators completed the test ban treaty.

The abrupt shift in the international atmosphere contributed to a debate in America about what its implications were, and about what additional steps, if any, should be taken. Young liberals seemed most willing to plunge ahead to try to end the Cold War: a group of students defied the official ban on travel to Cuba in the summer of 1963, and the Young Democrats of California resolved in September that America should recognize mainland China, improve relations with Cuba and East Germany, and withdraw its forces from Vietnam. At the other end of the political spectrum, conservatives tried to prevent Senate ratification of the Test Ban Treaty (it passed, 80 to 19, on September 24), criticized the grain deal with Russia, and denounced Kennedy in October for holding talks in the White House with a communist leader, Josip Broz Tito of Yugoslavia, while refusing to meet with a member of South Vietnam's ruling family. Conservative journalists nervously asked where the relaxation of tensions would end. Would Kennedy next follow Canada's example and sell grain to China? Would he seek to establish relations with Cuba?

When asked such questions at press conferences, Kennedy generally denied any change in policy toward other communist nations, and he disassociated himself from the Young Democrats' resolutions. Kennedy already viewed Goldwater as his likely opponent in the 1964 election, and he did not want to risk losing the middle ground in foreign policy to him. But there is considerable evidence that the president was thinking seriously about shifting U.S. policy on China and Vietnam—if not on Cuba—after his probable reelection. Roger Hilsman and some others at the State Department worked on developing a policy of greater flexibility toward China during 1962 and 1963, and Kennedy said at his last press conference on November 14, 1963, that the administration was "not wedded to a policy of hostility to Red China." When Quaker leaders visiting with Kennedy in the White House that summer urged him to improve relations with China, Kennedy listened sympathetically and responded, "You light a fire under me, and I'll move on it."

Similarly, Kennedy told Senator Mike Mansfield in early 1963 that he planned a complete military withdrawal from Vietnam after the election. "If I tried to pull out completely now, we would have another Joe McCarthy red scare on our hands, but I can do it after I'm reelected," he explained to presidential aide Kenneth O'Donnell after Mansfield departed. "So we had better make damned sure that I am reelected."

Although he insisted publicly throughout 1963 that America should not abandon its commitment in Vietnam, Kennedy made comments similar to those he made to Mansfield and O'Donnell to dovish Senator Wayne Morse and to presidential aide Michael Forrestal in the fall of 1963. Kennedy told Forrestal on November 21: "we have to start to plan for what we are going to do now in South Vietnam. I want to start a complete and very profound review of how we got into this country, and what we thought we were doing, and what we now think we can do. I even want to think about whether or not we should be there." The upcoming election prevented any "drastic changes of policy, quickly," Kennedy said, but he wanted to consider "how some kind of a gradual shift in our presence in South Vietnam [could] occur."

Equally persuasive testimony that Kennedy was thinking seriously about pulling U.S. troops out of Vietnam comes from Secretary of Defense Robert McNamara, who has told several fellow officials and interviewers that he and Kennedy jointly made the decision in October 1963 to remove all U.S. troops from Vietnam by the end of 1965. "I know for a fact that John Kennedy would have withdrawn from Vietnam," McNamara later told a colleague at the World Bank. He elaborated in an interview with biographer Deborah Shapley:

> I believed that we had done all the training we could. Whether the South Vietnamese were qualified or not to turn back the North Vietnamese, I was certain that if they weren't, it wasn't for lack of our training. More training wouldn't strengthen them; therefore we should get out. The President agreed.
>
> Then there was an argument over whether we should announce the decision. I thought the way to put the decision in concrete was to announce it. So we did [in a White House press release on October 2, 1963]. . . . Those who opposed the decision to begin the withdrawal didn't want it announced since they recognized, as I did, that if it were announced it would be in concrete.

To note that Kennedy and his defense secretary were thinking about removing the U.S. troops from South Vietnam does not prove that Kennedy would have done so if he had lived and been reelected. What he would have done can never be known. But it does suggest that, in the context of the administration's new self-confidence after the Cuban missile crisis, Kennedy was considering a shift away from some policies that had seemed appropriate in the frigid atmosphere of 1961. If so, his cautious, largely private shift on Asian policy may be seen as paralleling his emphatic, public shift on policy toward Russia.

Unfortunately, Kennedy did not share his private thoughts on Vietnam with his vice-president, Lyndon Johnson, or with his secretary of state, Dean Rusk, both of whom were more conventional Cold Warriors than Kennedy, especially in regard to Asia. The president from Massachusetts had not developed a close personal relationship with either of these sons of the South—then still a region that many Northerners considered inferior. As with Truman in April 1945, LBJ, who took power in November 1963, was relatively inexperienced in foreign affairs and ill-informed about the intricacies of his predecessor's policies.

Vietnam at Center Stage, 1964–1968

Although other issues existed, the five-year Johnson presidency was dominated by race relations at home and Vietnam abroad. On the one, Johnson reacted with both compassion and substantial effectiveness; on the other, he responded with neither imagination nor common sense. His policy of sharply escalating the U.S. military involvement in Indochina, after running as a man of peace in the 1964 election, alienated many liberals, and his apparent determination to pursue victory in Vietnam regardless of the consequences alienated allies in Western Europe and strained relations with Russia and China. But this was by no means a totally negative period in East-West relations, for both America and Russia were interested in maintaining at least some of the momentum for improved relations begun in 1963, and pressures built within the U.S. to try to develop a more constructive policy toward Beijing.

Why did Johnson and the chief foreign policy advisers that he kept on after Kennedy's death—Rusk, McNamara, and national security adviser McGeorge Bundy—decide in early 1965 to begin bombing North Vietnam and to send substantial numbers of U.S. combat troops to fight in South Vietnam? Although the administration frequently deceived the public and withheld information about specific military operations (e.g., the Gulf of Tonkin incident off North Vietnam in August 1964 and the secret bombing of Laos from the mid-1960s through the early 1970s), it was quite open about the basic reasons for sending hundreds of thousands of U.S. troops to Indochina. In its view, it was doing precisely what Eisenhower and Kennedy had done: helping the South Vietnamese government defeat the communist insurgents, and thereby demonstrating that America "keeps its commitments" and that "aggression doesn't pay." More broadly, it was following the Cold War policy of containing communism and upholding what it considered to be the proper balance of power in Southeast Asia. U.S. power—notably America's overwhelming technological superiority over North Vietnam—should enable the United States to achieve these goals, officials reasoned.

The argument of the preceding paragraph—that Johnson and his top advisers made the decision in early 1965 to change the character of the U.S. involvement in Vietnam—is only partially accurate. Although Johnson listened to his advisers and adopted some of their suggestions, the decision was Johnson's alone to make, and he made it. In a 1993 interview Bundy commented that the president himself made the decision to turn Vietnam into America's war. Bundy also argued that he, Rusk, and McNamara would have supported Johnson if he had decided against America's taking over the war—a decision that Bundy believes Kennedy probably would have made had he lived because of his greater skepticism about the prospects for victory and his greater doubt about whether victory in Vietnam was vital to America's standing as leader of the free world. Ignoring Bundy's warnings at the time, Johnson also alienated many members of Congress in 1965 by unilaterally changing the original intent of the Gulf of Tonkin resolution—to warn North Vietnam not to challenge the U.S. advisory mission in Vietnam—into an assumed congressional approval of the huge expansion of the U.S. role in the war.

Perhaps the clearest statements of Johnson's position were contained in a speech he gave at Johns Hopkins University on April 17, 1965, and in a special message to Congress four weeks later. "Our objective is the independence of South Viet-Nam, and its freedom from attack," Johnson said in his speech. "We want nothing for ourselves—only that the people of South Viet-Nam be allowed to guide their own country in their own way." American intervention was justified because "North Viet-Nam has attacked the independent nation of South Viet-Nam" and because North Vietnam's leaders "are urged on by Peking." In the president's view, the stakes were much larger than simply the fate of South Vietnam: people from West Berlin to Thailand counted on America's keeping its commitments.

"The aim [of the communists] in Viet-Nam is not simply the conquest of the South, tragic as that would be," Johnson asserted in his message to Congress asking for $700 million in additional appropriations for the war. "It is to show that the American commitment is worthless. Once that is done, the gates are down and the road is open to expansion and endless conquest." Citing the Cold War experience in places like Iran, Greece, and Korea, Johnson insisted that "the American people . . . have learned the great lesson of this generation:

wherever we have stood firm aggression has been halted, peace restored and liberty maintained."

The greatest error Johnson made in the spring of 1965 was to base his policy less on the concrete realities of the situation in Vietnam and the marginal U.S. interests there than on the alleged aims of international communism and on painful memories of past experiences at home and abroad. Given the Sino-Soviet split and Ho Chi Minh's partly nationalist brand of communism, to speak of an international communist movement bent on "endless conquest" showed limited insight into the situation in Vietnam. The communist leadership in Hanoi capitalized on the long-standing determination of Vietnamese nationalists to end foreign domination, and on the general perception of the Americans as colonial successors to the French. The U.S.-backed government in Saigon suffered from the overwhelming U.S. presence and tried vainly to compensate by sheer military force for what it lacked in political appeal. In this situation Ho and his colleagues, although dependent on aid from both Russia and China, were nevertheless the only credible liberators of Vietnam in the eyes of millions of their compatriots. Their objective, widely shared, was to remove U.S. power from South Vietnam and unite the country.

Johnson's Cold War mentality and fear of renewed McCarthyism as influences on his policy in 1965 emerged graphically in a subsequent interview with political scientist Doris Kearns:

> . . . everything I knew about history told me that if I got out of Vietnam and let Ho Chi Minh run through the streets of Saigon, then I'd be doing exactly what Chamberlain [British prime minister in the late 1930s, who became the symbol of appeasement] did in World War II. I'd be giving a big fat reward to aggression. And I knew that if we let Communist aggression succeed in taking over South Vietnam, there would follow in this country an endless national debate . . . that would shatter my Presidency, kill my administration, and damage our democracy. I knew that Harry Truman and Dean Acheson had lost their effectiveness from the day that the Communists took over China. I believed that the loss of China had played a large role in the rise of Joe McCarthy. And I knew that all these problems, taken together, were chickenshit compared with what might happen if we lost Vietnam.

Although Johnson and other officials offered plausible explanations for their prowar stand, the greater reality for most policymakers by 1966 or 1967 was a sense of anguish and disappointment that,

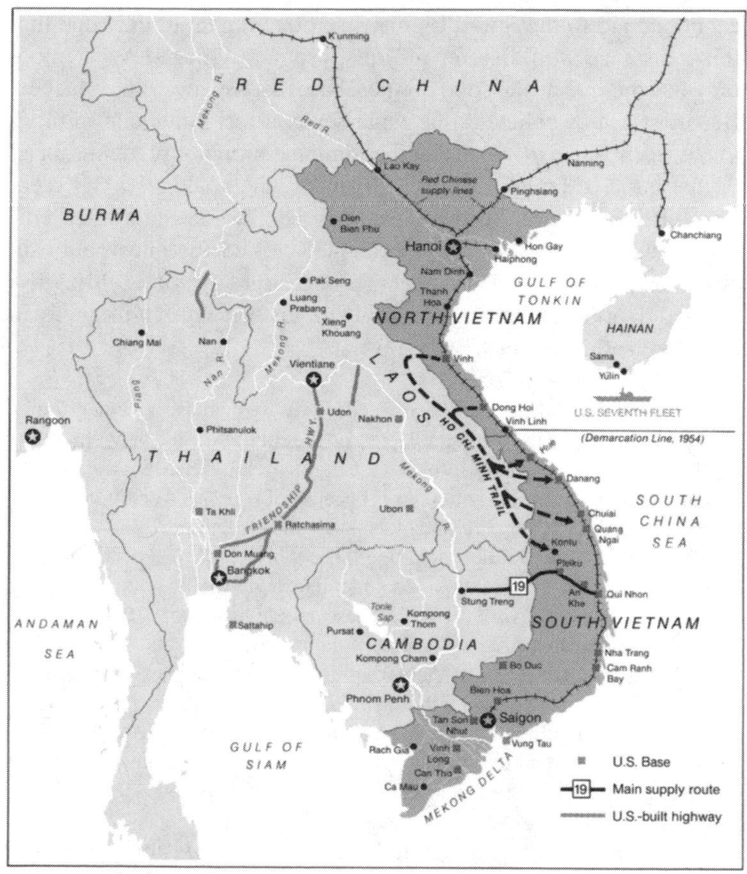

despite the military escalation, the war was continuing with no end in sight. "I didn't want to bomb Hanoi; I didn't want to withdraw," McNamara recalled. "I didn't have all the answers. All I knew was we were in a hell of a mess." But McNamara and other officials remained publicly optimistic about the "progress" America and its allies allegedly were making toward winning the war.

Most critics of the U.S. intervention did not question Johnson's sincerity, and they also acknowledged that there had been times and places in which American firmness in defense of Western interests had been justified. Many even supported the sending of weapons and economic aid to the South Vietnamese government in the hope that this assistance would foster reforms, promote village-level democracy, and thus create the solid political base that the government lacked. But most critics believed that large-scale, direct American military involvement was a mistake, that the administration was plunging ahead on the basis of faulty premises. To many, the analogy with Korea, often cited by the administration, was especially misleading. The editors of the *New Republic*, for example, viewed the intervention in Korea as justified to check Soviet aggression "operating through a puppet" North Korean regime. But the historical circumstances in Vietnam were "very nearly the reverse":

> On the heels of the Japanese surrender, the Vietnamese assumed the right of self-determination and declared the independence of Vietnam. If they do not now fully possess the right of self-determination and enjoy independence as a nation it is because of actions taken by France and the United States. Pleading the cause of self-determination for the Vietnamese in the South (excluding those who refuse to accept a government installed and maintained under a foreign shield—they have no rights) we have deprived the Vietnamese people as a whole of that right and preserved an artificial division of their nation. . . .
>
> We have sent an army to Vietnam to force a settlement of a civil war on our terms, and we have done so without any mandate from any government that could conceivably be regarded as representative of Vietnam and without any mandate from the international community. . . . [W]hat we have done in Vietnam is to commit aggression.

This view of the situation in Vietnam was increasingly common among liberals and Asian specialists by 1965 and 1966. Indeed, the speakers at "teach-ins" about the war and rallies against the war often made precisely these points. In their view, the tragedy was not simply that the Johnson administration was misguided in its heavy-handed policies, but rather that the entire thrust of U.S. policy toward Vietnam since World War II had been wrongheaded and perhaps evil. It had been wrong to aid the French in trying to maintain their Indochinese colonies, to assist in setting up a separate government in Saigon, to send the CIA and U.S. military "advisers" to shore up this corrupt and dictatorial regime, and now to dispatch the latest in American military technology (except for nuclear weapons) to blow up and burn helpless civilians as well as those who understandably opposed U.S. policies. And if America had been so consistently opposed to allowing the Vietnamese to establish their independence and work out their own internal affairs, then perhaps the entire U.S. policy toward developing nations since the beginning of the Cold War required a searching reexamination.

The collapse of the Cold War consensus, to which Johnson and Rusk still appealed, occurred on several levels. There was what might be called polite dissent, which involved raising questions and expressing concerns about U.S. policy in Asia without challenging most earlier Cold War policies. Many of the academics and former officials who testified at the Senate hearings on Vietnam and on China in 1966 would fit roughly into this category, as would respected senators like J. William Fulbright (Dem., Ark.) and newspapers like the *New York Times*. Then there was insistent dissent, like that found in the pages of liberal magazines or in meetings of liberal organizations like Americans for Democratic Action, which strongly opposed the war and supported U.S. recognition of mainland China. And finally there was uncompromising dissent, to be heard at antiwar rallies and to be read in publications of Students for a Democratic Society and other left-wing organizations. To these critics on the radical left, the fundamental problem was capitalism, and Vietnam was only one example of what capitalist nations would do to destroy socialist movements and protect potential markets and sources of raw materials.

Ignoring its strident opponents, the Johnson administration responded to its moderate critics in Congress and in the press by insisting that they were entirely wrong about Vietnam, that it was necessary to stand firm there to demonstrate America's resolve to defend freedom wherever it was threatened. The administration was not clear about precisely who the enemy was—North Vietnam, China, or simply communism—but it was determined to defeat it. And regarding the calls for better relations with China, the administration insisted by 1966 that it was initiating modest first steps to improve relations, but that the Chinese were responding with unrelenting hostility. In taking these Cold War stands, the Democratic administration could count on strong but increasingly silent support from Republicans and conservative Democrats in Congress, who together assured passage of all appropriations bills to cover the burgeoning costs of the war.

While consistently escalating the war in Vietnam until March 1968, the administration pursued a contradictory policy toward China. On the one hand, it made conciliatory overtures, as in Hilsman's speech in San Francisco in December 1963 and Johnson's call in April 1965 for a "freer flow of ideas and people between mainland China and the United States." Both publicly and in meetings with Chinese representatives in Warsaw, the administration assured Beijing that its objectives in Asia were limited and that it favored increased contacts between the two countries.

On the other hand, U.S. officials warned the public that a China armed with even primitive nuclear weapons—that nation conducted its first nuclear test in August 1964—was a greater threat than Russia; the U.S. insisted on keeping Taiwan in the UN and maintaining its defense arrangements with Jiang Jieshi's government; and the U.S. repeatedly implied that China was the prime culprit in Vietnam. High officials like Rusk and National Security Adviser Walt Rostow harbored a long-standing hatred of China, and Rusk in particular went out of his way to insult the proud Chinese by repeatedly referring to their capital by its former name, "Peiping." In his memoirs, Johnson referred to China only in negative terms, failed to mention any U.S. initiatives for better relations, and advanced the fanciful notion that China in 1965 was on the verge of dominating the entire region by means of a "Djakarta-Hanoi-Peking-Pyongyang axis."

Even if the administration had sent more consistently conciliatory signals to Beijing, it is not clear that relations could have been improved as long as America was expanding its military involvement along China's southern border. In their public statements Chinese leaders expressed the fear that America might widen the war to include their country, and they warned the United States that an invasion of North Vietnam would lead to Chinese intervention. In the mid-1960s China sent military and economic aid (including military personnel) to North Vietnam, and Chinese and U.S. warplanes occasionally exchanged fire and inflicted casualties in or near Chinese air space. Despite such incidents, the Johnson administration avoided the kinds of provocations that had led to the large-scale Chinese intervention in Korea fifteen years before.

China's militant verbal support for world revolution, the principal ideological underpinning for its feud with Russia, also hindered Sino-American rapprochement. The same U.S. officials who had been worried in 1961 about Khrushchev's support for "wars of national liberation" found confirmation for America's hardline stance in Vietnam in Lin Biao's statement in 1965 advocating "people's war" in developing nations in order to defeat "U.S. imperialism and its lackeys." As this statement suggests, the rhetoric pouring forth from Beijing between 1963 and 1968 was as bitterly anti-American as ever, and the Cultural Revolution, beginning in 1966, caused so much turmoil in China that serious Sino-American negotiations probably could not have occurred even under more favorable international circumstances at least until 1968. From the administration's viewpoint, the Chinese seemed as determined to remain isolated from America as they were to perpetuate their bitter feud with Russia.

Although Russia sent substantial military aid to North Vietnam, especially after the bombing of the north began in 1965, neither side allowed U.S.-Soviet relations to deteriorate to anything approaching the continuing hostility in Sino-American relations. Johnson and Rusk wanted to maintain the process of patient negotiations with Russia, which had borne fruit in the summer of 1963, and Khrushchev's successors—party leader Leonid Brezhnev and Premier Alexei Kosygin—also were interested in improved relations with the West. While U.S. leaders were anxious to demonstrate that the Vietnam War was not blocking progress toward détente with Russia, Soviet leaders had to be careful not to give the appearance that they were selling out the interests of a beleaguered communist nation, North Vietnam, in order to further their relationship with Washington. The result was a more subdued and cautious process of accommodation than might have occurred without the U.S. escalation in Vietnam, but one which still yielded significant results.

When U.S.-Soviet relations were acrimonious, as they were in 1950 and again in 1961, American leaders tended to use their nation's superior wealth and technology to improve their position in the strategic arms race. When these relations were fairly conciliatory, as they were between 1963 and the early 1970s, the emphasis was less on winning the race than on setting limits to it. This period saw two important U.S. initiatives in the latter direction: a treaty, initiated in 1964 and signed in 1968 by many nations, including Russia and America, to prevent the spread of nuclear weapons to nations other than the five that already had them; and an effort, started in 1967, to limit the number of offensive ICBMs and defensive antiballistic missiles (ARMs) that each side could deploy. Although the strategic missile and ARM agreements (known together as SALT I) were not signed until 1972, Johnson began the negotiating process that led to them.

One reason Soviet leaders were cautious in responding to U.S. initiatives on arms control was that, until the late 1960s, Russia was well behind America in offensive strategic weapons. Although Brezhnev and Kosygin wanted improved U.S.-Soviet relations, they also were determined to end the disparity between the two sides' nuclear capabilities, thus lessening the likelihood of another humiliation, such as the resolution of the Cuban missile crisis, and achieving international acceptance of Russia as the full strategic equal of America. As late as 1965, Russia had an estimated 262 ICBMs to America's 854, 155 strategic bombers to America's 738, and 107 submarine-based missiles to America's 464. As a result of U.S. restraint after 1967 and its own efforts to achieve parity, by 1969 Russia actually led in ICBMs, 1,198 to 1,054, though it trailed in the number of warheads these missiles could carry, 1,326 to 1,710. While the West maintained a comfortable lead in deliverable warheads during the 1970s, the Soviets were close enough to equality to enter into arms control negotiations with reasonable confidence.

Johnson boasted in his memoirs that America and Russia signed a larger number of "significant agreements" during his presidency than they had in the previous thirty years. The proud Texan habitually exaggerated, but it is true that the two nations concluded a steady stream of modest agreements that helped to maintain the constructive atmosphere in U.S.-Soviet relations. There was a treaty formalizing the pledges of the two nations not to station nuclear weapons in space; there was the U.S.-Soviet Consular Convention, which facilitated travel and other activities in each country; and there were agreements on such diverse subjects as returning astronauts who might accidentally land on foreign soil and prescribing what U.S. and Soviet fishing fleets had a right to catch in each other's territorial waters. The cultural exchange agreement was renewed in 1964 despite some pressure in both countries to cancel it, and roughly 16,000 U.S. tourists visited Russia in 1966. None of these things by itself was earthshaking, but all of them together, combined with progress on arms control and relative Soviet restraint on Vietnam, suggested a more constructive and stable relationship than the two superpowers had experienced before 1963.

The fact that crises in the Middle East in 1967 and in Czechoslovakia the next year did not lead to wider conflict underscored the value of the generally positive atmosphere in U.S.-Soviet relations. Tensions had been rising in the Middle East between Israel, heavily backed by the U.S. government and most American Jewish organizations, and Egypt and Syria, armed by Russia. In May 1967 President Nasser of Egypt, amid signs of impending hostilities between Israel and his ally Syria, closed the Gulf of Aqaba to Israeli shipping and obtained the removal of the UN peacekeeping force, which ever since the 1956 invasion had patrolled Egyptian territory in the Sinai along the Israeli border.

Both Russia and America feared the outbreak of a war that they could not control and that might lead to superpower confrontation; thus, while the Russians were urging caution on Nasser, both Johnson and French President Charles de Gaulle (a supplier of aircraft to Israel) were admonishing Israel to show restraint. De Gaulle, who earlier had urged Kennedy not to make the same mistake France had made in becoming involved militarily in Indochina, told Israeli Foreign Minister Abba Eban that his nation should not start a war. "You will be considered the aggressor by the world and by me," the French leader warned. "You will cause the Soviet Union to penetrate more deeply into the Middle East, and Israel will suffer the consequences. You will create a Palestinian nationalism, and you will never be able to get rid of it."

Spurning all this advice and not informing Washington of its plans, Israel conducted a preemptive attack on Egypt and Syria on June 5, 1967. Within six days it had won a smashing victory over those two nations and Jordan, seizing large chunks of their territory. During the fighting Johnson and Kosygin used the "hot line" to exchange assurances of nonbelligerency, and Johnson carefully informed the Russians in advance about U.S. troop movements in the area, as in the aftermath of Israel's sinking of an American warship. After the end of the Six-Day War, Russian leaders backed the Arabs in angrily denouncing Israel's refusal to withdraw from the lands conquered during the fighting, and they also found themselves having to replace much of the military equipment lost by Egypt and Syria in the war. But as de Gaulle had warned, Russian influence in the region increased, for America appeared to many Arabs as an accomplice in Israel's conquests.

Despite the situation in the Middle East and the continued heavy U.S. involvement in Vietnam, Kosygin accepted an invitation to meet with Johnson in late June 1967 at a college in Glassboro, New Jersey, to discuss current world problems. Although the meetings between the two leaders were cordial, it was a measure of the element of strain in U.S.-Soviet relations during the Vietnam War that Kosygin refused to hold the meetings with Johnson either in Washington or at Camp David.

This Soviet reticence diminished after the signing of the nonproliferation treaty on July 1, 1968. Within weeks of that event, Soviet leaders invited Johnson to come to Russia in early October to inaugurate formal talks on strategic arms limitation. After discussing the invitation with Rusk and Rostow on August 19, the president decided to accept and to issue a news release on the subject two days later. On August 20, however, on learning that Soviet troops had invaded Czechoslovakia, Johnson felt compelled to postpone planning for the visit to Russia and to go on national television to denounce the Soviet move and to demand the withdrawal of all Warsaw Pact forces.

The Soviets invaded Czechoslovakia for many of the same reasons that had led them to crush the rebellion in Hungary twelve years before. During the spring and summer of 1968 a new Czech government under Alexander Dubcek had been acceding to popular demands for broadening civil liberties, allowing greater freedom of the press, and permitting noncommunists to participate more actively in politics. Recently released Soviet sources suggest that Russian leaders also were concerned about growing West German financial and political influence in Eastern Europe, especially in Prague; one motive for intervening, therefore, was to make sure that Czechoslovakia did not end up in the West German orbit. From the Russian viewpoint, the events in Czechoslovakia—like those in Hungary earlier—threatened the continuation of the communist system throughout Eastern Europe and even in Russia itself. Like U.S. leaders, Soviet officials during the Cold War lived in fear of falling dominoes.

Although Soviet purposes in 1956 and 1968 were quite similar, both their approach and the U.S. response were more restrained than in the Cold War atmosphere of 1956. They took the trouble this time to bring units from East Germany, Poland, and Hungary with them—a demonstration of Warsaw Pact solidarity. Also in contrast to Hungary, the Soviets knew in advance that the Czechs would not offer significant armed resistance to a military intervention. Finally, through a special meeting between Ambassador Dobrynin and President Johnson, Russian leaders made a point of assuring the president of the importance they attached to constructive U.S.-Soviet relations.

By the mid-1960s the U.S. government had shifted its basic policy toward Eastern Europe from urging "liberation" by dissidents in each country—a policy whose unreality had been fully revealed in 1956—to "building bridges" of trade and cooperation with the increasingly independent communist governments there. This fundamental departure affected America's response in 1968. Although the administration welcomed the liberalization in Czechoslovakia, it carefully avoided depicting the situation in Cold War terms until after the actual invasion. Even then, its reaction, though sharp, was brief—unlike the years of diplomatic ostracism of Hungary after 1956. Within a few months after the invasion the administration was eager to get on with the SALT negotiations. Johnson, who had invested considerable effort and political capital in improving U.S.-Soviet relations, felt rebuffed when the Kremlin turned down his offer to meet with Soviet leaders in Geneva before Christmas. The Russians apparently had decided that it would be prudent to wait until after the new Republican administration assumed power in January 1969.

Toward a New Balance of Power, 1969–1972

U.S. foreign policy from 1969 until the mid-1970s was directed by two bold, controversial leaders, President Richard Nixon and his chief national security adviser, Henry Kissinger. A native Californian and opportunistic politician, Nixon rose to national prominence as an opponent of domestic communists and liberals during the late 1940s, and he was known during his eight years as Eisenhower's vice-president as a staunch Cold Warrior. Although he was defeated for the presidency in 1960 and for governor of California in 1962, Nixon returned to prominence in the Republican party after Barry Goldwater's defeat in 1964 by campaigning tirelessly in behalf of GOP candidates and by emphasizing his middle-of-the-road position within the party. When the Democratic party splintered in 1968 under the strains of Vietnam and domestic polarization, Nixon was able to mount a successful campaign for the White House. His remark in 1969 that "flexibility is the first principle of politics" was clearly exemplified in his foreign policy—especially by the startling shift in his approach to Russia and China during his presidency.

According to Elliot Richardson, a high administration official, Nixon was "a man of remarkable intelligence . . . as well as quickness of mind" who "had it within his grasp to be our greatest post–World War II president." But Nixon's "realism tilts toward cynicism," and his many good qualities could "give way very quickly to manipulation and ruthlessness." These qualities of mind and character also describe Kissinger, a Jew born in Germany and educated at Harvard whose background stood in stark contrast to Nixon's. Both men also were deeply suspicious, even of close associates, and both shared a seemingly insatiable drive for power. "If he were ten percent less brilliant and ten percent more honest," a family friend said of Kissinger, "he would be a great man."

Nixon and Kissinger shared an interest in broad conceptual approaches to foreign policy, and both spent considerable time during the Kennedy-Johnson years reflecting upon the limits of the Cold War approach in dealing with the major communist powers. In an article in *Foreign Affairs* in October 1967, for example, Nixon noted that "the role of the United States as a policeman is likely to be limited in the future," and argued that "we simply cannot afford to leave China forever outside the family of nations. . . ." Such public comments from the leader of the Republican party would have been unthinkable a decade before.

As John G. Stoessinger has pointed out, Kissinger's conception of great power politics was based on three main assumptions: first, to quote Stoessinger, "to be secure, a peace must be based on a negotiated settlement, with all sides in equilibrium, rather than on a victor's peace"; second, the leading power (in this case, America) must give the chief rival power (in this case, Russia) a tangible stake in improved relations; and third, to maintain equilibrium or balance in the system, a balancer is required to "throw his weight on the weaker side whenever an imbalance occurs and by so doing restore the equilibrium and maintain the peace." In Kissinger's view, America should play the key role of balancer, working to increase Russia's stake in the international system while simultaneously increasing China's ability to serve as a counterweight to Russian influence in Asia. In addition to America, Russia, and China, a resurgent Europe and Japan completed the pentagonal structure of power. Reflecting this viewpoint, Nixon remarked in 1971 that "it will be a safer world if we have a strong, healthy United States, Europe, Soviet Union, China, [and] Japan, each balancing the other. . . ."

Recognizing that U.S. power was more limited than it had been immediately after World War II, Nixon and Kissinger sought to establish a "structure of peace" in which common interests and incentives for conciliatory behavior would be emphasized, and ideology and instinctive hostility—so important in the thinking of John Foster Dulles and Mao Zedong in the 1950s—would be played down. Convinced that both Russia and China would have to play a constructive role if this new balance of power was to succeed, the Nixon administration moved toward better relations with both countries, thus transforming the Cold War. But while they achieved many of their goals in foreign policy, the new leaders' decision to continue the Vietnam War, combined with the unlawful means they often used against their domestic opponents, ironically contributed to a result these proponents of presidential power abhorred: an increase in the ability and determination of Congress and other institutions in American society to influence the nation's foreign policies.

Before elaborating on Nixon's success in easing tensions with Russia and China, let us examine his less successful policy in Indochina.

While domestic issues like race relations were important, Nixon was elected in 1968 primarily because of the public's disillusionment with the Vietnam War and with the turmoil that it stirred up at home. In September 1964, shortly before Johnson's landslide victory over Goldwater, Gallup's respondents had viewed the Democrats as the party best able to maintain peace by the margin of 43 to 20 percent. Due to the escalation in Vietnam, the Republicans had taken an eight-point lead by June 1966, and the month before the 1968 election they led by 37 to 24 percent. During the campaign Nixon naturally encouraged the view that the Republicans could end the war, and he claimed that he had a plan for doing so, which he would implement if elected. Neither supporters nor opponents of the war knew what Nixon's plan was, however, because he refused to discuss details on the grounds that he did not want to jeopardize the Vietnam peace talks, which recently had begun in Paris.

Upon his inauguration Nixon had a golden opportunity to end the direct U.S. military involvement in Vietnam, either immediately or in a phased withdrawal to be completed within a few months. The president could have announced that America had done all that anyone reasonably could expect it to do, and he could have quoted Kennedy's remark in September 1963 that success in the war ultimately depended upon South Vietnam's performance and not America's military assistance. Instead, Nixon tragically became the fifth consecutive president determined to prevent a communist victory in Vietnam's civil war.

Like his four predecessors, Nixon was more concerned about the possible impact of failure to "help" Vietnam on conditions in America and elsewhere than he was about the situation in Vietnam itself. As he told a journalist in May 1969, "We would destroy ourselves if we pulled out in a way that wasn't really honorable." Kissinger agreed, noting in an article that same year that "what is involved now is confidence in American promises." In an article in the *New Republic* in August 1980, Kissinger acknowledged that he had been wrong in 1966 to advocate a continuation of the war, that America probably should have cut its losses and gotten out. But when they took office, Nixon and Kissinger reiterated the stale Cold War view that America had to remain in Vietnam until "peace with honor" was achieved.

What the new leaders in Washington seemed unable to understand was that the Viet Cong and the North Vietnamese already had made too many sacrifices—and had too good a prospect of winning—to be willing to end the war by accepting the legitimacy of the U.S.-backed South Vietnamese government. In their view, America could have peace by withdrawing its forces, or it could seek to defend its honor by remaining in Vietnam. But no matter how much it bombed and threatened, it could not achieve peace with honor, as Nixon defined the phrase.

In a letter to the president in August 1969, shortly before his death, Ho said that he was "deeply touched at the rising toll of death of young Americans who have fallen in Vietnam by reason of the policy of American governing circles." But he insisted that if U.S. leaders wanted to "act for a just peace," they would have to "cease the war of aggression and withdraw their troops from South Vietnam, and respect the right of the population of the South and of the Vietnamese nation to dispose of themselves, without foreign influence." As former U.S. official Townsend Hoopes observed in 1970, "The one thing we can negotiate at this stage of the war is the manner of our going."

After four years of intense fighting and domestic controversy under Johnson, numerous public opinion polls showed that most Americans by 1969–70 were eager to have the war ended, even if the United States lost. But Nixon gave them exactly four more years of war: direct U.S. military involvement ended when the so-called peace agreements were signed in January 1973. Although he was under substantial domestic pressure to end the war quickly, Nixon tried bolder and riskier tactics than Johnson had used to try to force the Viet Cong and the North Vietnamese to give up the fight. Nixon tried to threaten Hanoi into suing for peace in 1969, and he also told Russian leaders that progress toward détente depended upon their success in getting the North Vietnamese to accede to U.S. demands. When these and other gambits failed, Nixon asserted that his policy of "Vietnamization"—turning over more of the ground fighting to South Vietnam while gradually withdrawing U.S. troops—was succeeding.

Showing no concern about civilian casualties in public statements or in meetings with advisers, Nixon repeatedly ordered intense bombing raids in South Vietnam, North Vietnam, Laos, and, for the first time, Cambodia. While claiming that he was winding down the war, he infuriated his critics by dropping more tons of bombs throughout Indochina in four years than Johnson had done, sending U.S. troops into Cambodia in 1970, and mining the harbor at Haiphong and carpet-bombing suburbs of Hanoi two years later.

While Nixon and Kissinger were protecting America's "honor," an additional 20,553 U.S. soldiers were killed, an estimated 1 million Indochinese soldiers and civilians were killed, and millions more were wounded or turned into refugees. In Western Europe and elsewhere, America under Johnson and Nixon was gaining a reputation for ruthlessness and disregard for international opinion totally inconsistent with its earlier image as protector of the free world.

Even though Nixon's hard-nosed policies in Indochina may have won him some support among the so-called "silent majority," who disliked the radicalism and turmoil that marked America in the late 1960s, his administration clearly had a domestic price to pay for continuing the war long after it had lost the degree of support required in a democracy to sustain a viable military involvement abroad. The administration was confronted with widespread draft resistance and repeated peaceful demonstrations involving hundreds of thousands of Americans at a time, and it also faced a small minority determined to "bring the war home." Groups like the radical "Weathermen" faction of Students for a Democratic Society were responsible for bombings, broken windows, and other efforts to "trash" the establishment and hence to show solidarity with the Viet Cong and other Third World liberation movements.

More significantly, Congress was increasingly assertive, especially after the unexpected "incursion" into Cambodia led to nationwide protests and the killing of student demonstrators at Kent State University in Ohio and Jackson State University in Mississippi. In the wake of the invasion of Cambodia, the Senate repealed the Gulf of Tonkin Resolution of 1964, which had given the president the authority to wage war in Southeast Asia; and it also passed a watered-down version of a proposal to prohibit spending on military operations in Cambodia. Johnson's and Nixon's high-handed policies in Indochina led in 1973 to passage of the War Powers Act, which limited to sixty days a president's right to commit troops abroad without congressional approval.

Finally, the Nixon-Kissinger policies in Indochina contributed to the series of illegal activities that became known simply as "Watergate." Irritated by leaks to the press in the spring of 1969 about the secret bombing of Cambodia, the administration began wiretapping the home phone of Morton Halperin, an official on Kissinger's National Security Council staff. Subsequently, the wire-tapping included respected journalists, including columnists Joseph Kraft and Jack Anderson, who were publishing information on foreign affairs that was embarrassing to the administration. In the summer of 1971, after former Pentagon official Daniel Ellsberg released the government's secret history of the Vietnam War to the press, the White House took the step that led directly to the incident at Watergate a year later: it established a secret dirty-tricks group called the "plumbers," composed largely of former CIA operatives. On September 4, 1971, members of this group conducted an illegal break-in at the office of Ellsberg's psychiatrist in order to try to locate material to discredit Ellsberg. The following June several of the "plumbers" were surprised and captured during a break-in at the headquarters of the Democratic National Committee at the Watergate apartments in Washington, thus setting in motion the stunning series of revelations that led to Nixon's resignation in disgrace in August 1974.

Whereas much of the public and many members of Congress had acquiesced in deception and killing on a large scale in Indochina from 1964 to 1972, in 1973 and 1974 most were unwilling to look the other way while Nixon sought desperately to conceal his involvement in the violation of civil liberties at home. Unchecked government power growing out of the Cold War—visible earlier in the activities of intelligence agencies and now in the excesses of the "plumbers"—was claiming its most prominent victim.

In fairness, it is important to note that, like Johnson in 1964, Nixon received more than 60 percent of the popular vote in the 1972 election; and that his and Kissinger's imaginative policies toward Russia and China, combined with real progress by October 1972 in winding down the U.S. involvement in Vietnam, contributed to his landslide victory. In Nixon and Kissinger, the leaders in Moscow and Beijing found Americans who spoke the understandable language of balance of power and who avoided proclaiming that their nation had the right to rule abroad because of its moral superiority. At a time when conditions within all three nations were favorable for improved East-West relations, Soviet and Chinese leaders discovered practical, hard-nosed U.S. officials with whom they could strike deals.

As both the lengthy Nixon and Kissinger memoirs make clear, U.S. relations with Russia between 1969 and 1972 were extremely complicated. There was an assumption, carried over from the 1963–68 period, that continued improvement in relations was in the interest of both countries. But there also was a determination on each side that the other would have to pay an adequate price for specific gains in bilateral relations. To the Soviets, for example, America would need to show restraint in Vietnam; to the Americans, Russia would need to help in achieving mutually acceptable settlements in such places as Vietnam and the Middle East. Perhaps because Moscow seemed more eager than Washington to improve relations, U.S. leaders stuck more consistently—though often unsuccessfully—to their policy of "linkage," the idea that progress in one area depended on progress in others. People living through this period and reading headlines about the ultimate successes in U.S.-Soviet relations had little idea how much posturing and hard negotiating went into the agreements that were concluded in 1971 and 1972.

Although there were U.S.-Soviet agreements on numerous minor issues similar to those negotiated during the Johnson years, the most important agreements involved lessening tensions in Europe, stabilizing the strategic arms race, and increasing U.S.-Soviet trade. In the first area, West German Chancellor Willy Brandt took the lead and the Nixon administration, despite some misgivings, followed. After West Germany formally agreed in August 1970 to recognize the Oder-Neisse line as the permanent border between East Germany and Poland, East-West negotiations proceeded rapidly toward normalization of Western access to, and rights in, West Berlin (completed in April 1971) and the establishment of full "inner-German" relations between East and West Germany (completed in December 1972). The Berlin issue, which earlier had been a barometer of the Cold War atmosphere, finally had been eased substantially through negotiations.

The U.S.-Soviet strategic arms limitation talks (SALT) proved more difficult for many reasons, not the least of which was the momentum of the arms race itself. Before one new development in missile technology could be fully understood, a second was declared technically feasible and a third, even more lethal, was on the drawing boards.

Another issue was what to include and what to omit from the treaty: should medium-range U.S. missiles deployed in Western Europe and capable of reaching Russia be included, for example, or should the negotiations be limited to long-range missiles? Although the talks began in November 1969, it was not until May 1971 that a breakthrough involving a key compromise by each side was announced. Russia agreed to ignore the thousands of nuclear weapons America and its allies could deliver from Western Europe and nearby waters, and America granted the Soviets a 3-to-2 edge in the number of ICBMs. The actual SALT I agreements, one setting five-year numerical limits on ICBMs and the other permanent limits on ABMs, were completed and signed in Moscow during Nixon's historic visit—the first by an American president in peacetime—in May 1972.

As in most important international negotiations, success required persistence, an atmosphere of mutual respect, and key concessions by both sides. Over the objections of "hawks" in the Pentagon and in Congress, Nixon insisted that the U.S. goal in the nuclear arms race should be "sufficiency" rather than overwhelming superiority. Now that the Soviets had pulled relatively even in strategic arms, it would have been expensive for America to have tried to maintain a large lead. As Nixon and Kissinger realized, it also would have been self-defeating, for the Soviets could match America missile for missile, thus increasing the risk of total annihilation if all-out war between the two nations ever occurred.

Kissinger masterfully orchestrated the negotiations—minimizing bureaucratic delays in Washington, educating the Russians on arms control issues, and at times bypassing the official SALT negotiators in order to deal directly with the Kremlin. Soviet leaders also helped make agreement possible by not insisting on restraining the Americans' technological superiority in such key areas as missile launching submarines and MIRV (multiple independently targeted reentry vehicle) missiles, which, by allowing America to fire several warheads from one ICBM, offset Russia's numerical advantage. A complicating factor for the Russians was that, with the continuing Sino-Soviet split, they had to be prepared to defend themselves simultaneously against China and the Western alliance.

The Russians were eager to increase U.S.-Soviet trade, especially in such areas as foodstuffs and high-technology items, which could improve their production of consumer goods. Despite pressure from liberals in Congress and from the business community, Nixon and Kissinger moved slowly in this area. "I do not accept the philosophy that increased trade results in improved political relations . . . ," Nixon told a National Security Council meeting in May 1969. "Better political relations lead to improved trade." As he noted in his memoirs, Kissinger also believed in linking progress on trade to progress in other areas, and he acknowledged that there was dissatisfaction within the State and Commerce departments in regard to this stance.

Because the two top leaders steadfastly maintained their position, the breakthrough on U.S. trade with Russia occurred only after the SALT treaty and other steps toward détente had been taken at the Moscow summit. That summer the administration permitted the Soviets to begin making large purchases of American grain, and on October 18 a significant trade agreement was signed in which Russia was offered most-favored-nation treatment (that is, the lowest regular tariff rates) and Export-Import Bank loans in exchange for gradual repayment of $722 million in World War II debts. Although this liberalized trade program soon ran into roadblocks in Congress, U.S.-Soviet trade grew from $220 million in 1971 to $2.8 billion in 1978. The administration's structure of peace had acquired another important building block.

One of the last agreements signed by Nixon and Brezhnev at the Moscow summit was a declaration on "basic principles" guiding U.S.-Soviet relations. Listed first was their "common determination that in the nuclear age there is no alternative to conducting their mutual relations on the basis of peaceful coexistence," followed by the equally vague agreement to avoid the "development of situations capable of causing a dangerous exacerbation of their relations." Arms limitation, economic and cultural ties, and other constructive goals were mentioned. The Kennedy, Johnson, and Nixon administrations—and their Soviet counterparts—already had proceeded far along this road toward improving relations and ending the Cold War. But even in the euphoria of 1972, one key question remained: Was it possible to maintain the momentum of détente between these two great political and military rivals?

Although the Moscow summit in May 1972 resulted in numerous agreements, the highlight of Nixon's presidency almost certainly was his trip to China three months earlier. Like the trip to Moscow, this dramatic encounter between countries lacking formal diplomatic relations was three years in the making, with the decisive breakthroughs occurring in 1970 and 1971. But whereas the expanded détente with Russia seemed a logical outgrowth of the substantial improvement in U.S.-Soviet relations after 1962, America and China seemed as far apart on the basic issues of Taiwan and U.S. power in Asia when Nixon became president in 1969 as they had been when he became vice-president in 1953. Given the record of two decades of bitter Sino-American hostility, it is not surprising that Nixon felt justified in proclaiming, in a toast during his last evening in Beijing, "This was the week that changed the world."

As in U.S.-Soviet relations, there was no straight line toward inevitable rapprochement running from Nixon's inaugural address to his journey to China. Instead, there was much hesitation and uncertainty on both sides in 1969 and 1970. "The new Administration had the general intention of making a fresh start," Kissinger recalled. "But in all candor it had no precise idea how to do this and it had to take account of domestic realities, not the least of which was Nixon's traditional support among the conservative 'China lobby' that had never forgiven Truman and Acheson for allegedly betraying Chiang Kai-shek [Jiang Jieshi]." The Chinese—still in disarray from the excesses of their "Great Cultural Revolution"—also lacked clear direction in 1969, as when they abruptly canceled meetings with U.S. representatives in Warsaw on February 18, two days before they were scheduled to begin, and unleashed a propaganda attack against the Nixon administration. Throughout 1969 the issue of whether to pursue a moderate or a hardline policy toward the United States became enmeshed in a power struggle within the Chinese leadership, with the moderate forces led by Zhou Enlai generally on top by the end of the year.

Contributing greatly to the possibility of improved relations with America was the durable Sino-Soviet split that, in addition to the usual vitriolic rhetoric, resulted in 1969 in military clashes at several points along China's long border with the Soviet Union. In a secret July 1969 report, Chinese officials stated that their former ally, Russia, posed "a more serious threat to our security" than America did. In its struggle against the "Soviet revisionists," China obviously needed at least diplomatic support.

Yet Nixon's bold policies in Indochina—especially the invasion of Cambodia in 1970, which Mao denounced—increased the difficulty of maintaining the momentum toward détente. Indeed, until it became clear in late 1970 that the U.S. definitely was lessening its military involvement in Asia, the prospects for a genuine improvement in Sino-American relations remained in doubt. In a real sense, therefore, the Chinese were playing a linkage game of their own: let the U.S. show progress in ending the involvement in Indochina and indicate a willingness to discuss Taiwan, and we will welcome its leaders in Beijing.

If Mao and Zhou considered improved Sino-American relations to be in China's interest, Nixon and Kissinger agreed for reasons of their own. As Kissinger noted in his memoirs, "Nixon saw in the opening to China a somewhat greater opportunity than I to squeeze the Soviet Union into short-term help on Vietnam; I was more concerned with the policy's impact on the structure of international relations." But both leaders agreed on the basic point "that if relations could be developed with both the Soviet Union and China the triangular relationship would give us a great strategic opportunity for peace." Stated bluntly, America as balancer would be able to play the two communist rivals off against each other. Moreover, improved relations would placate the many American liberals who had been calling for years for improved relations with China but who in 1969 and 1970 were concentrating their energies on denouncing Nixon's continuation of the war in Indochina. Finally, an opening to China would help to assuage the public's deep longing for peace, cast Nixon in a starring role as chief peacemaker, and thus assist in ensuring his reelection in 1972.

Although there were many signals in 1969 and especially in 1970 indicating that both sides would welcome an improvement in relations, perhaps the single most important U.S. move was Nixon's public use of the term "People's Republic of China" twice in October

1970. No previous president had referred to mainland China by its official name, and Nixon used it both in a press conference and in formally greeting the visiting president of Rumania in late October. Privately, Nixon told President Nicolae Ceausescu that America and China could exchange high-level representatives, and Ceausescu agreed to convey this information to Beijing. In addition to the "Rumanian channel," Nixon also used Pakistani President Yahya Khan to convey messages directly to Beijing. These initiatives soon bore fruit, for Zhou told Yahya on December 9 that Nixon's representative would be welcomed in Beijing to discuss Taiwan, and Mao told journalist Edgar Snow on December 18 that Nixon himself would be welcome to come. By the following May, Nixon privately had agreed to accept China's formal invitation to visit Beijing, and Kissinger was to go there in July to make arrangements for the visit.

Arriving in Beijing secretly on July 9, 1971, Kissinger quickly began his talks with Zhou, whom Kissinger later described as "one of the two or three most impressive men I have ever met." In their lengthy conversations the two leaders worked on developing mutual confidence and sketching out the two nations' general outlook on world affairs. Wishing to build a positive atmosphere for future negotiations, they avoided wrangling over controversial issues like Taiwan and Vietnam. In fact, the future of Taiwan was discussed only briefly and in generalities. "There is turmoil under the heavens," Zhou remarked at one point, "And we have the opportunity to end it." Kissinger remembered being "elated" as his plane left Beijing for Pakistan on July 11.

Although many Americans had sensed that something important was brewing when the Chinese invited an American ping-pong team to visit China the previous April, there was still genuine surprise when Nixon went on television on July 15 to announce that he would be visiting the People's Republic "before May 1972" in order to "seek the normalization of relations between the two countries and also to exchange views on questions of concern to the two sides." Expecting an adverse reaction in Russia, Taiwan, South Korea, and Japan, none of which were consulted or informed in advance, Nixon promised that the shift in policy "will not be at the expense of our old friends" and "is not directed against any other nation." Ecstatic that his policy was succeeding, Nixon ignored demonstrators chanting "Get out of

Vietnam" as he left the television studios, and proudly introduced Kissinger to startled patrons at a restaurant in Washington where the presidential party celebrated the breakthrough on China.

Given the dramatic announcement in July 1971, combined with the mounting international pressures since the early 1960s for Beijing's admission to the United Nations as the only lawful government of China, it is not surprising that the new, hastily improvised U.S. proposal that both Chinese governments should have seats in the United Nations was not accepted in the General Assembly that fall. When Beijing continued to refuse to sit in the United Nations as long as Jiang's government on Taiwan was represented, the General Assembly, despite strenuous U.S. diplomatic efforts, expelled Taiwan and admitted the People's Republic by a vote of 76 to 35. While remnants of the once-powerful "China lobby" denounced Nixon's alleged treachery toward Taiwan, most politicians and commentators praised the administration for recognizing realities in Asia, which previous leaders since 1949 had chosen to ignore. Partially reflecting the highly favorable image of China in the media, public opinion polls showed overwhelming support for Nixon's policies.

Like Khrushchev's visit to America in 1959, Nixon's visit to China in February 1972 was one big media event. A planeload of journalists accompanied U.S. officials to Beijing, and the three leading television networks competed with each other to provide the "best" coverage of the visit. In a sense, the most obvious shift in the technology of television paralleled the shift in the Cold War: whereas coverage before 1963 was in stark black-and-white, by the Nixon years most Americans were viewing world affairs in lifelike color. Even though the negotiations were private, and the networks thus devoted much time to mundane details of life in China and Nixon's visit to the Great Wall, the coverage received high ratings. More than at any other time in his presidency, Nixon came across to the public as a statesman, a sagacious man of peace.

As U.S. officials had warned before the trip, the week of negotiations in Beijing involved much hard bargaining and little progress on the key issue separating the two sides, Taiwan. Indeed, the two nations issued separate statements on Taiwan near the end of the meetings. The Chinese insisted that Taiwan was "a province of China," that they had the right to "liberate" it, and that, to normalize relations with Beijing, America would have to sever diplomatic relations with Taiwan and remove all of its troops from the island. While officially taking note for the first time of Beijing's view that Taiwan was "part of China," U.S. leaders insisted that differences between China and Taiwan had to be resolved peacefully, and they promised vaguely that America would remove its troops from Taiwan "as the tension in the area diminishes."

In their joint statement, the two nations took the much more positive view that "the normalization of relations between the two countries is not only in the interest of the Chinese and American peoples but also contributes to the relaxation of tension in Asia and the world." In what Nixon considered the most important portion of the joint communiqué, both promised not to "seek hegemony in the Asia Pacific region" and to oppose efforts by other powers (meaning Russia) to do so.

Given agreement on these points, the cordial atmosphere throughout the talks, and lesser agreements in cultural and other areas, leaders on both sides considered the trip a good start toward normalizing Sino-American relations. After some additional progress during the Nixon years, full diplomatic relations were established by new U.S. and Chinese leaders on January 1, 1979. As Walter Isaacson has observed, much of the significance of the rejuvenated Sino-American relationship lay in the fact that it "gave both of the world's communist giants an incentive to maintain better relations with the U.S. than they had with one another." In other words, it used the rivalry between these feuding neighbors—and each nation's desire for Western support in their feud—to contain the spread of communism, rather than relying solely on the power of the noncommunist world.

In achieving their goal of reducing East-West tensions while maintaining a central role for America in world affairs, Nixon and Kissinger—like Roosevelt during World War II—used the diplomacy of ambiguity. In contrast to some U.S. leaders earlier in the Cold War, the two statesmen were not interested in specifying which nations were America's friends and enemies. As Nixon commented in announcing his trip to China: "Any nation can be our friend without being any other nation's enemy." By keeping both traditional allies and adversaries off guard, U.S. leaders were able to maintain America's influence in world affairs at a time when its relative military and economic position was declining.

Nixon and Kissinger also realized that considerable ambiguity would be required to improve U.S. relations simultaneously with Russia and China. In dealing with Russia, they did not try to define in advance precisely what "détente" meant; nor did they risk the loss of negotiating leverage by giving the impression that America was overly anxious to improve relations. In dealing with China, they sought to create a favorable atmosphere by taking small steps and emphasizing common interests, rather than immediately tackling explosive issues like Taiwan. And when the question of Taiwan arose, they agreed in principle that Taiwan was part of China but postponed negotiations on details until all affected nations had had time to adjust to the new Sino-American relationship. Recognizing that international relations usually are more analogous to the subtle nuances of personal relationships than to the strict prescriptions of contract law, Nixon, Kissinger, and their Soviet and Chinese counterparts left a record of diplomatic achievement that would not be equaled until after Mikhail Gorbachev's rise to power in 1985.

Conclusion

An important irony runs through U.S. foreign policy during the 1963–72 period of the Cold War: at the same time that America was working to improve relations with Russia and China, it became deeply involved in a brutal war in Indochina fought ostensibly to prevent the spread of Russian and Chinese influence in Asia. I have advanced the familiar argument that Johnson acted foolishly in sending large numbers of U.S. troops to fight in Vietnam beginning in 1965 and that Nixon kept a substantial force there long after it became apparent to most observers that America would not achieve a military victory. Yet the Vietnam War may not have been entirely in vain, for Nixon and Kissinger might not have worked as hard as they did to improve relations with Russia and China if they—and many other Americans—had not learned from the Vietnam experience that the U.S. clearly was overextended in Asia.

A second paradox of this period is that, although it took until 1971 to establish effective bilateral communications with China, U.S. leaders actually felt more comfortable in their new relations with Beijing than they did in their long-standing relations with Moscow. Kissinger, for example, referred to the Moscow summit as "more random and jagged" than the one in Beijing, and he noted perceptively that "we were geopolitically too competitive with the Soviet Union" for a "common appreciation of the international situation" to emerge. Even though America and Russia had been negotiating seriously in many forums since the mid-1950s, the element of competition between the two superpowers could not be overcome even at the height of U.S.-Soviet détente.

A third paradox involves the nuclear arms race. During these years America and Russia negotiated the test ban treaty, the nonproliferation treaty, and the SALT I agreements. Yet the nuclear competition continued, with both sides increasing their arsenals of nuclear warheads and offensive delivery systems and—with the United States in the lead—adopting new weapons technology more and more difficult to limit effectively in any future agreement.

A final conclusion about these years is not paradoxical, for it seems as self-evident in great power relations as it is in personal or group dynamics. As leaders like Rusk, Kissinger, and Zhou knew, it takes hard work and imagination to bring about genuine improvements in great power relations; as in personal relationships, it takes only carelessness and posturing to set them back. As events between 1973 and 1984 showed, even the painstaking achievement of relative détente in which both sides had a stake was no guarantee that two nationalistic, ideologically opposed superpowers could maintain the upward trend.

CHAPTER FOUR

The Roller-Coaster Years, 1973–1984

In June 1973, Leonid Brezhnev and other Soviet leaders spent nearly two weeks in America, meeting with top U.S. officials and seeking to build upon the achievements of the Moscow summit the previous year. Although there were no new treaties the magnitude of SALT, Brezhnev and President Nixon did sign an agreement to try to negotiate a treaty in 1974 that would control the nuclear arms race. They also signed agreements in such diverse areas as oceanography, transportation, agriculture, and cultural exchange. Throughout his visit, Brezhnev emphasized the benefits of improved relations, especially in East-West trade and in arms control, and insisted that all problems in U.S.-Soviet relations could be solved as long as both parties did not seek unilateral advantage and were prepared to compromise. In private meetings with Nixon and Kissinger, the Soviet leader expressed deep concern about the situation in the Middle East, implying that a new war would erupt if a peace settlement between Israel and its Arab neighbors was not negotiated quickly. Overall, however, the 1973 summit was constructive, with both sides affirming their commitment to arms control, increased trade, and other components of détente.

In early October—less than four months later—Egypt and Syria attacked Israeli forces in lands that Israel had occupied six years earlier, thus initiating the fourth major Arab-Israeli war since 1948. Using largely Soviet equipment, Egypt and Syria gained the early advantage, but then Israel, aided by massive airlifts of U.S. supplies, fought back and threatened to rout the Arab forces. When Israel ignored UN ceasefire resolutions passed on October 22 and 23, Brezhnev sent an urgent letter to the White House on October 24 stating that America and Russia together should send troops to enforce the ceasefire. If the U.S. refused to act jointly, Brezhnev warned, the Soviets would be forced to "consider . . . taking appropriate steps unilaterally."

Viewing this message as an ultimatum, Kissinger quickly convened a special National Security Council meeting that Nixon, preoccupied by his Watergate troubles, did not attend. At this meeting it was decided to issue a DEFCON III (Defense Condition 3) military alert, which was only two steps away from war. Whether this alert altered Russian behavior is not known; but Russian troops were not sent to Egypt, and a ceasefire finally occurred after Kissinger exerted strong and repeated pressure on Israel. The main point here is that Brezhnev's letter and the U.S. response presented a much more somber view of U.S.-Soviet relations than the recent summit; indeed, it was the most serious confrontation since the Cuban missile crisis eleven years before.

The up-and-down effect produced by these two contrasting episodes occurred repeatedly in U.S.-Soviet relations between 1973 and 1984, thus evoking the image of a roller-coaster ride to characterize this era. In fact, given the frequency of leadership changes in both countries during these years—each had four different top leaders and the United States had six different secretaries of state—it might well be viewed as several roller-coaster rides. Compared with earlier years, both countries experienced greater uncertainty and inconsistency in foreign policy, and both possessed less relative power and less inherent respect in their alliance systems than they had in the early post–World War II period. But at least they stayed on the tracks in the most important sense: avoiding the nuclear war between them that could have ended modern civilization.

Although U.S. and Soviet leaders normally remained the leading actors in the Cold War, the roller-coaster years were characterized by increased assertiveness on East-West issues by governments and private citizens throughout Europe. From July 30 through August 1, 1975, for example, the leaders of thirty-five nations—including all European nations except Albania plus Russia, America, and Canada—met in Helsinki, Finland, to sign an agreement on European security and cooperation that had taken three years to negotiate. A product of détente in Europe, this agreement gave Russian leaders something they had long wanted: recognition of the legitimacy of both the communist governments of Eastern Europe and their nations' post–World War II borders. But in a section that made Soviet leaders uneasy, the agreement stipulated that all signatory nations had to respect their citizens' human rights. This section encouraged human rights' activists within the Soviet bloc and elsewhere and helped to make support for human rights in Russia and Eastern Europe a persistent theme of U.S. policy under Presidents Carter and Reagan. As historian Jussi M. Hanhimaki has noted, the Helsinki agreement is considered "an important milestone on the road to the demise of the totalitarian systems of the Soviet bloc."

Détente Bogs Down, 1973–1976

President Nixon's overwhelming reelection in November 1972, the Vietnam peace agreement the following January, and the strong commitment to détente in the Soviet leadership boded well for even greater improvements in East-West relations. Those most responsible for the day-to-day operation of foreign affairs in each country—Foreign Minister Andrei Gromyko in Russia and Henry Kissinger in the United States—were capable, experienced diplomats who sought improved relations. Yet the hopes of leaders in both countries were frustrated as often as they were fulfilled during these four years; and by 1975–76, U.S.-Soviet relations seemed to be heading slowly but steadily downhill.

Why did this unexpected shift in momentum occur? Why did U.S.-Soviet relations reach a plateau in 1972–73 and then begin to decline thereafter? A multitude of interrelated factors were involved, but seven seem especially important in understanding why détente bogged down during this period: 1) different understandings of détente among U.S. and Soviet leaders; 2) continuing superpower competition in the Third World; 3) the failure of the SALT process to slow the arms race significantly; 4) the breakdown of the Cold War consensus in U.S. public opinion, combined with failure to achieve a prodétente consensus; 5) a decline in effective presidential leadership coupled with increased congressional assertiveness in foreign policy; 6) the skill of Senator Henry Jackson (Dem., Wash.) and other opponents of détente in linking human rights, especially Jewish emigration, with trade issues, thus serving as a focal point for anti-Russian and anti-Kissinger sentiments; and 7) the presence of U.S.-Soviet relations as a major issue in the 1976 election. Thus, although the problems that U.S.-Soviet relations encountered resulted partly from the assumptions and actions of the leaders of both nations and from the generally competitive nature of world politics, internal U .S. attitudes and political practices also were deeply involved in the gradual shift away from détente.

1. Different understandings of détente. A couple entering a marriage with divergent assumptions about how the housework and finances will be handled is headed for trouble, and so are two nations with different outlooks that are trying to develop and sustain an improved relationship. Détente continued to be the official policy of both governments until late 1979 because both sought to reconcile, or at least to live with, their differences. But contrasts in their conceptions of détente harmed relations even during the hopeful years of the early 1970s. By mid-decade, harsh statements to the effect that the other was not "living up to détente" became common in each country.

John Lewis Gaddis has argued that Nixon and Kissinger saw détente as "yet another in a long series of attempts to 'contain' the power and influence of the Soviet Union, but one based on a new combination of pressures and inducements that would, if successful, convince the Russians that it was in their own best interests to be 'contained.'" Kissinger viewed détente as involving the need to "manage the emergence of Soviet power"—with America (i.e., Kissinger) doing much of the managing. This management would include agreements to limit the nuclear arms race; to increase trade, which U.S. leaders thought the Soviets wanted and needed more than Americans did; and to restrain interventions in the Third World, which was meant to apply especially to Soviet behavior.

Some U.S. officials—especially in the State Department—believed that improving U.S.-Soviet relations in such areas as arms control and trade were in America's national interest and, therefore, should not be tied to other issues (such as Soviet behavior in the Third World) in order to try to extract concessions. But Nixon and Kissinger, who had the dominant influence on U.S. policy, strongly believed in linkage. Thus, while there were many agreements normalizing U.S.-Soviet relations in this period, the administration's conception of détente largely meant using traditional carrot-and-stick diplomacy to influence Soviet foreign policy.

Not surprisingly, Soviet leaders viewed détente differently. They believed that détente had been made possible by the Soviet strategic buildup of the 1960s. As Brezhnev commented in 1975: "Détente became possible because a new correlation of forces in the world arena has been established. Now the leaders of the bourgeois world can no longer seriously count on resolving the historic conflict between capitalism and socialism by force." In contrast to Kissinger, Soviet leaders saw the main thrust of détente to be the management of America's decline from preeminence in world affairs to a position of rough equality with the U.S.S.R. Because of the Soviets' nuclear strength, America could no longer intimidate Russia, as it had done during the Cuban missile crisis, nor could it intervene with impunity in the Third World, confident that Russia could not react strongly.

Soviet leaders took great pride in SALT and other agreements of the early 1970s because they believed that they confirmed Russia's standing as a superpower deserving full equality with America in world affairs. Indeed, one of the recurring words in Soviet speeches and writings of the 1970s was "equal"—such as in "equal security" and "equal relations." To the Soviets, it was inappropriate for America to use linkage to extract concessions from a recognized superpower. What Russian leaders did not realize was that, in practice, Nixon and Kissinger—plus the large number of continuing Cold Warriors—were not prepared to grant Russia the complete equality that it considered its due. Moreover, in international as in interpersonal relations, "equality" is even more difficult to put into practice than it is to define.

Finally, the two nations disagreed in their understanding of the likely effects of détente on revolutionary change in the Third World. The Soviets insisted that détente could not halt the movement of history in the direction of socialism, a tenet of Marxist ideology that they believed was confirmed by the experience of the twentieth century. Largely for ideological reasons, they believed that Russia should aid Marxist governments and revolutionary movements throughout the world—a belief that, when implemented, not only angered U.S. officials but also drained scarce Soviet economic resources. U.S. leaders, in contrast, saw détente as leading to greater stability and the enhancement of what Kissinger called "American values." In seeking improved relations, neither side was about to change its basic ideology.

2. Continuing competition in the Third World. In the Basic Principles Agreement, signed at the Moscow summit in May 1972, U.S. and Soviet leaders pledged to "always exercise restraint in their mutual relations" and to resist the temptation to "obtain unilateral advantages at the expense of the other. . . ." Like some of the Yalta agreements, these and similar pledges had two key drawbacks: first, they were too general and idealistic to be implemented as long as both countries disagreed sharply on the rights and wrongs of particular conflicts; and, second, they could be quoted in an accusatory fashion by leaders of the two countries against each other and by opponents of détente against its supporters. Despite the Basic Principles Agreement and other affirmations of restraint and cooperation, the Cold War pattern of open or secret aid to governments or to revolutionary groups continued. From 1973 to 1976, U.S.-Soviet rivalry in the Third World occurred mainly in the Middle East, in Southeast Asia, and in Africa. On the U.S. side, this rivalry was managed mainly by Henry Kissinger, who became secretary of state as well as national security adviser in late 1973.

Even more than before the October 1973 Arab-Israeli war, America was the dominant outside power in the Middle East. America not only supplied large quantities of modern weapons to four major countries in the region—Israel, Egypt, Saudi Arabia, and Iran—but also, through Kissinger, played the leading role in the ongoing peace negotiations between Israel and its Arab neighbors. Russian leaders objected to their exclusion from the main developments in a region much closer to Moscow than to Washington. They also complained that Kissinger was ignoring the pledges of superpower equality—which indeed he was. But while Kissinger made some progress in disengaging hostile armies and in returning some captured land to the Arabs, no movement was made in the direction of providing either territory or political rights for the Palestinians. America was also unable to prevent an Arab oil embargo in response to U.S. support for Israel in the war and a sharp rise in oil prices thereafter that triggered a new round of inflation at home. In short, although Soviet influence in the Middle East declined, Kissinger made only modest progress toward a more general Mideast peace and proved unable to counter the oil producers' new assertiveness.

In Southeast Asia, America's allies in Indochina finally lost the war. Receiving some arms and economic assistance but no direct U.S. military support after January 1973, South Vietnamese troops fought on alone until Saigon fell to North Vietnamese and Viet Cong forces on May 1, 1975. The United States continued heavy bombing in Cambodia for seven months after ending its direct involvement in Vietnam; but Cambodia, too, finally was taken over in April 1975 by a local communist movement allied with China rather than with Russia. Laos, meanwhile, had come under the control of a communist party largely subservient to North Vietnam. As with the "fall of China" a generation before, conservatives argued that the "fall of Indochina" could have been avoided if the U.S. had shown greater resolve. On the other hand, many liberals were relieved that the war, which they believed America should never have entered, was finally over. As the major ally of North Vietnam, Russia could be viewed as the superpower winner in the conflict. But except for receiving the abandoned U.S. naval base at Camranh Bay, what Russia really acquired was a desperately poor and war-torn country that needed seemingly unlimited amounts of economic and military aid.

The area of greatest U.S.-Soviet tensions in the 1970s, at least from the American viewpoint, was Africa. During the administration of President Gerald Ford (August 1974–January 1977), East-West competition centered in Southern Rhodesia (later called "Zimbabwe") and Angola. Named for the famous British businessman and colonizer, Cecil Rhodes, Southern Rhodesia had long been ruled by its white minority with little interference from the nominal colonial ruler, Britain. In the 1960s, some factions of the indigenous tribal peoples, who made up well over 90 percent of the population, began to organize to achieve majority rule in the nation they called Zimbabwe. As guerrilla warfare between whites and blacks and tensions among various liberation groups intensified in the mid-1970s, America, Russia, and China all became involved in modest but significant ways.

In the early 1970s, the administration had showed little interest in Southern Rhodesia, but in 1976 Kissinger strongly supported Britain's effort to negotiate a transition to majority rule in that country, thereby avoiding serious conflict with either the black majority or with their supporters—the Chinese, the Russians, and other African nations. Skillful British mediation and U.S. support for peaceful change helped blacks and whites work out the details for elections and a black-led government in the late 1970s.

The situation in Angola proved more difficult to resolve and much more damaging to détente. In contrast to Britain's role in the crisis in Rhodesia, in Angola the colonial power, Portugal, pulled out of the country quickly in 1975. The result was a struggle for power among three major political groups: the National Liberation Front of Angola (FNLA), the Popular Movement for the Liberation of Angola (MPLA), and the National Union for the Total Independence of Angola (UNITA). Each of these groups had support in particular tribes, and each sought outside support in order to defeat its rivals and take power.

In retrospect, it probably would have been better for Angola if the major outside powers—China, Russia, America, South Africa, Zaire, and Cuba—had agreed to stay out of the civil war. But that would have been difficult to negotiate because of the rapidly shifting situation in Angola and because of bitter relations between China and Russia, on the one hand, and America and Cuba, on the other. Despite the advice of most middle-level officials in the State Department and CIA that the United States should not become involved in the conflict because it had no vital interests at stake, Kissinger persuaded President Ford that America should undertake CIA operations to counter Soviet moves.

As Georgi Arbatov's memoirs make clear, there also was considerable debate within the Soviet leadership about whether to involve Soviet and Cuban forces in the conflict. At one point Arbatov and an opponent, Andrei Alexandrov, debated the issue in Brezhnev's presence. Arbatov argued that Soviet military intervention would undercut détente and "restore the worst traditions of [Soviet] foreign military intervention in a completely new situation." Alexandrov countered with the claim that the Soviets had an "internationalist duty" to aid liberation movements in the Third World, and reminded Brezhnev that America frequently had intervened in the Third World. Although Brezhnev did not state his opinion at the time, Alexandrov clearly won this argument in practice.

From the U.S. viewpoint, Angola was damaging to détente because Russia's intervention was more forceful and successful than it usually had been in Third World conflicts. The faction that Russia and its ally Cuba supported, the MPLA, was largely successful in gaining power in 1975–76—and international acceptance as the lawful government—whereas Chinese aid to the FNLA and covert U.S. aid to both the FNLA and UNITA proved ineffective. Moreover, the tide turned in MPLA's favor after 250 Cuban military advisers arrived in Angola in June 1975 to instruct MPLA forces. When South Africa sent several thousand troops into Angola in October to assist UNITA, Cuba countered by using Soviet planes to airlift fourteen thousand of its troops to assist MPLA.

Because most black Africans detested South Africa for its white supremacist policies and for its occupation of Namibia (old Southwest Africa), black African governments generally viewed the Cuban-Soviet action as necessary to prevent the further spread of South African influence. But because Cuba was closely allied with Russia, without whose aid it would not have been able to intervene in Angola, many Americans saw the use of Cuban troops in Angola as a bold new form of Soviet imperialism and a challenge to America's standing in world affairs. Kissinger and many conservatives were angered when Congress, wary of foreign interventions in the wake of Vietnam and uncomfortable at finding America associated with white-supremacist South Africa, cut off U.S. aid to FNLA and UNITA in early 1976.

Soviet leaders considered their involvement in Angola as being consistent with détente. They insisted that they had as much right to assist "progressive forces" in the Third World as China, America, and South Africa had to help their factions. They also believed that they had been shunted aside in the Middle East and that letting the Chinese and Americans disregard their preferences in Africa would be a serious blow to their status as a superpower. Still viewing conflicts in the Third World largely in East-West terms, most Americans did not realize that Russia was intervening in Angola partly to defeat its bitter rival, China. In criticizing Russia's use of Cuban troops in Angola, Americans also did not note similarities with their own use of South Korean and other Asian troops in Vietnam that the Soviets might equally view as proxies.

Regardless of the merit of Soviet defenses of their own and Cuba's behavior in Angola, however, the fact remained that it proved helpful to antidétente forces in the U.S. It also led the Ford administration to abandon discreet talks with Cuba, begun in 1974, which might have led to a substantial détente in America's mini–Cold War with that country. Finally, the Soviet-Cuban success in Angola had fateful consequences for subsequent Soviet foreign policy, contributing substantially to the demise of détente. "After Angola, we went boldly down the path of intervention and expansion . . . ," Arbatov recalled. "It led us through Ethiopia, Yemen, a series of African countries, and, eventually, into Afghanistan."

3. The continuing arms race despite SALT. Like the U.S.-Soviet rivalry in the Third World, the continuing competition in strategic arms helped to undermine détente in the 1970s. In theory, the 1972 agreements should have led to the end of the nuclear arms race because (a) the antiballistic missile treaty sharply and permanently curtailed defensive systems, and (b) with neither side able to defend itself against a nuclear attack by the other, it should have been possible to freeze the number of offensive arms held by each side and eventually reduce them to a level sufficient to ensure mutual deterrence. Such, indeed, was to have been the goal of SALT II.

Why were the two sides not able to follow up their comprehensive agreement virtually abolishing defensive systems with an agreement effectively limiting offensive systems? Such an agreement would have brought the U.S.-Soviet nuclear arms race to an end, it would have eased the world's anxiety over the possibility of nuclear war, and it would have set an example for other actual or potential nuclear powers. But the nuclear arms race continued virtually unabated. Why?

In retrospect, it appears that the main reason was that the political will to end the arms race was lacking in both countries. Ending the offensive arms race would have required a confrontation by Nixon with the Pentagon, which was used to "staying ahead" of the Soviets technologically by ordering expensive new weapons systems from defense contractors, and a confrontation by Brezhnev with his defense ministry, which was accustomed to getting a large share of the budget for its contractors in order to "catch up" with America. Because these confrontations did not occur, SALT I and subsequent agreements, instead of limiting offensive arms significantly, largely ratified what each side was already planning to do to "modernize" its strategic forces. For each side, this meant improving the accuracy of its missiles (thus seeking the ability to launch a preemptive "first strike" to destroy the other side's ability to retaliate) and, equally important, putting multiple independently targetable reentry vehicles (MIRVs) on existing and new missiles, so that each missile now could carry several warheads instead of just one.

Thus, although the numbers of missiles and long-range bombers on each side were limited to 2,400 (including not more than 1,300 MIRVed missiles) at a meeting between President Ford and Premier Brezhnev at Vladivostok, U.S.S.R., in November 1974, the number of warheads these missiles and bombers could carry was not limited. By the time SALT I expired in 1977, America had roughly 8,500 warheads, compared to 5,700 in 1972. The Soviets had increased their warheads from 2,500 to 4,000, and, like the United States, had improved the accuracy of their delivery systems, thus increasing the threat to America's land-based missiles in the event of a preemptive attack.

The failure to make more progress in ending the arms race disappointed Nixon and Kissinger. Both were proud that SALT I established the goal of limiting competition in strategic weapons; both regretted that more was not accomplished before they left office. Kissinger believed that liberals did not understand the need for a strong defense while new limits were being negotiated, but he also chastised conservatives for failing to realize that arms control agreements could enhance U.S. security in the nuclear age. "One of the questions we have to ask ourselves as a country is what in the name of God is strategic superiority?" Kissinger commented in 1974. "What is the significance of it politically, militarily, operationally, at these levels of numbers? What do you do with it?" Nixon's remarks to Secretary of Defense James Schlesinger that same year struck a similar note: "Many of my friends are horrified at our even talking to the Soviet Union. But are we going to leave the world running away with an arms race, or will we get a handle on it?"

4. The lack of consensus in American public opinion. The 1970s saw the most extensive debate about the goals of U.S. foreign policy—and the appropriate means to achieve them—since the isolationist versus internationalist confrontation before Pearl Harbor. The belief in an activist, anticommunist foreign policy had been dominant from late 1946 until the mid-1960s. But the Vietnam War, together with Nixon's initiatives to improve relations with Russia and China, shattered the Cold War consensus and left a multitude of opinions about America's proper role in world affairs. The diversity of attitudes made it difficult for the administration to win broad public and congressional support for specific policies. Although public opinion polls showed that most Americans supported détente, many remained instinctively anticommunist and suspicious of Russia.

The ending of the Cold War consensus was most noticeable among the more knowledgeable and politically active segment of the population. Earlier, this broad grouping had been overwhelmingly supportive of Cold War policies, but by 1970 it had split into conservative internationalists on the one side and liberal internationalists on the other. Conservative internationalists tended to remain strongly anticommunist, anti-Russian, promilitary, and in favor of CIA and limited military interventions in the Third World to combat leftist movements. Liberal internationalists favored détente with Russia, arms control, lower defense budgets, much less military and CIA involvement in the Third World, support for human rights instead of right-wing dictators, and international cooperation in addressing such problems as economic development and environmental protection.

In Congress, the perspectives of conservative internationalists such as Senators Jackson and Strom Thurmond (Rep., S.C.) and liberal internationalists such as Senators Edward Kennedy (Dem., Mass.) and Charles Mathias (Rep., Md.) were so different that the Nixon, Ford, and Carter administrations could not expect unity or consistency in congressional votes on foreign policy. Similarly, after Vietnam the liberal *New York Times* and the conservative *Wall Street Journal* seldom agreed editorially on world affairs. Like most politically active people, both liberal and conservative internationalists had their share of inconsistencies: for example, liberals wanted strong U.S. support for human rights while deploring America's tendency to intervene in other nations' internal affairs, whereas conservatives sought increased budgets for defense and intelligence while cutting the cost of government and lowering taxes.

While the more politically active were dividing sharply in their views, the roughly one-half of the public who were less interested in and knowledgeable about world affairs tended to be suspicious of government—especially after Vietnam and Watergate—and of foreigners. Basically, as public opinion analyst William Schneider has pointed out, they favored both peace and military strength. They wanted better relations with the Russians but remained distrustful of them. They thought that the U.S. should stay out of foreign quarrels, yet they were sensitive to slights to America's pride. Because their views were volatile and not based on either a conservative or a liberal ideology, they could provide the swing votes in elections, going for liberal Democrats in one election and conservative Republicans in another.

In short, the Cold War consensus was not replaced by a new one, either in elite or in mass opinion. Neither prodétente nor antidétente forces dominated public opinion or Congress during the 1970s or 1980s, and presidents had to try to appeal to both conservative and liberal strands of thought, often at the same time. As Nixon and his successors learned, the climate of opinion did not facilitate a consistent, stable policy either toward Russia or toward the often baffling Third World, seen by some in purely Cold War terms and by others as having a wide range of essentially local problems with the need for peace and development as the one unifying theme.

5. The decline in presidential leadership in foreign policy. One of the central tenets of the Cold War consensus had been that the country should look to the president for leadership in foreign affairs, especially in standing up to communism. In the 1950s and 1960s, America's Vietnam policy had embodied this principle: Congress dutifully voted billions of dollars in aid for noncommunist Indochina, looked the other way while the CIA undertook extensive operations in the region, and then voted the money for Johnson's and Nixon's expensive war there. During the Nixon era, however, there was a barrage of revelations about dubious presidential actions and coverups of illegal activities. In his memoirs, Kissinger blamed the new congressional assertiveness in foreign policy, and the resulting decline in presidential authority, largely on Watergate. But it was not just Watergate that had brought about the change: it was the coverup of the My Lai massacre in Vietnam; the coverup and lying to Congress (which Kissinger participated in) about the bombing of Cambodia; news reports, which turned out to be accurate, about the participation of the CIA and U.S. companies in efforts to prevent the elected president of Chile from taking power; and the growing sense that Nixon's and Kissinger's secrecy, their tendency to bypass State Department and other officials in making policy, and their general disregard for truth and morality were inconsistent with American ideals and thus required increased congressional supervision of foreign affairs.

The ending of the Cold War consensus in itself increased the need for greater give-and-take between the executive and Congress. But the actions of Nixon and Kissinger in Cambodia and elsewhere during their first term, many of which came to light after 1972, prompted congressional demands for a sharply increased role in foreign affairs. Applied to U.S.-Soviet relations, the new mood on Capitol Hill meant that any administration proposal would be subject to intense scrutiny and that the Nixon-Kissinger conception of détente would not necessarily be endorsed by a newly skeptical Congress.

6. Senator Jackson's congressional assault on détente. In 1919–20, a Republican senator from Massachusetts, Henry Cabot Lodge, orchestrated the forces that defeated President Wilson on the issue of U.S. entry into the League of Nations. In 1973–75, a Democratic senator from Washington, Henry Jackson, played a similar role in undermining détente with Russia. Like Lodge, Jackson had served in the

Senate for many years at the time of his challenge to administration policy; he was the second-ranking member of the Senate Armed Services Committee, which oversees the Pentagon's budget. A skillful legislator, he knew how to make things happen in Congress; he also had close ties to the Pentagon, defense contractors, organized labor, and the Jewish community. A conservative internationalist with presidential ambitions, Jackson detested the U.S.S.R. and believed that it should be approached from a position of military strength and not through trade, arms control, or other components of détente. Kissinger remembered Jackson as a "fierce negotiator" and a "master psychological warrior," and he commented with his famous dry humor that a meeting with Jackson in March 1974 was "the beginning of a dialogue that made me long for the relative tranquility of the Middle East."

Jackson's greatest success in undermining détente came in his persistent assault on U.S.-Soviet trade. Jackson knew that increased trade was an important component of détente to the Soviets, who wanted access to U.S. technology and credit to improve their economy. Jackson also knew that, in order to defeat the administration on this issue, he would need the votes of some liberals, both because liberals held the balance of power in Congress and because some conservatives would support the increased trade favored by most U.S. business groups. Accordingly, Jackson embraced the idea of linking congressional support for equality in trade—symbolized by the granting of most-favored-nation tariff status to Russia—to Soviet concessions on Jewish emigration, a concept embodied in the Jackson-Vanik amendment to the trade bill that worked its way through Congress in 1973–74. Despite business opposition, some conservatives voted for Jackson-Vanik because, like Jackson, they disliked both détente and the U.S.S.R.; and many liberals voted for it because they deplored antisemitism in Russia and considered freedom to emigrate to be a basic human right.

Both the administration and Soviet leaders strongly opposed Jackson-Vanik and other efforts to limit trade. Nixon and Kissinger supported increased Jewish emigration and, in general, more Soviet respect for human rights. But they argued that these goals were more likely to be achieved through quiet diplomacy and tacit understandings than through congressional pressure. They also thought that U.S. leaders should be cautious about seeking to change the other superpower's domestic policies and that linkage should be applied to Russia's international behavior, not to its internal affairs. For their part, Soviet leaders had already begun to permit increased Jewish emigration, but they denounced the idea of quotas imposed by Congress as meddling in their domestic affairs. When Congress finally passed a trade bill in December 1974 that included the Jackson-Vanik Amendment and set a limit of $300 million on U.S. credits to Russia without congressional approval, the Soviets informed U.S. leaders that they would not implement the provisions of the 1972 trade agreement. And as Kissinger had predicted, they also cut back sharply on Jewish emigration. "I think détente has had a setback," Kissinger commented.

Aided by Richard Perle, a hard-working member of his staff whom opponents called the "Prince of Darkness," Jackson also worked persistently to undermine public and congressional support for arms control agreements. He argued in 1972 that SALT I gave the Soviets the advantage and got an amendment through the Senate stating that all future treaties would have to give America numerical equality in strategic launchers. When Kissinger and Ford gained Soviet acceptance of that principle in the Vladivostok agreement in 1974, Jackson and Perle denounced the agreement because (a) the numbers were too high and (b) the Soviets had more heavy missiles than the United States. In fact, America had chosen not to build heavy missiles, though it would be free to do so under the agreement. Moreover, Vladivostok gave the U.S. the possibility of continued strategic superiority—assuming that the concept had any meaning at the existing levels of destructive potential—because U.S. forward-based systems (bombers and missiles in Europe and the Mediterranean) were not counted as part of the 2,400 limit, whereas the Soviets had no similar forward-based systems.

Jackson and his allies in the Pentagon and in the press were not interested in an evenhanded analysis of the strategic balance. They wanted to push ahead with new U.S. weapons systems and saw the SALT process as undermining support for defense expenditures. Assisting them was the momentum of new technology, which now made it possible for the U.S. to deploy cruise missiles (low-flying missiles that could elude Soviet radar) that, because of their small size, would be difficult to verify and hence to include as part of arms control agreements. The Soviets also had new weapons, including the so-called Backfire bomber. Also assisting opponents of arms control was the public's continuing ignorance of the details of the strategic balance, which permitted conservatives to argue (as the liberal Kennedy had done in 1960) that America was falling behind Russia and that the SALT process had given the Soviets the advantage. The fact that the two nations' force structures were very different, with America having most of its nuclear warheads on submarines and bombers while the Soviets had most of theirs on land-based missiles, also made comparisons difficult. Finally, the fact that both sides were modernizing their forces showed that SALT had not slowed the offensive arms race significantly. But instead of urging new agreements with qualitative as well as quantitative restrictions, conservatives sought to cast doubt on the entire SALT process. This combination of factors, plus fear that the Pentagon and Congress would not support a treaty involving concessions by both sides, made it impossible for Kissinger to conclude a SALT II agreement in early 1976. In a real sense, therefore, Jackson had won at least a partial victory against arms control that accompanied his success in restricting trade.

7. Détente as an issue in the election of 1976. Nineteen seventy-six was the year of the outsider in American politics. There were plenty of experienced insiders who wanted to be elected president that year—President Ford for the Republicans and Senator Jackson and others for the Democrats—but many of the votes and headlines went to two men with no experience in Washington: an actor and former California governor, Ronald Reagan, for the Republicans; and a peanut farmer and former Georgia governor, Jimmy Carter, for the Democrats. Voters seemed to be looking for new faces unassociated with either the Vietnam War or Watergate. Reagan totally opposed détente and Carter appeared to support it while criticizing its implementation; both cast doubt on the wisdom of the approach by their sharp attacks on Ford and Kissinger.

While Carter moved steadily toward the Democratic nomination with his good political organization and his calls for morality in public life, Ford faced a tough fight for the nomination. An effective speaker who could warm the hearts of conservative audiences, Reagan found that Ford was most vulnerable among Republican voters on foreign policy issues, especially those involving the alleged weakness of the administration on U.S.-Soviet relations and on defense. So Reagan went on the attack. "Let us not be satisfied with a foreign policy whose principle accomplishment seems to be our acquisition of the right to sell Pepsi-Cola in Siberia," Reagan told cheering students in New Hampshire. "Under Kissinger and Ford, this nation has become Number Two in a world where it is dangerous—if not fatal—to be second best," he stated in Florida, and continued, "There is little doubt in my mind that the Soviet Union will not stop taking advantage of détente until it sees that the American people have elected a new President and appointed a new Secretary of State." In reply, Ford defended his foreign policy and accused Reagan of oversimplifying reality; but he also announced that he was dropping "détente" from his vocabulary.

The race turned out to be very close: Ford won most of the primaries in the Northeast and Midwest, but Reagan had the upper hand in the South and West. In late July, Ford had a slight lead in delegates, but the undecided delegates held the balance of power. At the Republican national convention in August, Ford won by the slim margin of 1,187 to 1,070. But he had to accept a platform that, on foreign policy, read like some of Reagan's speeches: "In pursuing détente we must not grant unilateral favors with only the hope of getting future favors in return."

Having barely escaped becoming the first sitting president in the twentieth century to be denied the nomination of his party, Ford now faced an uphill struggle against Carter. Although Ford was able to close the gap in public opinion polls as the campaign progressed, Carter possessed the advantage that had helped Reagan: he could remain on the offensive, whereas Ford had to defend his policies. And Carter did not have to be consistent. He could accuse Ford of giving away too much to the Russians while at the same time saying that Ford had not tried hard enough to get a new SALT agreement. Still, Ford might have won a narrow victory if he had not made the enormous error, during the second televised debate, of insisting that there was "no

Soviet domination of Eastern Europe." This was a statement certain to anger Americans of East European descent and to renew doubts about Ford's intelligence.

Carter won the election with roughly 50 percent of the popular vote to 48 percent for Ford. But during the campaign, neither of the candidates had offered much guidance for the future of U.S.-Soviet relations. As in many election years, there was much politicking—but little substance—in U.S. foreign policy in 1976. Détente clearly was on hold, but military technology and the size of the arsenals on both sides were moving forward.

Carter Rides the Roller Coaster, 1977–1979

As a statesman, Jimmy Carter is remembered largely for his achievements outside the area of U.S.-Soviet relations. He is especially known for the Panama Canal treaties of 1977, which showed that politically charged issues can be resolved through negotiations, and for the Camp David accords of 1978, which produced peace between Egypt and Israel. His administration also established full diplomatic relations with the People's Republic of China, negotiated skillfully for a comprehensive treaty to update the law of the seas, and worked hard to improve the human rights situation in many countries and to prevent the spread of nuclear weapons to nations that did not already possess them. These and other efforts to create a more peaceful and just world order have given Carter greater admiration from some scholars of world affairs than he received from the American public at the time.

Yet Carter has not been widely praised for his overall handling of U.S.-Soviet relations. His vision was lofty: he said in his inaugural address that, at the end of his presidency, "I would hope that the nations of the world might say that we had built a lasting peace, based not on weapons of war but on international policies which reflect our own most precious values." He also promised that his administration would "move this year a step toward our ultimate goal—the elimination of all nuclear weapons from this earth." Lamentably, Carter did not come close to achieving either the goal for the end of 1977 or the one for the close of his presidency. Instead, U.S.-Soviet relations under Carter started off poorly in 1977, recovered just enough to permit the signing of the SALT II treaty in June 1979, and then shifted to bitter hostility when the Soviet Union invaded Afghanistan six months later.

Although Carter alone did not end détente—Soviet and Cuban actions in the Third World and the growing influence of Cold Warriors at home played their part—the president was so inconsistent in his policies and so inept in his political leadership that he also certainly contributed to the downturn in relations from 1977 through 1980. Lacking a clear sense of what he most wanted to achieve and how to achieve it, Carter zigzagged and waffled while losing support both at home and abroad. The president's domestic approval rating in the Gallup poll stood at 67 percent in July 1977, 39 percent in July 1978, 29 percent in July 1979, and 21 percent (an all-time low for the post–1945 presidency) in July 1980. In Britain, long America's closest ally, 62 percent of respondents in a 1979 poll doubted "the ability of the United States to deal wisely with present world problems."

The difficulties in U.S.-Soviet relations during Carter's first year began, before the inauguration, with his selection of Cyrus Vance to be his secretary of state and Zbigniew Brzezinski to be his national security adviser. Vance, a mild-mannered, modest man who avoided the spotlight, had served effectively in the Democratic administrations of the 1960s. Vance believed that difficulties in U.S.-Soviet relations could be worked out on a case-by-case basis and that most of the problems in the Third World had largely local roots and should not be blamed on Russia. A liberal internationalist, Vance also opposed linkage, especially on arms control, which he considered to be clearly in the national interest of both nations.

In many ways, Brzezinski was the opposite of Vance. Called by reporters the "Polish Kissinger," Brzezinski in fact had several similarities to his famous predecessor. Both were immigrants (Kissinger from Germany, Brzezinski from Poland) who still spoke with accents; both were respected political scientists at Ivy League universities; and both were highly ambitious men who loved to talk with reporters and be in the limelight. But Brzezinski differed from Kissinger in being instinctively anti-Russia and pro-China. A conservative internationalist whose views on U.S.-Soviet relations had changed little since the 1950s, Brzezinski also lacked Kissinger's sense of grand strategy.

Journalist Elizabeth Drew wrote in 1978: "Of all the many people I have discussed the subject of Brzezinski with, hardly any have used the word 'thoughtful.'"

In his memoirs, Carter wrote that he had been warned of some of Brzezinski's character traits—his aggressive ambitiousness and the possibility that "he might not be adequately deferential to a secretary of state"—before he appointed him. But Carter liked Brzezinski as a person and respected his intellect, and he thought that he could permit Brzezinski and Vance to state different opinions because "the final decisions on basic foreign policy would be made by me in the Oval Office." In fact, however, Brzezinski repeatedly sought to overrule the State Department and to win Carter's support for his ideas or, as in the case of China policy, to seize control of decision making. Moreover, the two men's advice often was incompatible. Yet Carter, with his lack of experience in foreign affairs, often did little more than try to split the difference between them, thus contributing greatly to the inconsistency and incoherence in U.S. policy during these years. Finally, the persistent leaking of conflicting viewpoints to the media by Brzezinski and his staff and by the State Department added to the perception of an administration in disarray.

The incoherence in policy toward Russia was evident during the administration's first few months in office. Carter wanted to carry out his campaign pledge by making human rights a new pillar of U.S. foreign policy. He also wanted to move forward rapidly to achieve a new arms control agreement to replace SALT I, which was to expire in October 1977. With the euphoria that accompanied his becoming president, Carter seemed unconcerned that Soviet leaders would be angered by his stance on human rights. He also brushed aside warnings—including one by Soviet Ambassador Anatoly Dobrynin in a meeting with Carter on February 1, 1977—that officials in Moscow would reject outright his new approach to arms control. Their memoirs make it clear that Vance largely disagreed with Carter's confrontational approach during his first few weeks in office, whereas Brzezinski welcomed it.

Carter began to anger Soviet leaders on human rights when, shortly after his election in November, he sent a telegram of support to Soviet dissident Vladimir Slepak. Carter then instructed Vance to meet in

December with an exiled dissident, Andrei Amalrik; shortly after Carter's inauguration, the State Department praised another leading dissident, Andrei Sakharov, and Carter sent a letter of support to Sakharov in mid-February. In a letter to Carter dated February 25, 1977, Brezhnev denounced the president's correspondence with Sakharov, "a renegade who proclaimed himself an enemy of the Soviet state," and insisted that he would not "allow interference in our internal affairs, whatever pseudo-humanitarian slogans are used to present it."

With the atmosphere thus poisoned, Carter decided to send Vance and chief arms negotiator Paul Warnke to Moscow in late March with a proposal for deep cuts in offensive weapons. Brezhnev and Gromyko gave the two envoys an icy reception and publicly ridiculed their proposal for deep cuts. Because these cuts would affect Soviet land-based missiles significantly while requiring few changes in the U.S. force structure and because the Soviets had insisted that negotiations should proceed along the lines established previously at Vladivostok and pursued thereafter by Kissinger and Gromyko, it is remarkable that Carter thought that he had any chance of getting his proposal accepted. It also appears that the president did not think through either the negative impression a public defeat on this issue would make at home or the effects of his proposal on Soviet attitudes toward him. Carter's decision to ignore the results of the SALT talks between 1972 and 1976 astonished and infuriated Russian leaders.

From here it was a long, slow ride back up the roller coaster until SALT II was finally signed more than two years later. Carter wanted to have a summit meeting to exchange views with Brezhnev in 1977, but the Soviet leader refused to meet until SALT II was ready for their signatures. Meanwhile Carter continued to give the impression of inconsistency in his defense policies. He supported some weapons programs that the conservatives wanted—cruise missiles, a counterforce capability for the land-based Minuteman III, and the Trident submarine—but angered them when he canceled two other potential weapons—the B-1 bomber and the neutron (enhanced radiation) bomb, which would kill people while doing less damage to property than other nuclear weapons. Liberals were upset because defense spending was increasing, despite Carter's campaign pledge to cut it, but

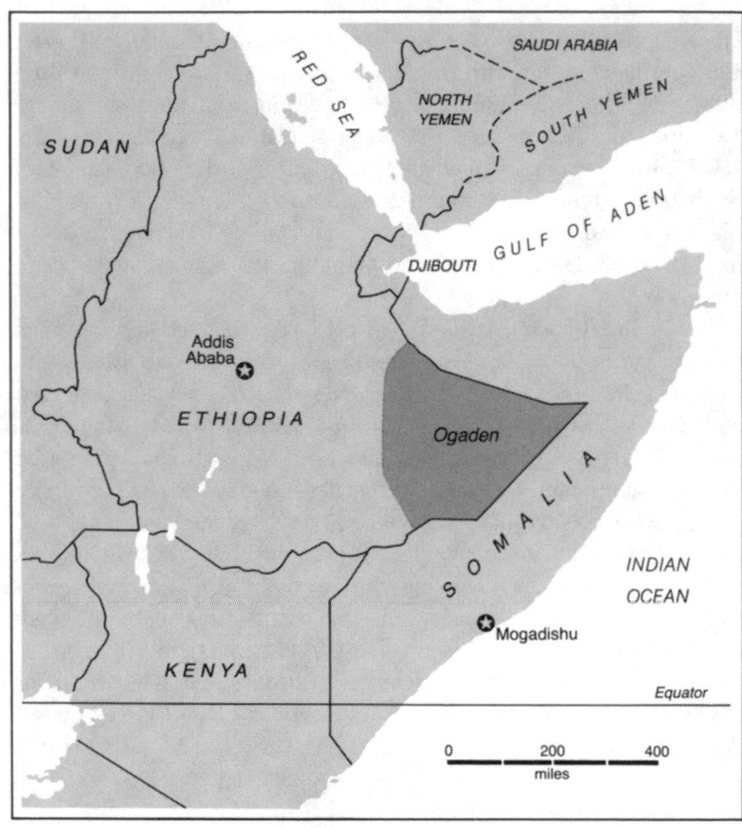

conservatives did not think that it was growing rapidly enough and gave Carter no credit for his strategic modernization programs.

In addition to human rights and arms control, two other major issues harmed U.S.-Soviet relations and stirred disputes within the administration. The first of these was the continuing superpower rivalry in Africa, now centered in the Horn of Africa, an area in the northeast corner of the continent close to the strategic Middle East. In this poor and ethnically divided region, America had provided Ethiopia with military and economic aid since 1953, and Russia had supplied arms to Somalia beginning in 1963, receiving a naval base on the Somali coast in return. Somali leaders wanted to annex the Ogaden region of Ethiopia, a sparsely populated, largely desert area inhabited mainly by ethnic Somalis. When a Marxist coup and resulting civil war occurred in Ethiopia in 1974, Somali ambitions to seize the Ogaden increased. U.S. aid to Ethiopia continued after the coup, but relations became strained, and in December 1976 Ethiopia signed an agreement with the U.S.S.R. to receive Soviet weapons. The Carter administration stopped military aid to Ethiopia the following May, and, when Soviet-Somali relations cooled in response to Moscow's new friendship with Ethiopia, the United States in July 1977 "agreed in principle" to help Somalia obtain weapons for defensive purposes.

At that very moment, however, Somali troops were in the Ogaden helping local guerrillas oust Ethiopian troops from the area. As the Somalis won more and more territory, Soviet-Somali relations deteriorated further, with a complete break occurring in November. The Soviets and Cubans then provided major support to Ethiopia: roughly $1 billion in Russian weapons and twelve to seventeen thousand Cuban troops were airlifted to the country. Between January and March 1978, an Ethiopian-Cuban offensive routed the Somalis from the Ogaden and returned the region to Ethiopian control. At that point the war ended, and the crisis gradually subsided.

The events in the Horn of Africa ignited a bitter dispute within the Carter administration. Brzezinski viewed the situation largely in East-West terms. He believed that the Somali-Ethiopian war posed "a potentially grave threat to our position in the Middle East, notably the Arabian peninsula." He thus wanted Carter to take forceful actions, including sending an aircraft carrier task force to the region and warning the Soviets and Cubans that their actions were causing a serious crisis in U.S.-Soviet relations that could prevent progress on other issues such as arms control. Vance and others in the State Department, however, saw the situation as essentially a local conflict. They believed that the U.S. should not send arms to Somalia as long as Somali troops were inside Ethiopian territory and that America "should continue to work with our European allies and the African nations to bring about a negotiated solution of the broader regional issues." In short, so long as Ethiopian and Cuban troops did not invade Somalia, America should limit its involvement and not attempt to link the situation to other East-West issues.

In this conflict within the administration, Secretary of Defense Harold Brown sided with Vance, and so largely did President Carter. But Brzezinski still made his influence felt. He leaked his views to the press repeatedly, and he also was "very gratified" when Carter spoke forcefully on the issue in a meeting with a member of the Soviet politburo in January 1978. And when Gromyko proposed a "joint U.S.-Soviet mediation effort," Brzezinski helped to ensure that Carter rejected it. Finally, having lost the battle for a policy of linkage within the administration, Brzezinski went public on March 1 with the statement that "linkages may be imposed by unwarranted exploitation of local conflict for larger international purposes." Vance, who believed that a successful outcome of the conflict in the Horn was being achieved, was furious. He responded on the next day that there was "no linkage" between events in the Horn and SALT. But the damage had been done: opponents of détente such as Jackson and Paul Nitze were almost certain to quote Brzezinski in their effort to defeat a SALT II treaty.

Although Brzezinski lost out on overall policy toward the Horn of Africa, he succeeded in setting the direction of U.S. policy toward China from 1978 onward. The Carter administration was united in wanting to achieve normal diplomatic relations with mainland China. But Vance and Brzezinski disagreed on whether the major U.S. objective in normalizing relations was (a) to continue the triangular relationship established by Kissinger, with America as the evenhanded balance between Russia and China, or (b) to develop a de facto alliance with China against Russia. Vance argued vigorously for the first viewpoint, while Brzezinski worked steadily for the second. Carter does not appear to have recognized how much he was leaning toward Brzezinski's view; but in sending him to Beijing in May 1978 (against Vance's strongly stated wishes) and in subsequent actions, the president clearly was "playing the China card" against Russia.

During his trip to Beijing, Brzezinski did everything he could to please the Chinese leaders. He told them that the U.S. accepted their conditions for normalization; he shared sensitive military information with them; and he stressed repeatedly the evil nature of the U.S.S.R. and the threat that "the polar bear" posed to peace. His toasts at the formal dinners were almost as anti-Soviet as those of the Chinese. At one dinner he stated that "the United States recognized and shared China's resolve to 'resist the efforts of any nation which seeks to establish global or regional hegemony'"—hegemony being a code word for Soviet aggression in the standard Chinese denunciation of Russia. Upon his return, Brzezinski told a reporter that the trip was intended to "underline the long-term strategic nature of the United States' relationship to China."

While Carter was pleased with the progress that Brzezinski had made toward normalization, Soviet leaders were deeply concerned. An editorial in *Pravda* on May 30, 1978, stated that Brzezinski "stands before the world as an enemy of détente." *Pravda* also blamed China, stating on June 17 that "Soviet-American confrontation . . . is the cherished dream of Beijing." On the whole, U.S. officials were not displeased by the Kremlin's anger and concern: perhaps it would make Soviet leaders more eager to conclude the SALT negotiations and more inclined to show restraint in the Third World.

Secret Sino-American negotiations proceeded during the summer and fall, and on December 15, 1978, both nations announced that full diplomatic relations would be established on January 1, 1979, followed by a visit by Vice Premier Deng Xiaoping to Washington at the end of the month. Deng used the occasion, and the heavy media coverage it received, to denounce the U.S.S.R. Despite Vance's appeal for evenhandedness in dealing with Russia and China, Carter agreed to include "hegemony" in the joint communiqué issued at the end of the visit. Deng was playing the American card—his desire for a Sino-American alliance against Russia—at least as effectively as Brzezinski had played the China card in Beijing the previous summer.

The SALT II agreement, signed by Carter and Brezhnev in Vienna on June 18, 1979, was the high point of U.S.-Soviet relations during the Carter years. As in 1972, when Brezhnev went ahead with the summit despite the U.S. mining of Haiphong's harbor, Soviet leaders signed the SALT II treaty despite all the recent U.S. actions that, in their view, were undermining détente. But this time U.S. leaders, with little public or congressional enthusiasm for the treaty, were unable to persuade the Senate to consent to its ratification. Indeed, the signing of SALT II by an aging, sickly general secretary and an unpopular president did little if anything to slow the downward slide in U.S.-Soviet relations.

The treaty itself was too detailed and too technical to be understood fully by the average citizen or, for that matter, by the average senator. Essentially, however, it limited each side to a total of 2,400 strategic launch vehicles until the end of 1981, and to 2,250 from then until the treaty expired at the end of 1985. Limits also were put on the number of MIRVed land-based missiles (820), on the total number of MIRVed land-based and submarine launched missiles (1,200), and on the total number of these MIRVed missiles and heavy bombers equipped with long-range cruise missiles (1,320). The U.S.S.R. still had the advantage in the number of land-based missiles and the size of the deadly payloads they could deliver to U.S. targets, but the U.S. led in the number of weapons, submarine-based weapons, cruise missiles, and the forward-based systems that remained outside SALT. The treaty permitted one new land-based missile system for each side. As in previous arms control negotiations, SALT II basically let each side do what it was planning to do anyway. But at least it put limits—admittedly very high ones—on the nuclear arms race, and it called for further negotiations to achieve significant cuts in the arsenals on both sides.

Partly in order to try to convince conservative senators that it was tough on defense, the administration urged Congress to approve funds for the deployment of a new land-based missile, the MX, at the same time that it submitted the SALT treaty for the Senate's approval. It also proceeded, in conjunction with its NATO allies, to move toward the deployment of highly accurate Pershing II and cruise missiles in Western Europe to counter Russia's new intermediate-range missiles, the SS-20s. The new U.S. deployments would not be made if Russia could be persuaded to remove its SS-20s—or if the growing peace movement in several NATO countries could stop them.

It seems unlikely that SALT II would have passed the Senate even without the Soviet invasion of Afghanistan at the end of 1979. Carter's political standing was too low, U.S.-Soviet relations were too strained, and conservatives were too opposed to the entire concept of détente (which arms control had come to symbolize) for the administration to muster anywhere near the two-thirds vote required to win Senate approval. If the same treaty had been negotiated in 1977, when Carter was at the height of his popularity, it might well have passed. But by June 1979, the next presidential campaign was approaching, and most Republicans were not about to ratify an arms control agreement that might help an unpopular president win reelection. Most liberals probably would have voted for it, though many were disappointed that it did not do enough to end the strategic arms race.

Thus SALT II remained unratified, widely denounced by conservatives and given lukewarm support at best by liberals. Ironically, however, it was largely observed by both governments even after it expired in 1985, thus suggesting that it was more balanced and practical—or at least more in tune with the realities of U.S.-Soviet relations and the wishes of defense establishments on both sides—than critics at the time acknowledged.

The Third Dangerous Phase, 1980–1984

If the signing of SALT II can be considered a modest improvement in U.S.-Soviet relations, Russia's invasion of Afghanistan, beginning in late December 1979, created the worst setback since the Cuban missile crisis or even since the Korean War. The invasion and the U.S. response, Raymond Garthoff has observed, "marked a watershed in American-Soviet relations, sharply dividing the previous decade of détente (admittedly, faltering badly by that time) from the ensuing years of containment and confrontation." The unexpected Soviet invasion added an ominous new layer to the tensions that were building in East-West relations in the late 1970s, and precipitated a third dangerous phase in U.S.-Soviet relations that spanned Carter's last year in office and most of Reagan's first term.

Why did Russia make this move, which was almost certain to be viewed with alarm in the West as well as in the Middle East? And why did the Carter administration make a hardline response to Soviet intervention in a country on Russia's southern border?

As with most great power interventions in small countries, the Soviets said that their sending of troops to Afghanistan was a defensive move. They long had had interests there, but these grew sharply after a coup in April 1978 that brought the Marxist People's Democratic Party of Afghanistan (PDPA) to power in the capital, Kabul. When the new government tried to bring about land reform and other social changes in the conservative Muslim countryside, armed resistance developed. And when the PDPA chose to try to crush this resistance by air raids and other military tactics, the Soviet-backed government rapidly lost much of its limited popular support.

Brezhnev explained in June 1980 that Russia "had no choice but to send troops" in order to "preserve the gains of the April [1978] revolution." Brezhnev and other Soviet spokesmen also argued, with some justification, that their bitter enemy China, plus the U.S. and pro-U.S. Middle Eastern countries, were providing aid to the insurgents in 1979. The "unceasing armed intervention and far-reaching implications of the conspiracy of the external forces of reaction," Brezhnev commented on January 12, 1980, "created a real danger of Afghanistan losing its independence and being turned into an imperialist military bridgehead on our country's southern borders." Brezhnev also insisted that Russia had no "expansionist plans in respect to . . . other countries in that area."

In short, Brezhnev appeared to believe that Afghanistan had been within the Soviet sphere of influence since 1978 and that intervention was necessary to preserve the Marxist revolution against domestic and foreign enemies. In discussions within the Soviet government, however, some high-ranking officials argued that this traditional Muslim country was not ready for socialism and that the intervention would do serious damage to the Kremlin's relations with Western Europe and the U.S.

To U.S. officials and ordinary citizens alike, the Soviet move, far from being defensive, was a brutal invasion of an independent country, and the Soviets needed to be punished for it. Moreover, the timing was extremely poor. American pride had suffered a severe blow when, less than two months earlier, Iranian revolutionaries had seized the U.S. embassy in Teheran and taken more than fifty Americans hostage. Carter was under tremendous pressure to get the hostages back quickly or, if negotiations failed, to take military action against Iran. Moreover, the Marxist-dominated Sandinistas had come to power in July in Nicaragua and were developing close ties with Cuba; a controversy had developed in August and September about whether Russia had combat troops in Cuba and, if so, what the U.S. response should be; and price increases by the Organization of Petroleum Exporting Countries (OPEC) that U.S. leaders opposed publicly were again causing inflation at home and suggesting U.S. impotence abroad. Now Russia was using its troops outside the Warsaw Pact area for the first time since World War II in order to shape Afghanistan's internal affairs. While one could argue about the Soviet role in Angola or Ethiopia, the invasion of Afghanistan provided concrete evidence to support conservatives' warnings about "Soviet expansionism." Thus, even if Carter personally had favored a milder response, politically the 1979 chain of events and the effectiveness of the conservative critique of his earlier policies gave him virtually no choice but to take a strong stand against Russia.

The administration's hardline response was both rhetorical and substantive. Carter and Brzezinski denounced the Soviets repeatedly over the next several weeks, saying that they were lying about their motives for invading Afghanistan. Carter also insisted that the Russian action "could pose the most serious threat to peace since the Second World War." Vance supported Carter's view that the Soviet invasion was "unacceptable" and that a strong U.S. response was required. But while Vance thought that Moscow's "immediate aim was to protect Soviet political interests in Afghanistan which they saw endangered," Brzezinski, now clearly Carter's chief adviser, believed that the Soviet action was "not a local but a strategic challenge." Carter agreed with Brzezinski, and in his State of the Union message to Congress in January 1980 included a statement that quickly became known as the Carter Doctrine: "An attempt by any outside force to gain control of the Persian Gulf region will be regarded as an assault on the vital interests of the United States of America, and such an assault will be repelled by any means necessary, including military force."

The administration quickly decided on a series of measures designed to punish the Soviets for "their attempt to crush Afghanistan." On January 3, 1980, Carter asked the Senate to delay consideration of the SALT II treaty. The next day he announced several additional punitive measures. These included such economic measures as embargoes on the selling of grain and high-technology goods to Russia and such other actions as U.S. withdrawal from the 1980 summer Olympics in Moscow and the curtailment of cultural and scientific exchanges. The grain embargo was far from complete: 8 million tons were sold in accordance with a 1975 agreement, and the Soviet government was able to replace much of the 17 million tons that the United States held back by purchasing grain from Argentina and other nations, despite Carter's appeals to them not to increase their sales. In all, the State Department and the National Security Council came up with about forty steps the U.S. could take to punish Russia, and most of these were implemented. But several, including the Olympic boycott and the grain embargo, were controversial. The eventual Republican candidate for president, Ronald Reagan, told farmers that the embargo was hurting them, not the Russians, and that he would lift it if he became president.

Like previous Cold War crises, Afghanistan encouraged military approaches to containment and higher defense budgets. Carter asked Congress to approve increased defense spending (a growth of 5 percent above inflation) and registration of eighteen-year-old males to make possible a rapid military buildup or a return to the draft. Combat readiness for existing forces was improved, and a Rapid Deployment Force that could intervene in the Persian Gulf or elsewhere was organized. The administration offered increased aid to Pakistan and other nations in the region and began close military collaboration with China. On July 25, 1980, Carter signed Presidential Directive 59, which put increased emphasis on targeting Soviet nuclear forces—a step widely seen as threatening the concept of mutual deterrence. Quickly leaked to the press, PD-59 epitomized Carter's hardline stance during his last year in office. The president who had criticized Americans' "inordinate fear of communism" in 1977 had been transformed into a Cold Warrior.

In many respects, the election of 1980 was a replay of 1976. As Ford had done with Reagan in 1976, Carter fought off a challenger from within his own party, Senator Edward Kennedy, to win the nomination. As with Ford, détente was no longer part of Carter's vocabulary. Like Carter four years earlier, Reagan won his party's nomination by defeating candidates—notably George H. W. Bush—who had considerable experience in Washington. During the fall campaign, the basic question was the same as in 1976: could an unpopular incumbent president, forced to defend his policies, defeat an outsider who was personally appealing but who lacked experience in national or world affairs?

Like Carter in 1976, Reagan offered a positive vision of America as a nation of virtuous, old-fashioned patriots. He also promised to balance the budget, cut taxes, end inflation, strengthen the military, and "stand tall" against the Russians and Iranians (who still held the hostages). The situation was complicated by the presence of a significant third-party candidate, liberal Republican John Anderson, but the answer the voters gave was the same as in 1976: by a margin of 51 percent for Reagan to 41 percent for Carter, they elected a new president.

Historical analogies always are imperfect, but it seems fair to say that Reagan's rhetoric and policy toward the U.S.S.R. and its allies during his first term (Jan. 1981–Jan. 1985) bore considerable resemblance to the approach of one of Reagan's favorite presidents, John F. Kennedy. Like Kennedy, Reagan and his advisers saw Russia as an obvious and immediate threat to world peace and stability, and they viewed Soviet expansionism in the Third World with particular alarm. Reagan, too, harbored a deep-seated hatred of Castro's Cuba and of revolutionaries in Latin America with ties to Castro. Both presidents sponsored a major buildup of U.S. military power that eased public and congressional concerns about American "weakness." And both, after acting and talking tough during their first years in office, moved toward a more conciliatory relationship with Russia that—perhaps partly because of the presidents' earlier toughness—gained widespread public support.

Many differences could be cited, including the presence of more moderates on U.S.-Soviet relations in the higher echelons of the Kennedy administration and the fact that, with memories of Vietnam fresh in people's minds, Reagan was extremely reluctant to send U.S. troops into extended combat abroad. One other difference especially contributed to the tense atmosphere of the early 1980s: during his first few years in office Reagan repeatedly questioned the legitimacy of the "evil empire," including the legitimacy of communist rule in

Russia itself as well as the extension of Soviet power into Eastern Europe and elsewhere. To the aging and fearful Soviet leaders who still had painful memories of the Nazi attack during World War II and who had been taught to believe the Marxist-Leninist axiom about inevitable "imperialist" hostility, these criticisms, combined with the rapid U.S. military buildup, raised concerns about whether Reagan might choose to start a war to destroy their system.

Reagan did not want war. But he did put the Soviets on notice from the start that the era of détente was over, to be replaced by determined containment of Soviet power. The president set the tone in his first press conference. He said that Russia had used détente as "a one-way street. . . to pursue its own aims," including "the promotion of world revolution and a one-world Socialist or Communist state," and that Soviet leaders "reserve unto themselves the right to commit any crime, to lie, to cheat, in order to attain that."

With Reagan's approval, the hardline secretary of defense, Caspar Weinberger, made it clear that the administration intended to ask Congress to appropriate unprecedented sums—the most important request was for $1.6 billion over five years—to regain American's "margin of safety" (superiority). The money went for new and existing strategic programs, including the B-1 and B-2 ("Stealth") bombers, and for expensive conventional programs such as expanding the navy from roughly 450 to 600 ships. Reagan also received large increases for the CIA and other intelligence agencies, partly to aid anti-Russian forces in Afghanistan and other Third World nations. Only for Central America—where Reagan wanted large sums to try to defeat the leftist insurgency in El Salvador and to help opposition forces topple the Marxist government in Nicaragua—did Congress appropriate significantly less money than the administration requested and limit Reagan's freedom of action in foreign affairs.

To Russian leaders, U.S. military superiority would mean their inferiority, an outcome they vowed to prevent. Moreover, the Soviets were frightened by loose talk emanating from the Pentagon about the development of nuclear "war-fighting strategies" and the firing of nuclear "warning shots" during crises. One general went so far as to claim that most Americans could survive a nuclear attack if there were "enough shovels" to dig backyard bomb shelters. Such seemingly ludicrous statements, combined with growing public awareness of the almost unimaginable devastation that was likely to result from an all-out nuclear war in the wake of the persistent buildup on both sides during the 1960s and 1970s, helped to fuel large antinuclear protest movements in the U.S. and Western Europe. As much as any specific action by America or Russia, the combination of the administration's frightening rhetoric and the equally scary warnings about nuclear war coming from the protest movements, from such best-selling books as Jonathan Schell's *The Fate of the Earth* (1982), and from such graphic depictions of the possible effects of nuclear war as the television film *The Day After* (1983) established the bone-chilling ambience of this third dangerous phase of the Cold War.

The loose talk about nuclear war suggested that the Reagan administration lacked direction, that its divisions and inconsistencies resembled those of its predecessor. To some extent that was true, especially on policy toward Central America, where the influence on policymaking of CIA director William Casey and zealous White House aides led first to such moves as the mining of Nicaragua's harbors by the CIA and ultimately to the major scandal of the Reagan years, the Iran-Contra affair of 1986–87. The administration also seemed rudderless and inconsistent on trade policy toward Russia: under pressure from Midwestern farmers and grain traders, it lifted the grain embargo that Carter had instituted, but then fought Western Europe's plans to build a pipeline to bring natural gas from the U.S.S.R. Reagan also was inconsistent in that he denounced and isolated communist dictators in the Third World (e.g., Fidel Castro in Cuba) but was more friendly to right-wing dictators (e.g., Augusto Pinochet in Chile) than Carter had been.

Otherwise, however, Reagan gradually developed a more consistent strategy for dealing with Russia and its spreading influence than critics at the time recognized. Administration officials called this strategy "negotiation from strength." Basically, it meant that the U.S. should negotiate on arms control only if its adversary recognized America's technological superiority and its right to match or exceed Soviet deployments in all potential military theaters. And, in Reagan's conception, America and its allies should negotiate to reduce—not just to limit—the number of nuclear weapons the two sides pointed directly at one another. Unlike his top advisers and Soviet leaders, who supported the existing practice of nuclear deterrence (often referred to as the "balance of terror"), Reagan believed that the ultimate goal should be to eliminate nuclear weapons entirely. In regard to the Third World, Reagan believed that, if given a choice, most people would choose democracy over communist dictatorship. Accordingly, the administration worked to limit the further spread of communism, to roll back some of the gains the Soviets had made in the 1970s, and ultimately to bring democracy and capitalism to the entire Third World. Overall, the administration believed that America should proclaim, loudly and proudly, that democratic capitalism was a far superior form of social organization than dictatorial communism; that, in Reagan's prescient words, communism eventually would be consigned to the "ash heap of history."

Most of the concrete results of Reagan's strategy—the 1987 treaty eliminating all intermediate-range missiles in Europe, for example, or the genuinely free elections in Nicaragua in 1990—occurred either during his second term or thereafter. During his first term, Reagan's main accomplishment was restoring the average citizen's pride in America that had been undercut by the Vietnam War, by Watergate, and by Carter's vacillation and apparent weakness. Through his policies and especially through his buoyant personality, Reagan at home personified an America on the rebound.

The president's optimism about the nation's future dominated public discussion even though the annual budget deficit jumped sharply as a result of the combination of the large tax cuts and the rapid doubling of defense spending that the administration pushed through Congress in 1981. Before Reagan, $50 billion deficits in peacetime were considered very large, but the tax cuts and defense increases, combined with steady growth in domestic spending, quickly pushed the deficits to $150 billion and beyond. As America borrowed huge sums from abroad to balance its burgeoning budget and trade deficits (the first helped to fuel the second), the nation shifted from being a creditor nation in 1981 to being the world's largest debtor nation by 1986.

In contrast to Reagan's popularity and his success in getting his program through Congress, his foreign policies generally failed to get other governments to change their behavior to conform to administration plans. Most nations had not bowed meekly to U.S. desires even at the height of the Cold War, and they certainly were not going to do so in the more diffused atmosphere of the early 1980s. Thus the limits of American power—a point that Nixon and Kissinger had grasped a decade before—were confirmed. These limits may be illustrated by looking briefly at U.S. relations in the early 1980s with Russia, Western Europe, and Central America.

Except for harsh rhetoric and a refusal to negotiate on arms control for more than a year, Reagan did not have a consistent policy toward Russia during his first couple of years in office. Broadly speaking, the administration was divided between those who favored careful negotiations with Russia and those who strongly opposed any serious efforts to deal with "the enemy." The first group was centered in the State Department and included Alexander Haig, who served as secretary of state until June 1982; his unusually able successor, George Shultz; and the director of the State Department's Bureau of Politico-Military Affairs, Richard Burt. The second, often more powerful, faction included Secretary of Defense Weinberger, who wanted nothing—especially arms control—to jeopardize his military buildup; Richard Perle, the former assistant to Senator Jackson who served as assistant secretary of defense for international security affairs; CIA director William Casey; and the assistant secretary of state (later national security adviser), William Clark.

The "two Richards"—Burt and Perle—tangled repeatedly on arms control issues, with Burt willing and Perle unwilling to try to come up with proposals that Soviet leaders might accept. Until mid-1983 Reagan preferred making speeches about the "evil empire" to imposing specific policies on his quarreling subordinates, with the result that the U.S. approach to the U.S.S.R. often featured more rhetoric than substance. Under pressure from West European leaders and from strong antinuclear movements in Europe and at home, the administration did begin negotiating with Russia in 1982. But Weinberger and

Perle won the internal debate in the sense that the U.S. proposals on nuclear weapons were so one-sided that Russian leaders were almost certain to reject them.

At first, Soviet leaders, thinking that Reagan's bark might be worse than his bite, sought to strike a deal with him. They had generally experienced steadier relations with Republican than with Democratic administrations, and thought that their relations with Reagan might follow this pattern. The succession of old and sickly Soviet leaders in the early 1980s—Brezhnev, Yuri Andropov, and Konstantin Chernenko—publicly supported improved U.S.-Soviet relations and urged Reagan to return to détente. Privately, it was learned later, they were so frightened by Washington's hardline policies and rhetoric that the KGB (Russia's main intelligence agency) was put on alert to prepare for a possible U.S. nuclear strike from 1981 to 1983. Another sign of dangerously high tension: Warsaw Pact forces were put on alert to prepare for war during a NATO training exercise in November 1983.

Faced with U.S. hostility, Soviet leaders showed their determination to remain a superpower and protect their interests. In the absence of arms control, they insisted that they would maintain military strength equal to America's. Despite veiled U.S. threats about Poland, where the Solidarity labor movement was challenging the government, the Soviets helped to ensure that communist rule was maintained. Nor did they withdraw from Afghanistan or end their alliance with Cuba, as the Reagan administration would have liked. In March 1982 Ambassador Dobrynin told Reagan that U.S.-Soviet relations were "at their lowest point since World War II."

Soviet leaders were deeply disturbed when Reagan, to the surprise of much of official Washington as well as his European allies, made a televised address to the nation on March 23, 1983, in which he called on U.S. scientists and engineers to develop defensive weapons that could make missiles carrying nuclear weapons "impotent and obsolete." To Reagan, this Strategic Defense Initiative (SDI) program would make real a large part of his "dream" to eliminate the threat of nuclear weapons. But as Secretary of State Shultz and others reminded him, even if "Star Wars" proved technologically feasible and then worked perfectly despite Soviet countermeasures—two very big ifs—

the Soviets still could use bombers and submarines posted close to America's shores to carry out a nuclear attack. Moreover, while research on defensive systems might be permissible under the 1972 ABM treaty, any effort to build and deploy them would violate the treaty. Despite these and other concerns expressed repeatedly by critics of Reagan's idea, Congress appropriated funds for SDI research throughout the remainder of the 1980s.

Angry that Reagan's move might end the relative stability of mutual assured destruction and fearful that the United States eventually might be able to start a war without the threat of large-scale retaliation (thus ending Russia's status as a superpower), Soviet officials reacted bitterly. The new leader, Yuri Andropov, said that the U.S. was embarking on "an extremely dangerous path," and charged that SDI was "a bid to disarm the Soviet Union in the face of the U.S. nuclear threat." For the next several years, Soviet leaders repeatedly raised concerns about "Star Wars" in meetings with U.S. officials, insisting that cuts in their offensive nuclear weapons would be impossible without strict limits on SDI. In the long run, some analysts have argued, "Star Wars" helped to end the Cold War by showing Soviet leaders how expensive it would be for their faltering system to keep up with America in the arms race. However one judges its long-term consequences, SDI's immediate result was to widen the existing chasm between the two countries.

One of the low points in postwar U.S.-Soviet relations occurred when a Russian military plane shot down a South Korean civilian airliner flying over Soviet territory on September 1, 1983. The plane was traveling from Anchorage, Alaska, to Seoul, South Korea. All 269 passengers and crew aboard, including 61 Americans, were killed. In a televised address to the nation on September 2, Reagan denounced the "Korean airline massacre" as a "crime against humanity" for which "there was absolutely no justification, either legal or moral. . . ." Other officials made similarly harsh statements, saying that the incident was typical of Soviet "barbarism." The Soviets responded that they believed the "intruder" had been a spy plane, and that they had shot it down only after it failed to respond to Soviet inquiries concerning its identification. They pointed out that U.S. reconnaissance planes resembling the downed Boeing 747 frequently flew in or near their airspace and that a Korean airliner previously had been forced to land while flying over Soviet territory.

In the ensuing weeks U.S. officials, realizing that they could not substantiate their claims that Russia had deliberately shot down a civilian airliner, softened their rhetoric. But Soviet leaders remained incensed that U.S. leaders had used the incident to make virulent charges against them, and their anti-American rhetoric increased. On September 28 Andropov issued one of the most strongly anti-American statements since the Stalin era. It accused America of pursuing a "militarist course" designed to achieve "dominant positions in the world without reckoning with the interests of other states and peoples." Soviet leaders apparently decided that the U.S. response to the airliner incident, combined with the continuing lack of progress on arms control, offered conclusive proof that there was no point in continuing to seek to improve relations. That December they withdrew from the arms control negotiations in Geneva.

During 1984 Secretary of State Shultz, with Reagan's support, helped to put U.S.-Soviet relations on a more hopeful path. Although Shultz believed firmly in "negotiation from strength," he let Soviet officials know throughout 1983 and 1984 that he believed improved relations were possible if the Soviets showed restraint in their behavior and if they focused on areas of possible agreement. In persuading Reagan to pursue this moderate approach, Shultz had a key ally in the president's wife, Nancy Reagan, who liked Shultz and helped to persuade Reagan in 1983 to shift the hardline national security adviser, William Clark, to a position in domestic policy. Domestic political considerations also pointed toward moderation: public opinion polls showed that most Americans disliked Reagan's bellicose rhetoric toward Russia and wanted improved U.S.-Soviet relations.

Partly as a result of Shultz's persistent efforts to convince Soviet leaders that America would negotiate in good faith, Foreign Minister Andrei Gromyko agreed to visit Washington in September 1984 to conduct talks with high U.S. officials for the first time since before the Soviet invasion of Afghanistan five years earlier. To the dismay of leading Democrats, who were trying to make the poor state of U.S.-Soviet relations a major campaign issue, Gromyko's visit suggested that the third dangerous phase in U.S.-Soviet relations might well be ending.

Like Soviet officials, West European leaders stood up to the Reagan administration when they disagreed with its policies. They reminded the president of their support for arms control as well as adequate defense expenditures, and they insisted that he follow through with NATO's pledge to try to remove the Soviet SS-20 missiles aimed at Western Europe through negotiations before installing new U.S. Pershing and cruise missiles in their countries. Reagan's response—agreeing to negotiate with the Russians and offering in November 1981 not to place any intermediate-range U.S. missiles in Western Europe if the Soviets dismantled theirs—helped to stem the growing influence of Europe's antinuclear movement.

While the United States and its NATO allies thus were able to patch over differences on arms control, conflicts relating to trade with Russia proved irreconcilable. To most West Europeans, economic détente should not be ended just because Russia did something they did not like. Thus, when Carter decided in the wake of Afghanistan to curtail sales of computers and other high-technology goods to Russia, Western Europe had continued its own trade with Russia and, indeed, had picked up much of America's previous business. Reagan opposed this trade and tried to stop some of it. U.S. officials also did not like the fact that West Europeans planned to lend Russia money and sell it equipment to help build a pipeline to supply natural gas from Siberia to their countries.

In the first half of 1982, the administration moved toward a confrontation with the West Europeans on the latter issue. When Reagan ordered foreign subsidiaries of U.S. companies not to sell equipment for the pipeline and prohibited foreign companies from using American equipment or technology in the project, the Europeans were furious. They saw their own sovereignty being threatened by these efforts to tell their companies what they could and could not do, and they pointed out that they had received the licenses to use the U.S. technology before Reagan was elected and thus were operating within their legal rights. As British Prime Minister Margaret Thatcher, normally a close ally, commented: "The question is whether one very powerful nation can prevent existing contracts from being fulfilled. I think it is wrong to do that." Eventually the administration backed down on this issue, and Shultz had to work to ease tempers and to reach some vague face-saving agreements for the U.S.

The Reagan administration also chose confrontation as the keynote of its policy in Central America and the Caribbean. Haig and other officials did not believe that Carter had been sufficiently forceful in dealing with this region, which Reagan described as a "Communist lake." The new administration ridiculed Carter's emphasis on human rights in Latin America as naive and blamed him for the rise to power of the Sandinistas in Nicaragua in 1979. Seeing a concrete opportunity to break with "the failed policies of the past" and to establish itself as a vigorous opponent of communism, the Reagan administration moved quickly to shape events in Central America.

At the time El Salvador was a small, poor country long ruled by and largely for the economic benefit of a wealthy elite. A Marxist-led revolutionary movement calling for greater economic equality had gained strength in the 1970s and was waging a guerrilla war against the government. Carter had sought to encourage land reform and to end the atrocities committed by right-wing death squads while also opposing the guerrillas. In contrast, Reagan initially ignored the unsavory record of the right, which included the death-squad murders of the Catholic archbishop Oscar Romero and of four American nuns working to help the poor. Instead, the administration focused on defeating the rebels.

To build a case for greater U.S. involvement, the State Department issued a "White Paper" in February 1981. It blamed "Cuba, the Soviet Union, and other Communist states" for El Salvador's political instability. This charge was a half-truth at best, for there were ample socioeconomic and political factors within El Salvador to spark and feed the flames of rebellion. U.S. officials also argued that Nicaragua and Cuba supplied arms and training to the leftist forces—an accurate charge that showed the connectedness of the Marxist movements in the Caribbean area. Under Reagan, U.S. aid to El Salvador increased, most of the economic and political inequities remained, and the guerrillas never came close to toppling the government.

Once the situation in El Salvador largely had stabilized, Reagan's main goal in the region—though not officially acknowledged until 1985—became the overthrow of the Nicaraguan government. Reagan did not like the Sandinistas' Marxist orientation, and he especially did not like their close ties with Cuba and Russia. To overthrow the Sandinistas, the administration tried almost everything it could think of except direct U.S. military intervention.

The administration was not lacking in persistence. It cut off aid to and trade with Nicaragua; it made it difficult for Nicaragua to obtain loans from international agencies; and it sent the CIA to mine Nicaraguan harbors and otherwise to disrupt the economy. Most important, it supplied weapons and money to an army of Nicaraguans in exile known as the Contras, sent U.S. forces to train them in Honduras, and persuaded wealthy conservatives and U.S. allies to supply additional arms and money to them. When Congress cut off U.S. aid to the Contras in 1984, Reagan's staff continued raising money from domestic and foreign sources and came up with a new scheme: giving the Contras some of the profits from the secret sale of U.S. arms to Iran.

Why did all these efforts fail to overthrow the Nicaraguan government? One reason was that the Sandinistas enjoyed considerable popularity, especially in the early years when generous aid from Western Europe, from the United States (before 1981), and from the Soviet Union and Cuba helped them to set up education, health, and land-reform programs that reached out to the common people much more than the previous dictator, Anastasio Somoza, had done. A second reason is that, with Soviet and Cuban support, they built up a large "people's army" to defend the revolution and fight the Contras.

Although the Sandinistas won a partially rigged election in 1984, their long-term prospects were shaky. Tight controls over the economy alienated many farmers and business people, quite a few of whom joined the Contras or left for the U.S. Real incomes were falling sharply by the mid-1980s, and three of the scourges of communist economies—shortages, rationing, and privileges for the party elite—were becoming commonplace. Moreover, Soviet leaders made it clear that economic aid would be limited: they had no interest in keeping the Sandinistas afloat with billions of rubles in economic aid each year, as they did in Cuba. Apparently unaware that communist economies lagged well behind capitalist ones in every part of the world where they had been imposed, the Sandinistas unwisely invited Cuban and Bulgarian officials to help them plan their economy.

To Reagan's dismay, the Sandinistas remained in power in Nicaragua throughout his presidency. But he did succeed in removing the Marxist government of Grenada in late 1983. This tiny island nation in the Caribbean received its independence from Great Britain in 1974. Its corrupt and repressive leader, Eric Gairy, was overthrown in a leftist coup in 1979 led by Maurice Bishop. The Carter administration was angered when Grenada (along with Nicaragua and Cuba) did not vote in the UN to condemn the Soviet invasion of Afghanistan, and both Carter and Reagan were upset by Bishop's close ties to Cuba. The leaders of several of the neighboring islands also disliked Bishop's disdain for democratic procedures and his connections in Cuba.

Why did the United States invade Grenada on October 25, 1983, and, having won a quick military victory against local and Cuban troops, install a pro-American government a few days later? A coup against Bishop by one of his assistants in mid-October had thrown the country into turmoil, prompting the leaders of neighboring countries to call an emergency meeting and ask for U.S. intervention. Moreover, as Shultz's memoirs make clear, officials were concerned about the safety of the more than eight hundred Americans enrolled in a medical school on the island. They feared that Grenada's upstart rulers might do what Iran's new leaders did in 1979: take Americans hostage. The third and perhaps most important reason was that U.S. leaders wanted to defeat and then expel the government's Cuban advisers and put Grenada back on the U.S. side. Such a move would show America's adversaries that Vietnam was history, that the U.S. again would fight to protect its interests and advance the cause of freedom in the world. The U.S. victory in Grenada, Shultz recalled proudly, "was a shot heard round the world by usurpers and despots of every ideology."

Following Grenada, Reagan's approval rating shot up and remained high until 1986. But 1984—like 1964 for Johnson and 1972 for Nixon—was Reagan's year of triumph. At home, the recession that had hurt his popularity earlier was over, and the economy was growing rapidly with minimal inflation. Abroad, U.S. policy had experienced both successes and failures, as usual, but Reagan (unlike Carter) seemed to know how to receive full credit for the successes and keep the failures from hurting him politically. Noting that mistakes did not seem to hurt Reagan, disappointed critics called him the "Teflon-coated president." Supporters of an effort to freeze nuclear weapons systems as a first step toward disarmament had gained considerable public support in 1982 and 1983, but they could not get leading Democratic presidential contenders to campaign actively on this issue because Reagan's "peace through strength" approach seemed more popular with the general public. Moreover, Reagan shrewdly softened his rhetoric toward the Soviets and reminded voters of his commitment to peace.

Although no Democrat stood much of a chance in 1984, the party virtually ensured a landslide Reagan victory by nominating Carter's vice-president, Walter Mondale, as its candidate. Most voters had vivid memories of inflation, the hostage crisis in Iran, and their general disappointment with Carter, and they overwhelmingly elected Reagan to a second term in November 1984.

Conclusion

Ordinary Americans following developments in U.S.-Soviet relations from 1973 through 1984 never knew quite what to expect. One week their president might be hailing a breakthrough in arms control or East-West trade, and the next week he might be denouncing Soviet involvement in some previously obscure Third World country or saying that U.S. troops had landed somewhere because of the threat posed by a nation that was receiving military aid from Russia. An article in the newspaper would say that the U.S. was ahead in the arms race, but on the next page there would be another news story warning that America was falling dangerously behind.

The reality beneath the confusing headlines was that there were elements of both competition and cooperation in U.S.-Soviet relations, as there had been throughout the Cold War. In the early 1970s, when détente was at its peak, an effort was made to strike a new, enduring balance between competition and cooperation in order to try to prevent the dangerously competitive behavior that had threatened to lead to war on several occasions between 1946 and 1962. In this narrow sense, détente appears to have succeeded: the two nations were able to keep further away from war during the crises of the twelve years after 1972 than they had during the crises of the twelve years before 1963.

Still, détente largely failed in the broader sense of establishing a relationship in which (a) the arms race and expenditures on defense would be brought under effective control; (b) competition in the Third World would decrease significantly; and (c) trade would increase steadily and stabilize U.S.-Soviet relations. The reasons détente failed are at once complex and simple: complex in that many factors were involved, but simple in that both nations continued to view the relationship in largely competitive and ideological terms. This was certainly true of the military establishments and their vocal supporters on both sides, which were not content with the destructive power and sophistication of the arsenals in 1972 but instead undermined the arms control process by using it as a pretext to push ahead with even more dangerous systems.

In the Third World, America had been more interventionist earlier in the Cold War, but to the dismay of U.S. leaders from Ford through Reagan, it was the Soviets who were more expansionist during the 1970s and early 1980s. "Our foreign policy [especially in the Third World] was unreasonably dominated by ideology," Ambassador Dobrynin recalled. Led by vocal conservatives like Reagan and Senator John Tower (Rep., Tex.), Americans understandably questioned détente when they saw Soviet influence growing in Asia, Africa, and Latin America. Although U.S.-Soviet trade never stopped entirely, it became a political football and thus did not contribute to long-term improvement in relations.

Disputes about human rights and about each side's interventions in the Third World showed that a large part of the competition in U.S.-Soviet relations during the Cold War grew out of ideological differences that the two sides ultimately could not compromise or ignore. Viewed from a post–Cold War perspective, Nixon and Kissinger were wrong to think that U.S.-Soviet relations could be managed from the top indefinitely, despite the fact that Soviet leaders were oppressing their own people and continuing to expand their country's unsavory influence outside its borders. It can now be seen that, despite upsetting Soviet and East European leaders and several U.S. allies in the Third World, Carter deserves credit for expressing his sincere concern about human rights abuses in communist nations as well as in nations ruled by right-wing dictatorships.

While some of Reagan's words and deeds needlessly increased tensions in the early 1980s, he was right to develop a forceful policy to challenge Soviet and Cuban expansionism and to deploy potent weapons in Western Europe to counter the Soviet SS-20s. Reagan made America appear hypocritical when he ignored human-rights abuses in nations friendly to the U.S. But he was still correct when he added his voice and authority as America's president to the voices of the brave dissidents in Russia, in China, in Eastern Europe, and in Cuba who were risking their lives to tell their rulers two important truths: communism was indeed an inherently dictatorial system, and the struggle between dictatorship and freedom was at the heart of the Cold War.

EPILOGUE

The Cold War Ends, 1985–1991

As the free world grows stronger, more united, more attractive to men on both sides of the Iron Curtain—and as the Soviet hopes for easy expansion are blocked—then there will have to come a time of change in the Soviet world. Nobody can say for sure when that is going to be, or exactly how it will come about, whether by revolution, or trouble in the satellite states, or by a change inside the Kremlin. . . . I have a deep and abiding faith in the destiny of free men. With patience and courage, we shall some day move on into a new era . . .

Harry S Truman's farewell address January 15, 1953

During the forty years from the mid-1940s through the mid-1980s, the Cold War melodrama, starring America and Russia but also featuring such colorful actors as China and Cuba, held center stage in world affairs. This melodrama was still going strong when Mikhail Gorbachev took power in the U.S.S.R. on March 11, 1985, and it would continue to attract audiences for several years thereafter. But the Cold War was soon eclipsed in the world's imagination by several compelling new dramas: Gorbachev's efforts to revitalize the socialist system in the Soviet system through *glasnost* (openness to public debate) and *perestroika* (restructuring of the economy); growing movements to overthrow the communist regimes in Eastern Europe; and, finally, the intertwined movements toward democracy and disintegration within the U.S.S.R. itself.

In the early 1980s Ronald Reagan, the former star of B-grade movies, had been the leading actor on the world stage. But as the new dramas grabbed the headlines, Gorbachev took over the starring role that Reagan had been playing and held it until a new Russian leader, Boris Yeltsin, pushed him aside in 1991. By then, however, one of Gorbachev's major goals, the ending of the Cold War, had been achieved—with assistance from leaders in America and in Western Europe, to be sure, but above all through his own vision and persistence.

Just as the Cold War began not on any one date but as the result of numerous Soviet and Western actions in the mid-1940s, so it ended in a long series of actions and events—resulting largely from "new thinking" in the U.S.S.R.—in the late 1980s and early 1990s. Of these, perhaps the five most important were unmistakable actions by leaders like Gorbachev and Foreign Minister Eduard Shevardnadze to stop repressing Soviet citizens and threatening other countries and thereby, in Gorbachev's words, to gain acceptance "as a country like the others in the West"; second, Soviet decisions to reduce both their nuclear and conventional forces, either through unilateral actions or through negotiations (e.g., the U.S.-Soviet agreement in 1987 to eliminate all medium-range missiles in the European theater); third, the Soviet decision in 1989 to let the people of Eastern Europe (including East Germany) determine their own futures, thus ending both communist rule in the region and the post–World War II division of Europe; fourth, Gorbachev's decision in 1990 to permit a reunited Germany to remain in NATO; and fifth, the failure of the coup attempt against Gorbachev and his reforms by conservatives in the Soviet Communist party in 1991, which finally ended the ideological conflict between totalitarian/communist Russia and democratic/capitalist America that had been the central component of the Cold War.

By exposing most Russians' hatred of communism and their appreciation of Yeltsin's outspoken opposition to the coup and to all communist leaders, including Gorbachev, the unsuccessful coup hastened the end of Gorbachev's rule—and the end of the U.S.S.R.—on December 25, 1991. Ironically, Gorbachev, a communist reformer but not a revolutionary, never intended to bring about either the end of communist rule or the breakup of the U.S.S.R.

History buffs and scholars long will be fascinated by the details of these and other developments. They will marvel that Reagan and Gorbachev seriously discussed the elimination of *all* their nations' nuclear weapons at a meeting in Reykjavik, Iceland, in October 1986. They will ponder how the communist regimes in Eastern Europe fell like coconuts in a hurricane in the fall of 1989, or how large numbers of East Germans went shopping in West Berlin that same fall when the Berlin Wall was torn down peacefully. They may even take seriously journalist George Will's bold observation, as these events were occurring, that 1989 was "the most startling, interesting, promising and consequential year, ever."

Another broad generalization appears to be valid: one Soviet leader, Stalin, did more harm to more people's basic human rights than anyone else in history with the possible exception of Adolf Hitler; another Soviet leader, Gorbachev, by reversing Stalinism and then finding himself swept along on a tide of change toward pluralist democracy that he proved unable to control, ended up restoring these rights to more people than any previous political leader. More than conciliatory speeches on both sides or widely praised arms control agreements, it was the blossoming of personal freedom and political democracy in the U.S.S.R. and in Eastern Europe that ended the Cold War.

Tentative answers to three questions about the Gorbachev years (1985–91) and about lessons from the Cold War will complete the discussion of this conflict and its aftermath in these pages—but not, I hope, in classes and in conversations in halls and dorm rooms.

1. Why did Gorbachev undertake such sweeping reforms in Russia's domestic life and foreign policy?

Stated simply, the answer that is often given to this question is that Gorbachev's main goal was to improve the Soviet economy and that he felt that he had to allow greater freedom in order to accomplish this goal. This answer contains considerable truth, but it is too narrow. In fact, since the Khrushchev years Gorbachev and other reformers had hoped that Russia would move from the totalitarian system entrenched under Stalin to a much more democratic and humane form of socialism. Thus Gorbachev genuinely believed in "revitalizing all of Soviet society," which included, among other things, respect for basic human rights, unprecedented freedom for the media, limited democratization in political life, and substantial shifts in the economy. These beliefs go far to explain why Gorbachev continued the process of change rather than re-imposing repression even after the seemingly uncontrollable momentum for change threatened his own power and that of the Communist party.

And why did he work vigorously to end the arms race with the West and to take other steps to end the Cold War? Again, the answer partly relates to his desire to improve the Soviet economy, which in his judgment required shifting the lion's share of the large percentage of the Soviet GNP that had been devoted to defense and to subsidies to allies abroad to meeting pressing domestic needs. But Gorbachev's vision extended far beyond concerns about Russia's economy. He believed that a "new world" was emerging, one that required nations to cooperate in developing methods to achieve "common security" rather than continuing to rely on ever more destructive weapons. As he said in a speech at the United Nations in December 1988, the world was entering "an era when progress will be shaped by universal human interests." This new era would require "the freeing of international relations from ideology" and "self-restraint" in order to end large countries' military interventions in smaller ones.

Given this perspective, it is not surprising that Gorbachev strongly supported strengthening the UN and increasing respect for international law. He also removed Soviet forces from Afghanistan and assisted in resolving several other regional conflicts, including the long war between the Sandinistas and the Contras in Nicaragua. Beginning in August 1990, Gorbachev worked with President Bush within the UN to condemn the Iraqi invasion of Kuwait and to take effective steps to reverse this obvious aggression. Many leaders have expressed noble sentiments about a more peaceful world, but few have matched their words with as many concrete actions as Gorbachev, who in 1990 became the first Soviet leader to receive the Nobel Peace Prize.

2. What role did the Reagan administration play in ending the Cold War?

This is likely to be a controversial question among Americans for many years to come, with conservatives and Republicans tending to emphasize the U.S. contribution and with liberals and Democrats tending to play it down. Recently released Soviet documents partially support both interpretations. They demonstrate, as conservatives argue, that Reagan's determination to use America's technological advantages to re-establish U.S. superiority in the nuclear arms race disturbed and challenged Russian leaders, and that Reagan's large-scale aid to anticommunist forces in the Third World raised the costs to the Soviets of maintaining their client states. The documents also support the liberal contention that Reagan's policies did not force Soviet leaders to abandon either the communist system at home or the Cold War competition in defense and foreign policy.

The difficulty in reaching a fully convincing answer is illustrated by the debate in America over whether Reagan's costly defense buildup in general, and the "Star Wars" program in particular, hastened or postponed the end of the Cold War. Several Reagan officials have argued that the buildup convinced Soviet leaders that it would be either futile (because of Russia's technological inferiority) or too expensive to try to maintain equality with America in the nuclear arms race. Others, including some members of Congress and some scholars, have argued that the buildup postponed the end of the Cold War, partly because the Soviets refused for several years to reduce offensive long-range missiles as long as America insisted on its right to deploy "Star Wars" weapons in the future. The most relevant testimony, that of former Soviet officials, is mixed: some affirm that the Reagan buildup contributed to "new thinking" on defense issues and a desire to end the competition in arms, whereas others insist just as strongly that the buildup did not help to end the Cold War.

The American who probably did the most to end the Cold War was Reagan's secretary of state, George Shultz, a professional economist with long experience in government service and international business. A skillful negotiator and a person of integrity and vision, Shultz earned Gorbachev's respect and friendship. A former professor who believed that repetition aids learning, Shultz repeatedly made the point in speeches and in personal meetings with Gorbachev that the world's prosperous economies were no longer largely separate entities based on heavy industry, but rather that they had become thoroughly interdependent as a result of modern electronic technology that had created a worldwide information network, a new "information age."

Shultz argued that totalitarian rule and isolation from the mainstream of economic and technological developments—both traditional Soviet practices—would only increase the growing gap between the relatively poor communist countries and the prosperous capitalist nations in Western Europe, North America, and East Asia. Moreover, the widespread desire for human rights and political democracy could not be denied indefinitely. "As the world gets smaller, the importance of freedom only increases," Shultz commented in 1986. "The yearning for freedom is the most powerful political force all across the planet."

Shultz was soon preaching to the converted. Awareness of the impact of the computer revolution had long motivated bright, observant young Soviet officials and critics to call for major changes in domestic and foreign policies. In his UN speech Gorbachev showed that he had absorbed the message: he argued that "the latest means of communication, mass information, and transportation" had turned the global economy into "a single organism, outside of which not a single state can develop normally. . . ." He said that Russia now sought to protect "citizens' rights . . . based on the rule of law." One statement in this speech, which paralleled Shultz's comment about the global "yearning for freedom," summed up what was occurring in Russia and Eastern Europe—and in Latin America and elsewhere—during the late 1980s: "The idea of the democratization of the entire world order has turned into a mighty sociopolitical force."

Before Gorbachev, Raymond L. Garthoff has noted, "Soviet leaders were committed to a historically driven struggle between two worlds until, in the end, theirs would triumph." By the late 1980s, Russian officials were articulating an entirely different worldview. The Cold War had always been a competition in ideas more than it had been a military confrontation, and Gorbachev was acknowledging that he and many of his compatriots now found fundamental Western ideas more persuasive than the "scientific" communist teachings that had shaped Russian history since 1917.

Observing this growing similarity of outlook (which included Gorbachev's renunciation of the Marxist-Leninist concept of "class struggle"), British Prime Minister Margaret Thatcher commented in November 1988, "We're not in a Cold War now." Gorbachev strongly agreed at a summit meeting with President Bush in Malta in December 1989: "We stated, both of us, that the world leaves one epoch of Cold War and enters another epoch. This is just the beginning . . . of our long road to a long-lasting peaceful period."

3. What lessons can be drawn from the Cold War years that might be helpful to U.S. policymakers and citizens in the future?

One lesson is that, whenever possible, the U.S. should be true to its own deepest ideals in formulating its foreign policy. Just as Roosevelt had been right to oppose the highly nationalist and racist expansionism of Germany and Japan before World War II, so Truman and his successors were correct to "contain" the remaining totalitarian power after 1945. "With the doctrine of containment [formulated in 1946 and 1947]," historian John Lewis Gaddis observed in February 2004, "the international system found itself on a trajectory for peace for the second half of the twentieth century." In other words, containment played to the West's strengths in economics, in human aspirations for individual freedom and democratic government, and in other areas; it proved to be a sensible, sustainable approach located between war with the major communist nations on the one hand and appeasement on the other.

Truman and his successors acted wisely in helping the nations of Western Europe and the noncommunist nations of East Asia achieve prosperity and democracy after World War II. But they went against U.S. ideals when they supported French colonialism in Indochina and when they undermined self-determination in Iran by sponsoring a coup there in 1953. This latter error was repeated several times, most notably when America tried to undermine a freely elected Marxist president in Chile in the early 1970s. U.S. presidents frequently were too quick to forgive abuses of human rights, or to ignore the postponement or rigging of elections, when these actions were undertaken by "our allies" in the Cold War.

A second lesson is that U.S. policy on each issue should be decided on its own merits after thorough study and discussion. Deductive reasoning—"all communists are evil, therefore all should be opposed by force"—is inferior to inductive, nuanced thinking. Efforts to link policies in different parts of the world should be avoided, as should efforts to send indirect signals that, in practice, are often misunderstood or ignored. To the extent that President Kennedy decided to dispatch U.S. military advisers to Vietnam in order to demonstrate "resolve" to Khrushchev after his failure at the Bay of Pigs, for example, he clearly erred.

A third lesson is that, whenever possible, U.S. leaders should consider carefully the views of allies—and gain support at the United Nations—before going to war. The contrast between the wars in Korea and Vietnam is instructive. After North Korea's invasion of South Korea in 1950, President Truman easily gained support from all of America's allies, including military aid from many of them, as well as from the UN Security Council. In greatly expanding the U.S. involvement in Vietnam in 1965, President Johnson ignored the cautionary warnings—and the refusals to provide assistance coming from many nations, including such key allies as Britain and France. Especially because the conflict in Vietnam was not a direct threat to U.S. security, Johnson should have paid more attention to these warnings—and also heeded his awareness that any effort to win approval at the UN for U.S. military action in Vietnam almost certainly would have failed. As journalist James M. Klurfeld wrote in 2004 but easily could have written at any time during the Cold War: "For all its military and economic power, the United States is not strong enough to police the world by itself."

A fourth lesson is that, in formulating foreign policy, presidents and their associates should respect Congress's powers under the Constitution, most notably its power to pass laws and thus to make an administration's actions legitimate. On most major issues relating to U.S.-Soviet relations that arose during the Cold War, Congress strongly supported the president. The record suggests that, when clear U.S. interests are at stake, presidents generally have received broad public and congressional support when they have openly sought it. Although Congress sometimes makes mistakes (e.g., the Jackson-Vanik amendment of 1974), efforts by officials to deceive Congress and the American people and to circumvent laws serve only to weaken the fabric of constitutional government. The secret bombing of Cambodia during the Nixon years and the Iran-Contra scandal of the Reagan era are cases in point.

A fifth lesson is that, in facing serious problems, U.S. leaders must avoid narrow partisanship and work together to solve them—as the Truman administration and Congress did in 1947–48 in developing the Marshall Plan to help restore prosperity in Western Europe. Overall, and despite making mistakes in particular situations, U.S. leaders during the Cold War did a creditable job of solving the problems that they considered most urgent: limiting the expansion of the U.S.S.R. and other communist nations, promoting prosperity in America and in the rest of the noncommunist world, and preventing World War III. Examples of contemporary global issues include terrorism, threats to the environment, and high levels of poverty and unemployment in many nations. The challenge for U.S. leaders throughout the twenty-first century will be to select the most urgent domestic and international problems, persuade the American public and Congress to support policies designed to address them, and then persist in working toward solutions both domestically and internationally. As Secretary of State Dean Rusk observed, "Every generation must find its own answers."

Today's problems are challenging. But are they any more daunting than the ones Western leaders faced in late 1945 when they confronted large areas of the world prostrate after a devastating war, colonized peoples clamoring for independence and prosperity, and a rising communist tide?

BIBLIOGRAPHICAL ESSAY

A comprehensive and critical bibliographical essay on the Cold War—one involving discussion of the thousands of books, articles, and available primary sources that have contributed to understanding this huge subject—would require another book longer than this one. Accordingly, I have limited myself primarily to books that I have found especially useful in preparing this study. In citing books that have been published in two or more editions, I generally have listed the most recent edition up through 2003.

By far the best bibliography of the Cold War—one that contains thousands of annotated entries—is Robert L. Beisner, ed., *American Foreign Relations since 1660; A Guide to the Literature,* vol. 2 (2003). A useful collection of bibliographical essays is Michael J. Hogan, ed., *America in the World: The Historiography of American Foreign Relations since 1941* (1995). Another fine resource, with many essays and suggestions for further reading on topics relating to the Cold War, is Alexander DeConde, Richard Dean Burns, and Fredrik Logevall, eds., *Encyclopedia of American Foreign Policy,* 3 vols. (2002).

For many thousands of government documents relating to U.S. foreign policy from World War II at least through the 1960s, students should consult the impressive series of primary-source books published by the State Department under the general title, *Foreign Relations of the United States.* Many other useful collections of government documents and essays on specific topics have been published over the past twenty years—in print, online, or both—by two nongovernmental organizations based in Washington, the National Security Archive and the Cold War International History Project.

General Works

Fifteen general studies that I found especially helpful in writing this book are Warren I. Cohen, *America in the Age of Soviet Power, 1945–1991* (1993); Richard Crockatt, *The Fifty Years War* (1995); Walter L. Hixson, *Parting the Curtain* (1997); Henry Kissinger, *Diplomacy* (1994); Robert J. McMahon, *The Cold War* (2003); Joseph S. Nye, Jr., *The Making of America's Soviet Policy* (1984); John Ranelagh, *The Agency: The Rise and Decline of the CIA* (1987); Peter W. Rodman, *More Precious than Peace* (1994); Tony Smith, *America's Mission* (1994); Odd Arne Westad, ed., *Reviewing the Cold War* (2000); Joseph G. Whelan, *Soviet Diplomacy and Negotiating Behavior* (1979); and John Lewis Gaddis, *We Now Know* (1997), *The Long Peace* (1987), *Strategies of Containment* (1982), and chapters 6–9 of *Russia, the Soviet Union, and the United States* (1990).

Other general accounts and collections of essays also were quite useful: George W. Ball, *The Past Has Another Pattern* (1982); George W. Breslauer and Philip E. Tetlock, eds., *Learning in U.S. and Soviet Foreign Policy* (1991); H. W. Brands, *The Devil We Knew* (1993); Seyom Brown, *The Faces of Power* (1983); McGeorge Bundy, *Danger and Survival* (1988); Lawrence Freedman, *The Evolution of Nuclear Strategy* (1981); John Lewis Gaddis, Philip H. Gordon, Ernest R. May, and Jonathan Rosenberg, eds., *Cold War Statesmen Confront the Bomb* (1999); Raymond L. Garthoff, *A Journey through the Cold War* (2001); Alexander L. George, et al., eds., *U.S.-Soviet Security Cooperation* (1988); Robert C. Grogin, *Natural Enemies* (2001); Jussi M. Hanhimaki and Odd Arne Westad, eds., *The Cold War: A History in Documents and Eyewitness Ac-*

counts (2003); Gary R. Hess, *Presidential Decisions for War* (2001); Robert Jervis, *Perception and Misperception in International Politics* (1976); Bennett Korvig, *The Myth of Liberation* (1973); Diane B. Kunz, *Butter and Guns* (1997); Walter LaFeber, *America, Russia, and the Cold War, 1945–2000* (2002); Geir Lundestad, *The American "Empire" and Other Studies of U.S. Foreign Policy in a Comparative Perspective* (1990); David Mayers, *George Kennan and the Dilemmas of U.S. Foreign Policy* (1988) and *The Ambassadors and America's Soviet Policy* (1995); Patrick M. Morgan and Keith L. Nelson, eds., *Re-Viewing the Cold War* (2000); Thomas M. Nichols, *Winning the World* (2002); Frank A. Ninkovich, *Germany and the United States* (1995); Thomas G. Paterson, *Meeting the Communist Threat* (1988); Ronald E. Powaski, *The Cold War* (1998); Jerel A. Rosati, *The Politics of United States Foreign Policy* (1993); Marc Tractenberg, *A Constructed Peace* (1999); Ralph K. White, *Fearful Warriors* (1984); and chapters 8–17 of Howard Jones, *Crucible of Power* (2001).

In addition to the Rodman book cited above, diverse perspectives on U.S. relations with the Third World are contained in Peter L. Hahn and Mary Ann Heiss, eds., *Empire and Revolution: The United States and the Third World since 1945* (2001); Gabriel Kolko, *Confronting the Third World* (1988); Geir Lundestad, *East, West, North, South* (1988); Douglas J. Macdonald, *Adventures in Chaos* (1992); and Mark Peceny, *Democracy at the Point of Bayonets* (1999).

The best overview of Soviet foreign policy during the early decades of the Cold War is Vladislav M. Zubok and Constantine Pleshakov, *Inside the Kremlin's Cold War* (1996). Two other valuable studies are Galia Golan, *Soviet Policies in the Middle East* (1990) and David Holloway, *Stalin and the Bomb* (1994). Insightful memoirs by high-level Soviet officials include Anatoly Dobrynin, *In Confidence* (1995); Andrei Gromyko, *Memoirs* (1989); Nikita Khrushchev, *Khrushchev Remembers* (1971), *Khrushchev Remembers: The Glasnost Tapes* (1990), and *Khrushchev Remembers: The Last Testament* (1974); and Albert Resis, ed., *Molotov Remembers* (1993). For information about the tens of millions of politically motivated murders, unjust imprisonments, and other violations of human rights committed by the U.S.S.R., China, and other communist governments, see Stephane Courtois, et al., *The Black Book of Communism* (1999).

General accounts on Chinese foreign policy and Sino-American relations include Stanley D. Bachrack, *The Committee of One Million* (1976); Gordon H. Chang, *Friends and Enemies* (1990); Warren I. Cohen, *America's Response to China* (2000); Rosemary Foot, *The Practice of Power* (1995); Chen Jian, *Mao's China and the Cold War* (2001); Robert S. Ross and Jiang Changbin, eds., *Re-examining the Cold War: U.S.-China Diplomacy, 1954–1973* (2001); and Nancy Bernkopf Tucker, ed., *China Confidential* (2001). For Sino-Soviet relations, see Odd Arne Westad, ed., *Brothers in Arms* (1998).

Six books on American public opinion that give substantial attention to Cold War issues are Gabriel A. Almond, *The American People and Foreign Policy* (1960); Robert Dallek, *The American Style of Foreign Policy* (1983); Ole R. Holsti and James N. Rosenau, *American Leadership in World Affairs* (1984); Leonard A. Kusnitz, *Public Opinion and Foreign Policy* (1984); Ralph B. Levering, *The Public and American Foreign Policy* (1978); and John E. Mueller, *War, Presidents and Public Opinion* (1973).

Prologue and Chapter One (1941–1953)

U.S.-Soviet relations during World War II are analyzed in Edward M. Bennett, *Franklin D. Roosevelt and the Search for Victory* (1990); Robert Dallek, *Franklin D. Roosevelt and American Foreign Policy* (1979); Robert A. Divine, *Roosevelt and World War II* (1969); Robin Edmonds, *The Big Three* (1991); John Lewis Gaddis, *The United States and the Origins of the Cold War* (1972); Lloyd C. Gardner, *Spheres of Influence* (1993); George C. Herring, Jr., *Aid to Russia* (1973); Robert C. Hilderbrand, *Dumbarton Oaks* (1990); Warren F. Kimball, *The Juggler* (1991) and *America Unbound* (1992); Steven Merritt Miner, *Between Churchill and Stalin* (1989); and Martin

Sherwin, *A World Destroyed* (1987). For U.S. attitudes toward Russia, see Ralph B. Levering, *American Opinion and the Russian Alliance* (1976). Vojtech Mastny, *Russia's Road to the Cold War* (1979), is a provocative analysis of Stalin's wartime foreign policies.

The scholarly debate on the origins of the Cold War was most intense during the late 1960s. The orthodox viewpoint, which tended to blame Russia, is epitomized in Arthur Schlesinger, Jr., "Origins of the Cold War," *Foreign Affairs* 46 (October 1967): 22–52. The revisionist viewpoint, which tended to blame America, is ably expressed in Barton J. Bernstein, "American Foreign Policy and the Origins of the Cold War," in Bernstein, ed., *Politics and Policies of the Truman Administration* (1970), pp. 15–77. The best brief analysis of the origins and early years of the Cold War is Ralph B. Levering, et al., *Debating the Origins of the Cold War* (2002). Another fine overview is Mark S. Byrnes, *The Truman Years, 1945–1953* (2000). Other excellent introductions to the period include a one-volume presidential biography by Donald R. McCoy: *The Presidency of Harry S Truman* (1984); and a two-volume presidential biography by Robert J. Donovan: *Conflict and Crisis* (1977) and *Tumultuous Years* (1983). The premier full-life biography is Alonzo L. Hamby, *Man of the People* (1995).

Partly because of the tendency to proceed from the assumption that either Russia or America was largely responsible for precipitating the Cold War, much of the writing on Cold War origins before 1970 was not as carefully researched and judiciously argued as the best writing was thereafter. An exception would be any of the many books on the 1940s by Herbert Feis, which, while written from a U.S. viewpoint, were based on thorough research in Western primary sources.

Drawing upon ample primary source materials, especially for U.S. policy, numerous books and articles published between 1970 and 1981 established a new standard for judging scholarly writing on the Cold War. These include: Diane Shaver Clemens, *Yalta* (1970); Lynn Etheridge Davis, *The Cold War Begins* (1974); Hugh De Santis, *The Diplomacy of Silence* (1981); John

Lewis Gaddis's superb 1972 book mentioned above; Lloyd C. Gardner, *Architects of Illusion* (1970); Gregg F. Herken, *The Winning Weapon* (1981); Bruce Kuklick, *American Policy and the Division of Germany* (1972); Bruce R. Kuniholm, *The Origins of the Cold War in the Near East* (1980); Geir Lundestad, *The American Non-Policy Towards Eastern Europe* (1975); and *America, Scandinavia, and the Cold War* (1980); Robert J. McMahon, *Colonialism and Cold War* (1981); Thomas G. Paterson, *Soviet-American Confrontation* (1973); Gaddis Smith, *Dean Acheson* (1972); J. Samuel Walker, *Henry A. Wallace and American Foreign Policy* (1976); Patricia Dawson Ward, *The Threat of Peace* (1979); and Daniel Yergin, *Shattered Peace* (1978).

Important works on the early Cold War years published since 1981 include H. W. Brands, *Inside the Cold War* (1991); Paul Boyer, *By the Bomb's Early Light* (1985); Jeffrey M. Diefendorf, et al., eds., *American Policy and the Reconstruction of West Germany* (1993); John Fousek, *To Lead the Free World* (2000); Marc S. Gallicchio, *The Cold War Begins in Asia* (1988); James L. Gormly, *The Collapse of the Grand Alliance* (1987); Peter Grose, *Operation Rollback* (2000); Fraser J. Harbutt, *The Iron Curtain* (1986); John Earl Haynes and Harvey Klehr, *Verona* (1999); Michael J. Hogan, *The Marshall Plan* (1987); Walter L. Hixson, *George F. Kennan* (1989); Howard Jones, *A New Kind of War* (1989); Lawrence S. Kaplan, *The United States and NATO* (1984); Deborah Welch Larson, *Origins of Containment* (1985); Robert J. McMahon, *The Limits of Empire* (1999); Robert L. Messer, *The End of an Alliance* (1982); James Edward Miller, *The United States and Italy* (1986); Wilson D. Miscamble, *George F. Kennan and the Making of American Policy* (1992); Chester Pach, Jr., *Arming the Free World* (1991); Thomas G. Paterson, *On Every Front* (1992); Robert A. Pollard, *Economic Security and the Origins of the Cold War* (1985); Thomas Alan Schwartz, *America's Germany* (1991); Avi Shlaim, *The United States and the Berlin Blockade* (1983); and Irwin M. Wall, *The United States and the Making of Postwar France* (1991).

The most impressive overviews of Truman's foreign policy are Randall B. Woods and Howard Jones, *Dawning of the Cold War* (1991), and Melvyn P. Leffler, *A Preponderance of Power* (1992). Important official records of the Truman years have been assembled in Thomas H. Etzold and John Lewis Gaddis, eds., *Containment* (1978).

The best analysis of Soviet foreign policy during the 1940s is the essay by Vladimir O. Pechatnov and C. Earl Edmondson in Ralph B. Levering, et al., *Debating the Origins of the Cold War* (2002). See also Francesca Gori and Silvio Pones, eds., *The Soviet Union and Europe in the Cold War, 1943–53* (1996); Vojtech Mastny, *The Cold War and Soviet Insecurity* (1996); Norman M. Naimark, *The Russians in Germany* (1995); Norman M. Naimark and Leonid Gibianski, eds., *The Establishment of Communist Regimes in Eastern Europe, 1944–1949* (1997); and William Taubman, *Stalin's American Policy* (1982).

Students of American diplomacy between 1945 and 1953 have been aided by numerous published memoirs and diaries. The following are valuable examples: Dean Acheson, *Present at the Creation* (1969); John Morton Blum, ed., *The Price of Vision: The Diary of Henry A. Wallace, 1942–1946* (1973); Charles E. Bohlen, *Witness to History* (1973); James F. Byrnes, *Speaking Frankly* (1947); Lucius D. Clay, *Decision in Germany* (1950); Clark Clifford, *Counsel to the President* (1991); Milovan Djilas, *Conversations with Stalin* (1962); W. Averell Harriman and Elie Abel, *Special Envoy to Churchill and Stalin* (1975); Joseph M. Jones, *The Fifteen Weeks* (1965); George F. Kennan, *Memoirs,* 2 vols. (1967, 1972); Walter Millis, ed., *The Forrestal Diaries* (1951); Walter Bedell Smith, *My Three Years in Moscow* (1950); and Harry S Truman, *Memoirs,* 2 vols. (1955, 1956).

For U.S. policy toward China, in addition to the general works cited above, see John Robinson Beal, *Marshall in China* (1970); E. J. Kahn, *The China Hands* (1976); Ross Y. Koen, *The China Lobby in American Politics* (1960); Gary May, *China Scapegoat* (1979); Ernest R. May, *The Truman Administration and China* (1975); David Allan Meyers, *Cracking the Monolith* (1986); Michael M. Sheng, *Battling Western Imperialism* (1997); William Stueck, *The Wedemeyer Mission* (1984); Nancy Bernkopf Tucker, *Patterns in the Dust* (1983); and Odd Arne Westad, *Cold War and Revolution* (1993). On U.S. policy toward Japan, see Michael Schaller, *The American Occupation of Japan* (1985); William Chapman, *Inventing Japan* (1991); Theodore Cohen, *Remaking Japan* (1987); John W. Dower, *Embracing Defeat* (1999); and Aaron Forsberg, *America and the Japanese Miracle* (2000).

A superb, concise discussion of U.S. policy toward Korea after 1945 and the Korean War is William Stueck's *Rethinking the Korean War* (2002). Other useful books on these subjects include Stueck's *The Road to Confrontation* (1981) and *The Korean War* (1995); Ronald J. Caridi, *The Korean War and American Politics* (1969); Bruce Cumings, *The Origins of the Korean War,* vol. 1 (1983) and vol. 2 (1990); Rosemary Foot, *The Wrong War* (1985) and *A Substitute for Victory* (1990); Sergei N. Goncharav, John W. Lewis, and Xue Litai, *Uncertain Partners* (1993); Jian Chen, *China's Road to the Korean War* (1994); Burton I. Kaufman, *The Korean War* (1997); James Irving Matray, *The Reluctant Crusade* (1985); John W. Spanier, *The Truman-MacArthur Controversy and the Korean War* (1965); and Shu Guang Zhang, *Mao's Military Romanticism* (1995).

Chapter Two (1953–1962)

A good place to begin is Eisenhower's memoirs: *Mandate for Change* (1963) and *Waging Peace* (1965). See also Peter G. Boyle, ed., *The Churchill-Eisenhower Correspondence* (1990). Solid general accounts (largely favorable to Eisenhower) include Charles L. Alexander, *Holding the Line* (1975); Stephen A. Ambrose, *Eisenhower: The President* (1983); and Robert A. Divine, *Eisenhower and the Cold War* (1981). On John Foster Dulles, see Richard H. Immerman, ed., *John Foster Dulles and the Diplomacy of the Cold War* (1990); and Immerman, *John Foster Dulles* (1999).

Books on Eisenhower's foreign policy published since the mid-1980s have benefited from the increased availability of declassified documents. Especially useful are the following: Robert R. Bowie and Richard H. Immerman, *Waging Peace* (1998); H. W. Brands, Jr., *Cold Warriors* (1988) and *The Specter of Neutralism* (1989); Jeff Broadwater, *Eisenhower and the Anti-Communist Crusade* (1992); Warren I. Cohen and Akira Iriye, eds., *The Great Powers in East Asia* (1990); Robert A. Divine, *The Sputnik Challenge* (1993); Raymond L. Garthoff, *Assessing the Adversary* (1991); Walter L. Hixson, *Parting the Curtain* (1997); Zachary Karabell, *Architects of Intervention* (1999); Robert J. McMahon, *The Cold War on the Periphery* (1994); Richard A. Melanson and David Mayers, *Reevaluating Eisenhower* (1989); Chester J. Pach, Jr., and Elmo Richardson, *The Presidency of Dwight D. Eisenhower* (1991); and Stephen G. Rabe, *Eisenhower and Latin America* (1988).

Russian foreign policy in the 1950s and early 1960s is described vividly in the three volumes of Nikita Khrushchev's memoirs, cited above. An excellent biography is William Taubman's *Khrushchev* (2003), which contains a good bibliography. Of the general works discussed above, two of the most insightful for this period are chapters 6–9 of Gaddis, *We Now Know,* and chapters 5–8 of Zubok and Pleshakov, *Inside the Kremlin's Cold War.*

Books focusing on particular aspects of U.S.-Soviet relations include Richard A. Aliano, *American Defense Policy from Eisenhower to Kennedy* (1975); Michael R. Beschloss, *Mayday* (1986); Campbell Craig, *Destroying the Village* (1998); Alexander L. George and Richard Smoke, *Deterrence in American Foreign Policy* (1974); and Yale Richmond, *U.S.-Soviet Cultural Exchanges, 1958–1986* (1987). American policy in the Middle East is analyzed in James A. Bill, *The Eagle and the Lion* (1988); Peter L. Hahn, *The United States, Great Britain, and Egypt* (1991); Diane B. Kunz, *The Economic Diplomacy of the Suez Crisis* (1991); and Wm. Roger Louis and Roger Owen, eds., *Suez 1956* (1989). A systematic study of the use of American military power abroad during the Cold War is Barry M. Blechman and Stephen S. Kaplan, *Force without War* (1978).

On economic issues, see Burton I. Kaufman, *Trade and Aid* (1982). Studies of U.S. policy in the Caribbean area include Nick Cullather, *Secret History* (1999); Piero Gleijeses, *Shattered Hope* (1991); and Richard H. Immerman, *The CIA in Guatemala* (1982). For policy toward Africa, see Richard D. Mahoney, *JFK: Ordeal in Africa* (1983) and Thomas J. Noer, *Cold War and Black Liberation* (1985). Two books that focus on U.S. policy toward Vietnam in the 1950s are David L. Anderson, *Trapped by Success* (1991) and Melanie Billings-Yun, *Decision against War* (1988).

Useful studies of U.S.-Chinese-Soviet relations include Warren I. Cohen and Akira Iriye, eds., *The Great Powers in East Asia,* 1953–1960 (1990) and Shu Guang Zhang, *Deterrence and Strategic Culture* (1992) and *Economic Cold War* (2001).

An early book on the threat of the Cold War to America's domestic institutions is Harold D. Lasswell, *National Security and Individual Freedom* (1950). Two representative works on the military-industrial complex are Fred J. Cook, *The Warfare State* (1962), and Carroll Pursell, Jr., ed., *The Military-Industrial Complex* (1972). Two excellent scholarly studies of the national security state are Aaron L. Friedberg, *In the Shadow of the Garrison State* (2000) and Michael J. Hogan, *A Cross of Iron* (1998). A careful study of the movement against nuclear testing in the 1950s is Robert A. Divine, *Blowing on the Wind* (1978). The domestic underpinnings of the Cold War are decried in Richard J. Barnet, *Roots of War* (1972); Richard M. Fried, *Nightmare in Red* (1990); Stanley I. Kutler, *The American Inquisition* (1982); Ann Markusen, et al., *The Rise of the Gunbelt* (1991); Seymour Melman, *The Permanent War Economy* (1974); Michael Parenti, *The Anti-Communist Impulse* (1969); and Arthur M. Schlesinger, Jr., *The Imperial Presidency* (1973). Balanced, persuasive studies of anticommunism include John Earl Haynes, *Red Scare or Red Menace?* (1995); Philip Jenkins, *The Cold War at Home* (1999); Richard Gid Powers, *Not without Honor* (1995); and Stephen J. Whitfield, *The Culture of the Cold War* (1996). The exposure of U.S. soldiers and civilians in nuclear testing is discussed in Howard Ball, *Justice Downwind* (1986); Carole Gallagher, *American Ground Zero* (1993); and Howard L. Rosenberg, *Atomic Soldiers* (1980). Allan M. Winkler's *Life under a Cloud* (1993) ably discusses public anxiety about nuclear weapons. Two excellent studies of African-Americans, race relations, and U.S. foreign policy are Mary L. Dudziak, *Cold War Civil Rights* (2000) and Brenda Gayle Plummer, *Rising Wind* (1996).

There is now an extensive literature on the foreign and domestic activities of American intelligence agencies during the 1950s and 1960s. Most valuable for students of the Cold War is John Ranelagh, *The Agency* (1987). Other useful books include Richard M. Bissell, Jr., *Reflections of a Cold Warrior* (1996); Kenneth Conboy and James Morrison, *The CIA's Secret War in Tibet* (2002); James Kirkpatrick Davis, *Spying on America* (1992); Peter Grose, *Gentleman Spy* (1994); Richard Helms, *A Look Over My Shoulder* (2003); Loch K. Johnson, *America's Secret Power* (1989); John Prados, *Lost Crusader* (2003) and *Presidents' Secret Wars* (1986); Thomas Powers, *The Man Who Kept the Secrets* (1979); Athan Theoharis, *From the Secret Files of J. Edgar Hoover* (1991); Evan Thomas, *The Very Best Men* (1995); and Gregory F. Treverton, *Covert Action* (1987).

Many early books on the Kennedy years were written either by members of the administration or by journalists. Books by officials (often with academic backgrounds) include Roger Hilsman, *To Move a Nation* (1967); Arthur M. Schlesinger, Jr., *A Thousand Days* (1965); Glenn T. Seaborg, *Kennedy, Khrushchev, and the Test Ban* (1981); and Theodore Sorensen, *Kennedy* (1965). Four stimulating books by journalists are Michael R. Beschloss, *The Crisis Years* (1991); Henry Fairlie, *The Kennedy Promise* (1972); David Halberstam, *The Best and the Brightest* (1972); and Richard Reeves, *President Kennedy* (1993). Deborah Shapley's fine biography of Robert McNamara, *Promise and Power* (1993), covers both the Kennedy and Johnson years.

Two insightful works on Kennedy's foreign policy are Lawrence Friedman, *Kennedy's Wars* (2000) and Marc Tractenberg, *A Constructed Peace* (1999). Other useful studies of this period include James Giglio, *The Presidency of John F. Ken-*

nedy (1991); Montague Kern, et al., *The Kennedy Crises* (1983); Michael E. Latham, *Modernization as Ideology* (2000); Herbert S. Parmet, *JFK* (1981); Thomas G. Paterson, ed., *Kennedy's Quest for Victory* (1989); Michael D. Shafer, *Deadly Paradigms* (1988); Robert M. Slusser, *The Berlin Crisis of 1961* (1973); and Stephen Weissman, *American Foreign Policy in the Congo* (1974). An interesting analysis of American attitudes toward Russia in 1961 is Stephen B. Withey, *The U.S. and the U.S.S.R.* (1962).

Two useful studies of American attitudes and policies toward Castro's Cuba are Thomas G. Paterson, *Contesting Castro* (1994) and Richard E. Welch, Jr., *Response to Revolution* (1985).On the Bay of Pigs invasion, see Trumbull Higgins, *The Perfect Failure* (1987); Peter Kornbluh, ed., *Bay of Pigs Declassified* (1998); Lucien S. Vandenbroucke, *Perilous Options* (1993); and Peter Wyden, *The Bay of Pigs* (1979).

The best short analyses of the Cuban missile crisis are chapter 9 of John Lewis Gaddis, *We Now Know,* cited above, and chapters 9–14 of the superb book on U.S.-Soviet-Cuban relations in the late 1950s and early 1960s, Alexander Fursenko and Timothy Naftali, *"One Hell of a Gamble"* (1997). An indispensable primary source is Ernest R. May and Philip D. Zelikow, eds., *The Kennedy Tapes* (1997). Other valuable accounts include Graham T. Allison, *Essence of Decision* (1999); Lawrence Chang and Peter Kornbluh, *The Cuban Missile Crisis* (1992); Raymond L. Garthoff, *Reflections on the Cuban Missile Crisis* (1989); Robert F. Kennedy, *Thirteen Days* (1971); Richard Ned Lebow and Janice Gross Stein, *We All Lost the Cold War* (1994); Philip Nash, *The Other Missiles of October* (1997); James A. Nathan, ed., *The Cuban Missile Crisis Revisited* (1992); and Robert Weisbrot, *Maximum Danger* (2001).

Chapter Three (1963–1972)

The improvement in U.S.-Soviet relations in 1963 is discussed in the Schlesinger and Sorensen books cited above, and in greater detail in Christer Jonsson, *Soviet Bargaining Behavior:*

The Nuclear Test Ban Case (1979); and Ronald J. Terchek, *The Making of the Test Ban Treaty* (1970). A good starting point for understanding Soviet foreign policy in the 1960s and 1970s is Anatoly Dobrynin, *In Confidence* (1995).

For the Johnson years, begin with the essays in three books: Warren I. Cohen and Nancy Bernkopf Tucker, eds., *Lyndon Johnson Confronts the World* (1994); Robert A. Divine, ed., *The Johnson Years,* vol. 1 (1986); and Diane B. Kunz, ed., *The Diplomacy of the Crucial Decade* (1994). For the administration's viewpoint, see Lyndon Baines Johnson, *The Vantage Point* (1971); and chapters 28–41 of W. W. Rostow, *The Diffusion of Power* (1972). Other useful memoirs include Clark Clifford, *Counsel to the President* (1991) and Dean Rusk, as told to Richard Rusk, *As I Saw It* (1990). Other valuable studies include H. W. Brands, *The Wages of Globalism* (1995); Warren Cohen, *Dean Rusk* (1980); Robert Dallek, *Flawed Giant* (1998); Thomas Alan Schwartz, *Lyndon Johnson and Europe* (2003); Randall B. Woods, *Fulbright* (1995); and Thomas W. Zeiler, *Dean Rusk* (2000).

The literature on the Vietnam War is voluminous. The study that provides not only the most thorough documentation but also repeated examples of the Cold War mindset is *The Pentagon Papers: The Senator Gravel Edition,* 5 vols. (1972). The best broad secondary studies are George C. Herring, Jr., *America's Longest War* (2002), and Robert D. Schulzinger, *A Time for War* (1997). Other works of unusual merit include David L. Anderson, ed., *Shadow on the White House* (1993); Michael Beschloss, ed., *Taking Charge: The Johnson White House Tapes, 1963–1964* (1997); Charles DeBenedetti, *An American Ordeal* (1990); David L. DiLeo, *George Ball, Vietnam, and the Rethinking of Containment* (1991); William J. Duiker, *U.S. Containment Policy and the Conflict in Indochina* (1994); Frances Fitzgerald, *Fire in the Lake* (1972); Ilya V. Gaiduk, *The Soviet Union and the Vietnam War* (1996); Lloyd C. Gardner, *Pay Any Price* (1995); Lloyd C. Gardner and Ted Gittinger, eds., *Vietnam: The Early Decisions* (1997) and *International Perspectives on Vietnam* (2000); Leslie Gelb with Richard K. Betts, *The Irony of Vietnam* (1979); Mark Jason Gilbert, ed., *Why the North Won the Vietnam War* (2002); Howard Jones, *Death of a Generation* (2003); George C. Herring, *LBJ and Vietnam* (1994); Townsend Hoopes, *The Limits of Intervention* (1969); David Kaiser, *American Tragedy* (2000); Stanley Karnow, *Vietnam* (1983); Jeffrey Kimball, *Nixon's Vietnam War* (1998); David W. Levy, *The Debate Over Vietnam* (1991); Guenter Lewy, *America in Vietnam* (1978); Fredrik Logevall, *Choosing War* (1999); Peter Lowe, ed., *The Vietnam War* (1998); Robert S. McNamara, *In Retrospect* (1995); Edwin Moise, *Tonkin Gulf and the Escalation of the Vietnam War* (1996); Neil Sheehan, *A Bright Shining Lie* (1988); Brian VanDeMark, *Into the Quagmire* (1991); and Qiang Zhai, *China and the Vietnam Wars, 1950–1975* (2000). U.S. involvement in Laos is discussed in Charles A. Stevenson, *The End of Nowhere* (1973), and in Fred Branfman's moving first-hand account, *Voices from the Plain of Jars* (1972). A controversial book on the Nixon administration's policy is William Shawcross, *Sideshow* (1978).

Perhaps the best overview of American policy toward China in the 1960s is James C. Thomson, Jr., "On the Making of U.S. China Policy, 1961–9: A Study in Bureaucratic Politics," *China Quarterly,* April–June 1972. Robert S. Ross, *Negotiating Cooperation* (1995), covers the years 1969 to 1989. Chen Jian, *Mao's China and the Cold War* (2001), contains an excellent analysis of Mao's rapprochement with Nixon.

Two superb general accounts of Nixon's foreign policies are Raymond L. Garthoff, *Détente and Confrontation* (1994), and Walter Isaacson, *Kissinger* (1992). Other useful studies include Seymour Hersh, *The Price of Power* (1983); Keith L. Nelson, *The Making of Détente* (1995); Roger Morris, *Uncertain Greatness* (1977); M. E. Sarotte, *Dealing with the Devil* (2001); and Robert Schulzinger, *Henry Kissinger* (1989).

Two detailed defenses of administration policy are Richard Nixon, *RN* (1978); and Henry Kissinger, *The White House Years* (1979). Other useful accounts by administration officials include Nathaniel Davis, *The Last Two Years of Salvador Allende*

(1985); Alexander Haig, *Inner Circles* (1992); and William Hyland, *Mortal Rivals* (1987).

Chapter Four and Epilogue (1973–1991)

Students of Soviet-American relations in the 1970s and early 1980s should turn first to Raymond L. Garthoff, *Détente and Confrontation* (1994) and Mike Bowker and Phil Williams, *Superpower Détente* (1988). Other valuable books with broad coverage of the period since the early 1970s include Coit D. Blacker, *Reluctant Warriors* (1987); H. W. Brands, *Since Vietnam* (1996); Alexander L. George, Philip J. Farley, and Alexander Dallin, eds., *U.S.-Soviet Security Cooperation* (1988); Nish Jamgotch, Jr., *Sectors of Mutual Benefit in U.S.-Soviet Relations* (1985); Richard A. Melanson, *American Foreign Policy since the Vietnam War* (2000); Matthew J. Ouimet, *The Rise and Fall of the Brezhnev Doctrine in Soviet Foreign Policy* (2003); Robert S. Ross, ed., *China, the United States, and the Soviet Union* (1993); Adam B. Ulam, *Dangerous Relations* (1983); and Sanford J. Ungar, ed., *Estrangement* (1985). Two interesting accounts of Soviet foreign policy by officials are Georgi Arbatov, *The System* (1992), and Arkady N. Shevchenko, *Breaking with Moscow* (1985). Robert M. Gates, *From the Shadows* (1996), offers a U.S. official's perspective.

For the years 1973–1976, see especially the Garthoff book listed above. Other useful books include the second and third volumes of Henry Kissinger's memoirs, *Years of Upheaval* (1983) and *Years of Renewal* (1999), plus Gerald Ford's memoirs, *A Time to Heal* (1979). On Vietnam and Cambodia see Arnold R. Isaacs, *Without Honor* (1983). On Angola see Piero Gleijeses, *Conflicting Missions* (2002); Arthur J. Klinghoffer, *The Angolan War* (1980); and John Stockwell, *In Search of Enemies* (1978). Other important works include Robert C. Johansen, *The National Interest and the Human Interest* (1980); Thomas W. Wolfe, *The Salt Experience* (1979); Thomas Franck and Edward Weisband, *Foreign Policy by Congress* (1979); Alan Platt, *The U.S. Senate and Strategic Arms*

Policy (1978); and Richard W. Stevenson, *The Rise and Fall of Détente* (1985).

The place to begin for the Carter years is Odd Arne Westad, ed., *The Fall of Détente* (1995), which should be supplemented by the Garthoff book cited above. The memoirs of the three principals are instructive, especially when read together: Jimmy Carter, *Keeping Faith* (1982); Cyrus Vance, *Hard Choices* (1983); and Zbigniew Brzezinski, *Power and Principle* (1983). Also helpful are Burton I. Kaufman, *The Presidency of James Earl Carter, Jr.* (1993); David S. McLellan, *Cyrus Vance* (1985); Jerel A. Rosati, *The Carter Administration's Quest for Global Community* (1987); Gaddis Smith, *Morality, Reason and Power* (1986); and Robert A. Strong, *Working in the World* (2000). On human rights see Joshua Muravchik, *The Uncertain Crusade* (1986) and Glenn Mower, Jr., *Human Rights and American Foreign Policy* (1987).

For arms control during the Carter years, see Dan Caldwell, *The Dynamics of Domestic Politics and Arms Control* (1991); Strobe Talbott, *Endgame* (1979); and Jonathan Haslam, *The Soviet Union and the Politics of Nuclear Weapons in Europe* (1990). On policy toward Central America and the Caribbean, see Anthony Lake, *Somoza Falling* (1989); David D. Newsome, *The Soviet Combat Brigade in Cuba* (1987); and Robert Pastor, *Not Condemned to Repetition* (2002). For the U.S.-Soviet rivalry in Africa, see Gerald J. Bender, et al., *African Crisis Areas and U.S. Foreign Policy* (1985). For Afghanistan, see Thomas T. Hammond, *Red Flag over Afghanistan* (1984), and National Security Archive, *Afghanistan* (1990).

The two best overviews of U.S.-Soviet relations in the 1980s are Don Oberdorfer, *The Turn* (1991) and George P. Shultz, *Turmoil and Triumph* (1993). Other useful books on the early 1980s include Laurence I. Barrett, *Gambling with History* (1983); Coral Bell, *The Reagan Paradox* (1989); Alexander Dallin, *Black Box* (1985); Beth Fischer, *The Reagan Reversal* (1997); Walter Goldstein, ed., *Reagan's Leadership and the Atlantic Alliance* (1986); Alexander Haig, *Caveat* (1984); David E. Kyvig, ed., *Reagan and the World* (1990); David S. Meyer, *A*

Winter of Discontent (1990); Eric J. Schmertz, Natalie Datlof, and Alexej Ugrinsky, eds., *President Reagan and the World* (1997); James M. Scott, *Deciding to Intervene* (1996); Strobe Talbott, *The Russians and Reagan* (1984); and Douglas C. Waller, *Congress and the Nuclear Freeze* (1987).

The literature on Reagan's military buildup and on related issues in nuclear strategy and arms control is voluminous. Some of the more useful works include Graham T. Allison, et al., eds., *Hawks, Doves, and Owls* (1985); Donald R. Baucom, *The Origins of SDI, 1944–1983* (1992); Barry M. Blechman, ed., *Preventing Nuclear War* (1985); William P. Bundy, ed., *The Nuclear Controversy* (1985); Paul M. Cole and William J. Taylor, Jr., *The Nuclear Freeze Debate* (1983); Tom Gervasi, *The Myth of Soviet Military Supremacy* (1986); George F. Kennan, *The Nuclear Delusion* (1983); Robert S. McNamara, *Blundering into Disaster* (1986); Edward Reiss, *The Strategic Defense Initiative* (1992); Jonathan Schell, *The Fate of the Earth* (1982); Paul B. Stares, *Space and National Security* (1987); Strobe Talbott, *Deadly Gambits* (1984); and Daniel Wirls, *Buildup* (1992).

The best overview of U.S. relations with Latin America in the 1980s is Thomas Carothers, *In the Name of Democracy* (1991). Clifford Krauss, *Inside Central America* (1991), offers a readable, balanced account of U.S. policy in Central America. Reagan's policies in the Caribbean and Central America are also discussed in Jack Child, *The Central American Peace Process, 1983–1991* (1992); Kenneth M. Coleman and George C. Herring, eds., *The Central America Crisis* (1991); Morris J. Blachman, et al., *Confronting Revolution* (1986); Robert Kagan, *A Twilight Struggle* (1996); William M. LeoGrande, *Our Own Backyard* (1998); Richard A. Melanson, *Revolution and Intervention in Grenada* (1985); Lester D. Langley, *Central America* (1985); and Bob Woodward, *Veil* (1987).

On changes in the U.S.S.R, begin with Raymond L. Garthoff, *The Great Transition* (1994) and Mikhail S. Gorbachev, *Perestroika* (1987). The collapse of communism and East-West relations in the late 1980s and early 1990s also are discussed in the Oberdorfer and Shultz books cited above, and in four other fine books based primarily on interviews: Michael R. Beschloss and Strobe Talbott, *At the Highest Levels* (1993); Robert G. Kaiser, *Why Gorbachev Happened* (1991); David Remnick, *Lenin's Tomb* (1993); and Hedrick Smith, *The New Russians* (1990). Other useful accounts include Coit D. Blacker, *Hostage to Revolution* (1993); Anatoly Chernyaev, *My Six Years with Gorbachev* (2000); Robert D. English, *Russia and the Idea of the West* (2000); Jack F. Matlock, Jr., *Autopsy of an Empire* (1995); and William E. Odom, *The Collapse of the Soviet Military* (1998).

Daniel Deudney and G. John Ikenberry, "Who Won the Cold War?" *Foreign Policy* 87 (Summer 1992): 123–38 provides a useful discussion of the debate over America's role in ending the Cold War. Other valuable works that reflect the sweeping changes taking place at this time include Graham Allison and Gregory F. Treverton, eds., *Rethinking America's Security* (1992); Andrei G. Bochkarev and Don L. Mansfield, eds., *The United States and the USSR in a Changing World* (1991); John Lewis Gaddis, *The United States and the End of the Cold War* (1992); Michael J. Hogan, ed., *The End of the Cold War* (1992); Steven Kull, *Burying Lenin* (1992); and Philip Zelikow and Condoleeza Rice, *Germany Unified and Europe Transformed* (1995).

INDEX

The Cold War: A Post–Cold War History, Second Edition
Developmental Editor: Andrew J. Davidson
Copy Editor and Production Editor: Lucy Herz
Proofreader: Claudia Siler
Indexer: Margie Towery
Printer: Versa Press, Inc.